THE
ANTHROPOLOGY
OF SEX

THE ANTHROPOLOGY OF SEX

Hastings Donnan
and
Fiona Magowan

Oxford • New York

English edition
First published in 2010 by
Berg
Editorial offices:
First Floor, Angel Court, 81 St Clements Street, Oxford OX4 1AW, UK
175 Fifth Avenue, New York, NY 10010, USA

Berg is the imprint of Oxford International Publishers Ltd.

Library of Congress Cataloging-in-Publication Data

Donnan, Hastings.
  The anthropology of sex / Hastings Donnan and Fiona Magowan.
    p. cm.
  Includes bibliographical references and index.
  ISBN 978-1-84520-113-5 (pbk.) — ISBN 978-1-84520-112-8 (cloth) 1. Sex. 2. Sex
customs. I. Magowan, Fiona. II. Title.
  HQ12.D56 2010
  306.709—dc22

                                                                2010014857

British Library Cataloguing-in-Publication Data

A catalogue record for this book is available from the British Library.

ISBN   978 1 84520 112 8 (Cloth)
         978 1 84520 113 5 (Paper)
e-ISBN   978 1 84788 763 4 (Institutional)
         978 1 84788 762 7 (Individual)

Typeset by JS Typesetting Ltd, Porthcawl, Mid Glamorgan
Printed in the UK by the MPG Books Group

www.bergpublishers.com

To Hannah, Lucy, Kate and Eve

CONTENTS

PREFACE

This book is about the experiences, feelings and meanings of sex within and across different cultures. Although sex is a biological urge, it is rarely experienced in the same way by people everywhere; it is differently practised and felt depending on the social and cultural settings in which it occurs. In order to stress this experiential aspect of sexual practice, we focus in particular on what people themselves say and do about sex and on how they understand and interpret it. At the same time we seek to remain sensitive to the wider global forces that increasingly shape, constrain and facilitate the exchange of sexual belief and practice and which have generated worldwide a greater awareness of sexual rights and possibilities.

Given its rich archive of sexual practices from around the globe, anthropology is well placed to provide such an account. However, our goal is not to provide a compendium or catalogue of sexual variety and difference. Rather, we have tried to sketch the general issues in the social study of sex and to locate ethnographic case studies within broader theoretical debates, at the same time as providing ethnographic context for issues often discussed only in the abstract. Anthropology is distinguished by its emphasis on the voices and experiences of those it studies and even if we sometimes stray beyond this to include other approaches, our central focus remains what ethnography can contribute to understanding the role of sex in different contexts from politics to play, commerce to consumption, and music to migration.

There are many ways in which we might have approached the writing of this book, almost as many ways as there are of engaging in the subject of its focus, and although we are unlikely to satisfy everyone, we do hope to stimulate some. We might have taken a chronological approach, reviewing how the study of sex developed in the discipline, or organized the material by region or by type of sexual practice. We have, however, adopted a thematic approach, which we hope has enabled us not only to highlight the many situations in which sex has a major role to play but also to stress the value of comparison, and the potential insights to be generated by exploring practices in one context (whether defined geographically, historically, politically, etc.) alongside those in another. We should also declare at the outset that, despite the apparent confidence of our title, this book does not claim to be *the* anthropology of sex. Given the diversity of sexual practice and interpretation, as well as the diversity of anthropology itself, it would be foolhardy of us to claim to be offering the definitive account. We hope, therefore, that it will not seem too misleading to learn here in the opening pages that, regardless of the Olympian pretensions of our title, the book's ambitions are somewhat more modest.

In a book of this kind that tries to gather together and evaluate the major research in the field there are necessarily many references and citations. We thought long and hard about how these could be best presented and considered listing all references in endnotes in order to improve the flow of the text. In the end, however, we felt that it more adequately acknowledged the work of those upon whose ethnography we draw to retain the references in the body of the text, and this is what we have done here.

The book's beginnings lay in a casual conversation over dinner between one of the authors and a well-known commissioning editor; as is so often the case with sex, one thing led to another, and what you have in your hand is the result. Kathryn Earle provided the initial push to get the project going and we are extremely grateful to her and to Anna Wright for seeing it through, as well as to Anna's predecessor at Berg, Hannah Shakespeare. We are similarly indebted to the two referees for their very helpful comments and incredibly prompt turnaround of the draft manuscript. Thank you also to Mary Warren for her careful and comprehensive handling of the index. Mention of writing a book about sex sometimes raised titters along the lines of 'suppose you need to do more research then'. We are consequently grateful to the many librarians who, with barely a flicker of an eyelid, met our requests for reading material with often colourful titles. Finally, we would like to note that this book is a joint project and that both of us should be considered as principal authors regardless of the order of names on the cover.

Hastings Donnan and Fiona Magowan

I SEXUAL ADVANCES

Sex is not the answer, sex is the question, yes is the answer

(Howard Hoffman)

TEASING OUT AN ANTHROPOLOGY OF SEX

This book examines how sex acts, sensuousness and sexual experiences are variously narrated and embodied across cultures. We approach the study of sex by drawing out the perspectives of those whose sex lives have been buried within ethnographic examples. Performative, experiential subjectivities are brought to the fore and thus our theoretical pretensions are primarily to highlight the positions and agendas of those being studied and to argue from their own understandings and interpretations. Rather than being a series of 'just-so' sex stories, this book tries to bring together critically and comparatively what people in other countries say and do about sex and how their perspectives relate to sexual theories developed by anthropologists and other social scientists of sex.

While this book is concerned primarily with sexual practices and experiences as expressed in sexual intercourse, sex acts are indicative of much broader societal concerns. Sex is both productive and reproductive of social identities that, in turn, are constrained by official and unofficial sexual contracts. However, our analytic emphasis is upon how practices surrounding sexual embodiment are at once emotional, social, political and physiological. In looking at sexual experiences, we acknowledge a problem of reductionism in that it could be argued that such experiences are confined to those engaged in them and, as a result, it sometimes appears as if scholars feel more comfortable with discussing sex and sexuality in terms of representations and identity constructions. Nonetheless, singular experiences of sex are derivative of a multiplicity of positions and perspectives that are intersubjectively embodied and circumscribed by socio-political, racial, national and legal concerns. The anthropology of sex is also the anthropology of religion, economics, politics, kinship and human rights, as we show throughout this book.

In early academia, the remit of anthropologists was not always clearly distinguishable from that of their neighbours in biology and sociology. Consequently, theoretical agendas in the study of sex have become blurred over time as similar concerns have been taken up across disciplinary boundaries. This means that our objective of analyzing ethnographic case studies by anthropologists is not straightforward, since the field of sex has grown and overlapped with other disciplines and so we have not been able (and nor would we wish) to avoid drawing upon theories of sexual experience and desire from other areas of the social sciences. Thus, while we have tried to attend mainly to anthropological studies of sex in this book, it has only been possible up to a point, since to ignore contemporary works by scholars from related disciplines would be to impoverish the scope of the arguments and insights that have been developed in other domains. This book tries to bring ethnographic cross-cultural analyses to the fore and to ground its themes in broad cultural comparators.

Many studies have viewed sex from a position of theoretical dominance, but this book comes at sex from underneath, privileging the views of those involved. The field of sex is huge and this book is necessarily one of limited ambition. We are aware that we have not tried to assimilate all the areas of sexuality (or sexual abstinence) that have been covered by sexologists, feminists and sociologists, or to synthesize the large arena of queer studies which now combines a range of disciplines and would require another volume devoted solely to this purpose to do it justice. We aim to review some of the approaches that anthropologists, for the most part, have taken to sex, focusing on what they have had to say about the sexual experiences of people from different cultures.

THE MEANING OF 'SEX'

The anthropological study of sexual intimacy and desire brings with it particular methodological problems that other areas of anthropological research do not encounter. One of the questions raised by personal experiences of sex is: how can we get inside the minds and bodies of those being studied? Sexual experiences are at the core of sexual identity, and yet accessing and appreciating the affective power of sexual experience are often the most difficult aspects of engaging with sexuality. The problem of obtaining information on sex acts is compounded by the fact that anthropologists cannot verify what their informants say, although some have tried to do so by way of asking their informants to draw sexual positions (e.g. Berndt 1976). Instead, sexual experience must be decoded through verbal and other symbolic attitudes, values and expressions. This is further complicated by the fact that the same act may have many different meanings.

Even in ethnographic accounts which relate the particularities of sexual activities, there is seldom first-hand reference to sexual experience per se but rather an analytical code about what sexuality means for those people and how it should be approached, often through gender constructs (Caplan 1987: 16). Speaking of gender models, Henrietta Moore (1994: 6) suggests that they come from an anthropological imagination of projection and introjection, identification and recognition and that much greater attention is needed to unravel imaginative fantasies about the anthropological self. Indeed, the same could be said about attending to sexual experiences which have sometimes reflected the passions, prudishness and pruriences of the anthropological imagination as much as of the people being studied.

Although there are many theorists who would argue for the inextricable nature of sex and gender (see MacKinnon 1982; Wilton 1996), we take the position that sex and gender should not be subsumed within each other, as some studies have done. Lesbian studies, for example, have been criticized for being asexual and for stressing gender at the expense of considering the sexual understandings and practices of lesbian life (Stone 2007; Wekker 2006). But there is a way of talking about sex and sexuality productively that both sheds light upon and advances gender arguments and vice versa. While many Euro-American scholars would find the work of some sex and gender theorists from other disciplines, such as MacKinnon (1982), Laqueur (1990), Butler (1990, 1993), Harding (1998) and Richardson (2000), useful starting points for theorizing sex in the West, and while we also refer to their work periodically in what follows, they are not the focus here, as the book is not about theorizing Western relationships between sex and gender per se. Instead, we aim to show how cultural difference generates multiple experiences and classifications of sex, rather than treating sex as a product of gender relations or indeed purely as mental or physical urges, as sexologists and psychologists have done previously.

The term 'sex' poses many problems before we even begin to discuss its embodiments. Anthropologists, feminists, sexologists, gender studies scholars and others use terms such as 'sex', 'gender' and 'sexuality' in quite distinct ways. As we have said, it is not our intention to examine all the debates around these terms. However, in collating and comparing particular debates within the literature on sex and gender, we recognize that authors employ these terms for different ends and it has been necessary to take account of some of their critiques in order to engage with the complexity they entail. What is clear in each case is that there is no consensus on what is meant by each of the terms. For example, while the concept of sexual rights is widely applauded, the term defines a wide range of activities and principles. Neither are sex accounts self-evident depictions of personal experiences; they are historical portraits of limited viewpoints that often frame theoretical concerns within a particular period. Thus, in this chapter we provide a review of key debates on sex conducted by some philosophers, sexologists, anthropologists and gender theorists, locating them in historical and cultural perspective to show how sex is a hotly contested practice.

SEX IN THE WEST

Sex has increasingly been put on show since it became an object of study in the social sciences from the end of the nineteenth and beginning of the twentieth centuries (Bullough 1994). Much early sex research took for granted the question of what is 'natural' about the sex act in terms of biological instincts and thus derived sexual abnormalities on the basis of deviation from the norm. The normative benchmark was heterosexual sex in which sexual desires were ascertained through a limited range of accepted practices. However, as diversity was socially engendered, this ensured that even so-called 'normal sex' was potentially ambivalent or even deviant. In order to understand the development of theories of normativity and deviance as critiqued by early anthropologists of sex, we must first appreciate the social and academic conditions of Western society in which these scholars were working.

Towards the end of the nineteenth century, Victorian morality operated a series of binarisms with regard to sexual norms, oscillating between social prurience and restraint set alongside possible promiscuity, and sexual privacy in the home compromised by potential corruption and vice in public spheres. Social purity movements in Britain sought to regulate this harmful divide in organizations such as the Vice Society, the Obscene Publications police squad and the initiation of the Contagious Diseases Acts in 1864, 1866 and 1869, which were instigated to deal with venereal disease in the armed services arising from liaisons with prostitutes (Weeks 1993: 84, 85). These acts brought into public view distinctions between acceptable and immoral acts which required further regulation. The suppression of legal places for sex, for example by closing Victorian brothels or outlawing prostitution, drove sex underground and increased the danger to prostitutes by putting them out on the streets and into the hands of ruthless customers, as have similar rulings in much later times and places, such as the prohibition on twenty-first-century sex workers in Sweden (see Kulick 2003a). Inevitably, the privacy of sex acts was one reason why sex was a subdued focus of scholarly analysis.

Yet, sex has always been viewed as a powerful force of social life by Western theorists. Sexologists were primarily concerned with the biological bases of sex but they did attend to social factors to a certain extent, including marriage rules, exogamy, incest and non-reproductive sex. The relationship between these 'scientific' accounts and the naturalness of sex was determined by the expectation that sex 'facts' could be deduced from the research. However, the essence of what was 'natural' became the foundation for anthropological critique in establishing what terms such as 'the body', 'nature' and 'sex' referred to. What was considered natural before the eighteenth century, i.e. that men and women were fundamentally the same with women's genitals on the inside and men's genitals on the outside, was challenged by the 1800s, as various writers posed sexual and racial differences between men and women on the basis of genital and bodily distinctions (Laqueur 1987; Martin 1989). At this time naturalists and scientists created the myth of the Hottentot apron, a large flap of skin which they believed hung from the navel of Khoi and San, a belief that was eclipsed when they had the opportunity to view the ritually elongated labia minora and enlarged buttocks of Saat-Jee (known as the Hottentot Venus or Sarah Bartmann), a San woman who was made to display her genitals for paying customers in London and Paris around 1810 (Lyons and Lyons 2004: 31–4).

Sexologist Havelock Ellis saw sex as the essence of life, which he analyzed as both biologically based and culturally relative. In its biological essence he considered that each person was suffused by sexual urges, erotic dreams, feelings and involuntary manifestations such as hysteria that were part of an individual 'auto-eroticism' (Ellis 1900; Ellis and Symonds 1897). He identified multiple varieties of sex practices for reproduction and pleasure, including 'coprophilia, undinism, sadism and masochism, frotage, necrophilia, transvestism (eonism), inversion and many others' (Ellis 1900, cited in Weeks 1993: 149). All these processes arose from impulses of arousal and release that explained whether the sexual act was an exaggeration or distortion of its social purpose for marriage and the family.

Still, the historical background of Victorian prudery became the sexual hallmark for classifying as unacceptable works of science that were seen to invite titillation, most notoriously those of 'armchair' theorists that included plates of bare-breasted natives in what came to be vulgarly referred to as 'tits and spears' ethnography. At the same time, early primitive porno-exotica captured one element of the nineteenth-century public and marked a departure from the more socially oriented focus on sex as incest, taboo and marriage exchange. Sex was subjected to a popularization and voyeurism of decadence and excess by the media that to some degree undermined the study of sex by researchers as well as their reputations and credibility. Social pressures and fears about damaged reputations thus affected anthropological and sexological research interests. Medical writings such as those by Krafft-Ebing (1931: 115) got away with 'it' by using Latin when sex was discussed. Others, such as Havelock Ellis, were not so fortunate and suffered the condemnation of their texts as obscene, because they were written in an accessible manner for the public rather than obscuring tantalizing details. Embarrassment over exposing and honing in on native sexual practices was also apparent in Malinowski's apology for including the word 'sex' in the title of so many of his books (Lyons and Lyons 2004: 10; MacClancy 1996: 26–7), though his academic interest in the topic does confirm the centrality of sex from the very beginning of the modern discipline.[1]

SEX-TALK AMONG EARLY ANTHROPOLOGISTS

In the early twentieth century Bronislaw Malinowski and Margaret Mead brought foreign sex home to British and American shores to show that the natives were 'like us', but only in some regards. Primitive sexuality thus claimed a field for itself set in opposition to Victorian prudery. It also offered those who desired to break loose from this prudery a means of doing so. In both cases, sex remained outside of mainstream topics of research and everyday conversation as it presented a threat to the morality of the nation. Portraits of primitive sex were framed in terms of Western notions of love and lust, but they were still seen as more emotionally provocative and licentious than sex in the West. At the apex of sexual excess were Africans, who were considered to be sexually 'rapacious and dominating' with exaggerated genital endowments that were not thought to be matched by their intellectual capacity (Lyons and Lyons 2004: 7). Ethnographic accounts of the time tended to expose primitive sex in a guise that reflected the sexual anxieties of anthropologists or public ideas about sex. Anthropological prudery was inevitable as scholars such as Morgan, McLennan and Lubbock were products of a society with sexual sanctions acting upon the nature of their prudish discussions (Lyons and Lyons 2004: 55). Victorian sexuality, like much of Victorian anthropology, was male biased and focused on men's views of women by men. Phallocentric theories predominated at this time, drawing evidence from Indian and Egyptian religion and ritual. One paper by Sellon (1863–4) examined male and female fertility sects for the worship of *linga* in which young women rubbed themselves against phallic objects, and other sects for the worship of *yoni* (Lyons and Lyons 2004: 58).[2]

While the public viewed sex as needing to be brought under moral wraps, psychiatrists and sexologists considered sex as contributing to physical illness or well-being. When further located in cross-cultural contexts, sexual practices were subjected to Western neuroses about superstition, religion and the animal urges of primitive sex. In order to secure its place and legitimacy in the scientific academy, anthropology was forced to turn its attention to more 'noble' causes than sex, and so, as sex moved to the margins of academic research, the acceptable framing of sexual topics was posed in terms of family, marriage, kinship and social structure. For instance, although there were many other aspects of sex that might have been studied, incest received disproportionate theoretical attention and we highlight some of the key issues here.

Anthropological and Western notions of kinship shaped early anthropologists' views of incest and adultery (e.g. Malinowski, Freud, Radcliffe-Brown, Murdock and Talcott Parsons). Taboos pertained primarily to the nuclear family unit of mother, father and children, though their precise explanation was often hotly disputed. It was posited that because siblings were in close contact with one another in their early years, they would develop feelings of 'positive' sexual aversion, which were then reflected in a culturally codified proscription:

> Generally speaking, there is a remarkable absence of erotic feelings between persons living very closely together from childhood … sexual indifference is combined with the positive feeling of aversion when the act is thought of… Hence their aversion to sexual relations with one another displays itself in custom and in law as a prohibition of intercourse between near kin. (Westermarck 1926: 80)

For example, amongst Mountain Arapesh children, familiarity was thought to breed sexual indifference, as evidenced in Mead's (1950: 43–4) descriptions of their relaxed emotional and sexual engagement:

> Four-year-olds can roll and tumble on the floor together without anyone's worrying as to how much bodily contact results. Thus there develops in the children an easy, happy-go-lucky familiarity with the bodies of both sexes, a familiarity uncomplicated by shame, coupled with a premium upon warm, all-over physical contact.

Mead (1950: 70) suggests that although these relationships are marked by carefree caress, they do not go further but lead to sex aversion between brothers and sisters. In Mead's account, sibling warmth and aversion teach Arapesh boys and girls how to respond to the other sex and develop acceptable child marriage relationships with other people.[3] In contrast to the Arapesh, Trobriand siblings enjoyed no such physical contact, for though they lived close together, they must 'not even look at each other' and 'the sister remains for her brother the centre of all that is forbidden' (Malinowski 1932: 440). This strict taboo against close sibling encounters contrasted with the fact that Trobrianders did not protect virginity generally and sexual relations were encouraged in free love in the institution of the 'bachelor house'.

Freud (1922: 177) challenged the naturalness of psychological responses to incest posed by Westermarck and taken up by Mead, arguing instead that desire is inherent from childhood and that it is only by stringent sanctions that incest is prevented from occurring. This is a view that continues to have popular resonance today, as John Hegley's (1997: 111) short poem 'First Sex' illustrates:

I was about six
the first time my mother told me
how it was bad to play with myself,
but I think she preferred it
to me playing with my sister.

For Freud there is no natural positive aversion but quite the opposite, the inevitability of an 'incestuous love-choice'. As a Zande proverb has it: desire for a wife begins with a sister. Fox (1980: 24) challenges both Westermarck and Freud, pointing out that familiarity is not the catalyst for aversion since brothers and sisters cannot be tired of sex as 'they haven't had any'. Rather, he posits that being allowed to touch, if only to a point, instigates negative feelings about extending physical contact with siblings. Equally, he argues that if siblings are sexually segregated in childhood, there may be greater temptation for them to explore the nature of the taboo at the onset of puberty since the rules of negative enforcement have not been learned, and thus physically separating children in childhood may increase the possibility of incest occurring (Fox 1980: 25–6).

Other anthropologists have compared adultery and incest to show that these were regulated because of their potentially negative impact on reproduction. Goody (1956) argues that in matrilineal societies the prohibition was not against sleeping with related women but was rather against sleeping with women responsible for reproducing the descent group – that is, your 'sisters' – while in patrilineal societies the opposite was true and it was sex with members' wives that was more strongly proscribed. Goody's point here, then, is that matrilineal and patrilineal societies were likely to have very different views on incest and on the sanctions which applied should anyone transgress. While patrilineal societies could be more relaxed about sex with sisters (since wives rather than sisters reproduced one's lineage), for matrilineal societies it was a major offence (since your sisters rather than your wives reproduced the group). In the case of adultery, the inverse was true, with the former more concerned about this kind of sexual offence than the latter. Goody thus cautions against assuming that Western classifications of incest and responses to it are necessarily shared everywhere else.

Paul Roscoe (1994) has critically evaluated an extensive range of biological, pyscho-logical and sociological approaches to incest. Critiquing and advancing Westermarck's theory in new directions, he argues that incest is an effect of 'familial amity' as seduction and intercourse are closely associated with aggression. Thus sexual activity is taboo for those family members with whom amity should be felt in order to maintain peaceable relations and group cohesion (Roscoe 1994: 50). The prohibition and avoidance of incest are symbolized by the prescription that 'those towards whom one does or should feel familial amity are those with whom one does not or should not have intercourse, and vice versa' (Roscoe 1994: 57). To engage in sexual relations with family members is an act of aggression which has the potential to weaken and destroy the family unit; thus incest is spoken of in the Sepik as a man 'spearing his sister or mother' (Roscoe 1994: 60). Despite a wide range of sanctions and prohibitions cross-culturally, incest is a frequent occurrence around the world. Arguing for the value of contemporary feminist and psychoanalytic approaches to incest in relation to historical ones, Meigs and Barlow (2002) consider that an integrated disciplinary approach is still needed to understand its full complexity.

SEX-TALK, PERFORMATIVITY AND RIGHTS

While we are quite familiar with the social construction of sex and gender today, we tend to forget that this paradigm has only been developed in the last twenty to thirty years. Foucault's reorienting of sexual discourse was notable for the way it transcended and resisted previous struggles over definitions of sexuality. By locating sex within institutions and discourses of power, whether religious, legal, medical or educational, Foucault decentred sex as an effect of repression or liberation. Foucault (1981: 7) recognizes that if sex is viewed as a means of liberating the self, then talking about it can be empowering because it places accounts of sexual experiences outside of its practices. Sexual discourse has various effects – simply by virtue of being able to talk about it, sex gains a power of its own which can confound what is considered acceptable or normative (Mottier 1998: 117). While we are primarily concerned in this book with exploring sexual acts and experiences, these are nonetheless embodied in the discourses that represent them, as 'there is no power relation without the correlative constitution of a field of knowledge that does not presuppose and constitute at the same time power relations' (Foucault 1979: 27). Through discourse, genitalia could become symbols of all-encompassing power. For example, sexual joking or teasing undermines and liberates as it plays with dominant sexual discourses by subverting these discourses for symbolic violation or victory. Far from distancing sexual affect through sex-talk, joking and taunts have deep emotional and erotic resonances. Annette Weiner (1988: 89) gives an example of how sexual teasing by Trobriand children and young people includes the taunts 'Fuck your mother' or 'Fuck your father', but to say 'Fuck your wife' (or husband) to anyone is among the most dangerous of verbal assaults. The sexual activities of a married couple should never be referred to and to make such reference will result in potential death. Sex terms like these which double as terms of verbal abuse derive their power by calling attention to that which should remain hidden or which is taxonomically anomalous. In Britain, for instance, some of these expressions use the names of animals that are close to humans, like cock or pussy, as 'obscene euphemisms for unmentionable parts of the human anatomy' (Leach 1972: 215).

In addition to verbal performance, anthropology has also turned to examining sex in broader domains around its sensory and bodily effects. Titillation and temptation have always been part of sex as spectacle, and ethnographic examples of sexual spectacles are many and diverse. To get at these effects Judith Butler (1990: 8) asks 'to what extent does the body *come into being* in and through the mark(s) of gender', and how does this relate to its constitution through 'sex'? In Butler's (1990: 25) terms, gender is 'performatively constituted by the expressions that are said to be its results' and, equally, sex requires some kind of *doing* in order to generate meanings around it. Within this paradigm, sex and gender are performed rather than presented – there is no a priori standard against which performances are measured; rather, sex acts and gender performances are multivocal and potentially contested arenas in which sexual meanings and sexual rights are determined.

Sexual rights and pleasures run through all strands of intimate relationships, and the tension between these two areas is perhaps most strongly evidenced in the area of marriage and the family. The right to sexual pleasure as part of mutual consent is generally assumed to be part of women's rights to reproduction, but this is not always the case. In some cultures, marital sex without consent is legal and women may be forced to have sex with their husbands. Such social expectations around marriage raise questions about women's rights to sexual pleasure.

Sexual practices outside the Western world have at times been held to account by the West in political wranglings over human rights, but it is a mistake to think that concern with sexual rights is only about an abuse of human rights. Feminists have long been involved in debates on sexual rights and these debates have had supporters from different positions. The 'sex-wars' of the 1970s split feminists into two camps – non-radical feminists, who were considered pro-sex and supported women's rights to pleasure, and radical feminist writers, who warned of sexual danger in relation to pornography; for a summary of these debates see Dworkin (1981) and MacKinnon (1982). However, the 'sex-wars' stereotyping of feminist debates ignores the fact that radical feminists also consider issues of desire and pleasure and, similarly, pro-sex feminists do not fit neatly into a single categorization that can encompass the complexity of all the issues involved. These debates have had ramifications for how other scholars have deconstructed sexual rights (Richardson 2000: 99), as we shall see in the discussion of female genital circumcision, rape, domestic violence and honour killings in chapters 7 and 8.

While the right to engage in sexual activity is constrained by law and assumes certain kinds of responsibilities on the part of the adults involved, individual expectations about rights and the legislation surrounding them do not always correspond with one another. Sexual rights to engage in certain sex acts under conditions of mutual consent may grate against ideas of personal freedom, where such acts are not supported by the law. For example, in 1990 eight men were convicted of conducting 'sensual sado-masochistic acts in private' because such activity was 'against the public interest' (Richardson 2000: 102). The relationship, then, between sexual rights and sexual pleasures is not straightforward. The laws around bestiality and zoophilia, for instance, have changed throughout history, reflecting conflicting and contradictory ideas about animal welfare, sexual transgression and permissible pleasures. Few anthropological studies of bestiality exist; psychologists have described the preferences of zoosexuals but they do not explain these trends more broadly (Beetz and Podberscek 2005). As Rebecca Cassidy (2009) shows, contextualized understandings are needed to appreciate the changing practices as well as the moral ambivalences that have underpinned the emergence of zoosex and its subsequent banning in America.

SEX DIFFERENCE

So far we have only discussed heterosexual theories and issues, but with the sexual revolution of the 1960s a burgeoning of interest in the complexity of sexuality seeped through the social sciences. It had taken a long time for scholars to come to full recognition of the sexual diversities that obtained within and across cultures, and trying to label these appropriately proved problematic. The word homosexuality was invented in 1869 by a Hungarian, Benkert, and adopted in English in the 1880s to 1890s (Weeks 1993: 21). Sexual variations then began to be labelled around the turn of the twentieth century, often couched in terms of medical disorders or pathologies. By the 1980s ideas about homosexuality had beome the focus of human rights debates and were part of broader political agendas about demarcating sexual difference. At this time, same-sex scholarship tended to emphasize categories and roles more than subjectivities and desires (see Murray 1997). The growing acceptance of homosexuality meant a shift not only in the fragmentation of sexual identities, for example lesbian, gay, transgender and queer, but also in the discussion of sexual practices and experiences.

As markers of desire, eroticism, libido, dominance or submission, male and female genitalia have taken on allegorical dimensions in the West, in part fuelled by the availability of the contraceptive pill, the rise of gay and lesbian political movements, the possibility of abortion and access to sex information through family planning clinics, the social acceptance of divorce, and increased sexual illness, especially the global AIDS epidemic from the 1980s onwards. The politicization of male and female genitalia in different kinds of sexual unions has also had consequences for the construction of masculinity and femininity. Social theory developed alongside these societal changes, bringing with it new thinking about sexual identities such as transgender, queer, bisexual and pomosexual (those who choose not to be labelled with any sexual orientation), largely from a gender perspective. Richardson (2000: 26), for example, considers how the anus is predominantly associated with gay male sex in the West, and thus penetration of the anus in homosexual sex and the vagina in heterosexual sex obscures the possibilities of lesbian sex and anal intercourse for heterosexuals. Others have argued that the realities of sex acts have the ability to confound essentialized, ideal types of heterosexual genital imagery. As Butler (1993) notes, the phallus does not necessarily belong to all men as women can have it too on their own terms. Claims that lesbian sex is less than 'normal' heterosexual sex are refuted by some scholars through the experience of the lesbian phallus, which is seen to displace the dominant position of heterosexual sex. However, Richardson (2000: 28) casts doubt upon this argument, suggesting that it takes much more than 'chicks with dicks' parodying the penis to usurp heterosexuality as an institution. Indeed, in her study of lesbian feminists in London in the late 1980s, Sarah Green (1997: 160) shows how their relationship with the wider lesbian and gay community exposed a politics of sexual diversity that allowed difference and individuality to challenge heteropatriarchal society. However, within lesbianism, disagreements between libertarians and revolutionary feminists, amongst others, around how sexual difference should be manifest and represented, underscored a wider discourse about whether it was possible to constitute 'authentic' identity and how a multitude of perspectives informed individual relationships with the 'community' (Green 1997: 174, 195–6).

There is plenty of evidence that other sexualities have always been part of the diversity of human sexual experience cross-culturally, not only in the West. Anthropologists have not been remiss in attending to the plethora of sexual divergences, including collecting data on pre-European-contact sex practices. For example, Evans-Pritchard (1970: 1429) details how, prior to European rule, it was customary among the Azande for military companies of bachelors who served at courts to take young boy-wives to satisfy their needs due to a shortage of women. These boys performed many of the duties of a wife and were considered to be married to their bachelors for the length of the union. Lesbianism was also practised, partly due to sexual deprivation, as the king would take a multitude of women only some of whom he could attend to, and adultery was punishable by death (Evans-Pritchard 1970: 1431). Such accounts of sexual diversity have more often than not been viewed through the lens of gender roles and social expectations or constraints rather than through the particularities of sexual experiences as desire, pleasure and pain, amongst other things. Few studies have tried to explain what homosexual practices actually involve, although one notable exception is Herdt's (1981) classic text on the Sambia of Papua New Guinea. Extending Mead's (1950) work *Sex and Temperament* on masculinities arising from dominant attitudes in Samoa, Herdt adopts a psycho-dynamic perspective that combines the projection of male fantasy, symbolic activity and subjective emotional experiences of Sambia boys in their ritual ingestion of semen during male initiation rites. Murray (1997: 4) reports, however, that other Melanesianists have refuted the presence of erotic feeling in these homosexual encounters.

Perhaps the most famous anthropological examples of a certain kind of homosexuality are those which adopt a cross-gender identity. The Berdache of Native North America have been extensively examined in terms of the variability of their dress and customs

(Devereux 1937; Greenberg 1985; Whitehead 1981). Comparisons have been made with cross-dressing practices from India in the form of *Hijras* who occupy various roles as transsexuals, transvestites, castrati and hermaphrodites (Nanda 1990); male actresses in Javanese theatrical troupes (Peacock 1968); and the Omani *xanith* of the Near East who dress as women and may marry whilst also taking a male role (see Wikan 1977, 1978). Unni Wikan instigated an ongoing debate about how best to describe the sexual particularities of 'third sexes and third genders'. The uniqueness of this condition and other kinds of third sex have sometimes been referred to by terms such as 'parody', 'fetish' and homosexuality, but these may not do justice to the cross-cultural phenomenon and they may certainly not account for the range of affective expressions involved. There has since been concerted discussion, review and critique of what third sexes and third genders entail and how members of the transgender community are themselves involved in a form of '"cultur-ing", creating new forms and seeing new relationships in social forms as identities' (Bolin 1996: 477). Homosexuality is so diverse in its scope and range that it has a recognized, often interdisciplinary, field of queer studies all of its own (see, for example, Boellstorff 2007a, 2007b; Halberstam 1998; Kulick 2000; Sedgwick 1985; Weston 1993).

SEX IN SPACE

It is clear that sexuality and social expectations determine where public and private boundaries lie, but these are continually challenged by newly emergent domains such as cybersex, television, magazines and the construction of a wide range of virtual communities. The Internet, for example, has opened up 'new possibilities for pornographic consumption, paedophilia, sex tourism and gender-bending and for sex without (real) bodies – virtual sex' (Harding 1998: 43). Sex is a product of individuals who in turn influence the possibilities of engagement in relation to constraints imposed by the regulators, an issue we return to in Chapter 8 on sexual politics and sexual rights.

One of the key issues around contemporary analyses of sexual practices is the problem of sexual space, and for this reason we devote the penultimate part of this chapter to an examination of the efflorescence of spaces in which new forms of sexual encounters occur. In all the varieties of sexual practice that we examine in this book, one reason sex is so titillating is that it entails degrees of danger, pleasure and risk depending upon the relationships involved and the way in which sexual geographies are determined. Private and public are regulated not merely by the exposure of body parts but by where, with whom, how and what kinds of sexual act/s are performed. Sex is, then, delimited by boundaries relating to the body *and* the spatially oriented arenas in which it occurs. Sex in public is highly transgressive, confounding the relationship between what is natural and what is acceptable, and rendering problematic public and private boundaries and the geographies they encapsulate.

While science-fiction writers have had fun speculating on futuristic forms of sex in 'outer space' (Hill 1978), the sex and space that were the focus of early social research were rather more down to earth. Drawing on the work of Robert Park, Ernest Burgess and others of the Chicago School on the zonal structure and organization of urban America in the 1930s and 1940s, initial studies of the relationship between sex and space documented how and where commercial sex fitted into the overall pattern and activities of city life. Some neighbourhoods came to be seen as 'deviant' because of the sexual services on offer there and were segregated socially and spatially as transient and liminal zones between the suburban expansion of middle-class America and the industrial and commercial zones of productive trade and commerce. Sociological research traced the organization of these zones by class, race and gender, as well as their spread and flux as cities developed and economies changed or as social reformers and moral crusaders struggled to clean up or close down the red-light districts and strip joints that they believed blighted their cities, like London's Soho, Boston's 'combat zone' and San Francisco's 'Barbary Coast', even if the outcome was often just to move the action somewhere else.

Simultaneously symbolic and material, space has physical and socio-cultural properties, both of which influence the kind of sex that is likely to arise. Although not self-evidently a sexual stimulant, space certainly seems to fuel the action, as couples who couple in aeroplane washrooms or in the beds (or wardrobes!) displayed in department stores attest. It can also, of course, inhibit and limit the sexual opportunities available. Not surprisingly, the size, form and character of a particular location, and whether or not it is classed as public, private or something in between, impinge on sexual exploits, structuring sexual possibility across a range of settings and generating complex sexual geographies and mappings of desire (Bell and Valentine 1995).

Richard Parker (1999) has mapped the 'topography of desire' for the Brazilian gay community, among whom, he says, the anonymity of urban social relations has resulted in an increasingly eroticized urban space in which impersonal homoerotic sex is possible in ways inconceivable in smaller communities (on the sexualization of cities in general see Bech 1999). Parker shows how sexual subcultures organized around male prostitution and hustling stake a claim to space in many Brazilian cities and subvert the dominant heterosexual norm. City parks, plazas and beaches all offer opportunities for homoerotic contact and every setting holds out the possibility of such encounters: 'Anyone who feels horny … just has to go down … to the street to pick someone up' (cited in Parker 1999: 55). Public transport is sexually charged for many gays and is central to the construction of homoerotic space: 'Everybody [who is gay] jokes about how rush hour is the best time to take the subway or the train. There are even special wagons at the end of the train that become almost exclusively queer … so much playing around happens that anyone who isn't gay knows to stay away from them'. Bus rides also hold out the promise of sexual play: 'I always try to catch buses that are superfull, and I let myself get into my own sexual craziness. I don't go looking for anyone – inside the bus I just let it happen' (cited in Parker 1999: 59, 60; for heterosexual sex in urban transport see Bech 1999: 219). Other public and semi-private spaces are similarly appropriated as gay, such as cinemas and male toilets, which offer the potential for intercourse and sexual play that is simultaneously clandestine yet only partly hidden (Parker 1999: 65).

Although it is not clear whether these street erotics are a consequence of homophobic discrimination that drives gays out into the dangers of the street or whether they represent a subversive and transformative 'queering' of urban space, sexual space in Brazil's cities is plainly contested and a focus for both dominant and subversive sexual forms that seek to define it as one thing or the other (Parker 1999: 63–4). Moreover, it is these street-level erotics that have made possible other ways of being gay in Brazil by providing the 'substratum' on which a commercial gay world has been built and in which gay sociability and sexuality can be enacted without fear or threat. Thus in Brazil we find the specifically gay spaces familiar from other parts of the globe, the 'wet' and 'dry' venues such as gay clubs, discos, backrooms, bathhouses and saunas. Here interaction is less restricted as it is no longer under potential public gaze, and it is possible for men to express new types of gay sociability and identity that incorporate global trends and tastes at the same time as being anchored in Brazilian homoeroticism.

While interaction may assume particular local forms in these venues, their architectural layout is similar whether in Sydney or São Paulo and their interior is designed to facilitate certain kinds of sexual activity. Hallways and stairwells may be narrow, for example, to encourage a bunching of bodily contact, and some rooms are suitable for couples whereas others invite more orgiastic combinations. Low lighting, dark walls, heavy curtains and the absence of clocks create a space 'out of time', while themed re-creations of the world outside – like the back of a pick-up truck or an industrial yard – offer theatrical settings for sex, as in the Sydney gay club 'Headquarters' which advertised itself as 'the amusement park where you are the ride' (Richters 2007: 282). Spatial and physical features such as steps, platforms, steam rooms, bathroom cubicles, video rooms, darkrooms and glory holes enable a range of practices such as fellatio or group sex, and Juliet Richters shows how it is the layout of Sydney gay clubs that shapes the sexual potentialities of gay encounters in these settings. The darkroom, for instance, with its almost complete absence of light, is 'a world of sensation, of touch, smell, taste' where everyday patterns of social interaction are disrupted and sex does not have to be negotiated but is spontaneous, sustained and collective in a 'Dionysian tumble of body parts' (Richters 2007: 287), like the 'delirium' of another club's 'prison room' with its multiple simultaneous and serial penetrations that deny differences of class, status and physical attractiveness (Lambevski 2005: 574–5). So, too, in Brazil the 'polymorphous and … orgiastic pleasures' of the darkroom re-create the activities of the street at the same time as they transform them by removing the dangers associated with gay sex in public space (Parker 1999: 81–2). While safety from violence is a key attraction of the darkroom, so also is the fact that in the shadows the 'game' of cruising is suspended, and even those without the confidence or good looks to negotiate sex can easily find a partner(s).

The sexual possibilities in lesbian bathhouses are similarly shaped by layout and design, which also strive to create an environment that is sexual but safe. Pussy Palace and SheDogs are two lesbian/queer bathhouses in Toronto which, to facilitate lesbian sexual play, modify the male bathhouse premises in which they periodically meet by providing themed 'warm-up' services that include a massage room, a 'chick-with-a-dick room', a 'butt plug room' and a 'Temple Priestess room' in addition to the open spaces, darkrooms and maze-like hallways already outlined above (Hammers 2009: 322–4). The emphasis here, however, is on sociability; rather than the impersonality of sexual encounters that seems to typify gay male venues, in the lesbian bathhouse personal relationships and intimate exchange generally precede any physical sexual involvement. Moreover, many participants come simply to watch and mingle. In contrast to the anonymity common in male clubs, then, the spatial organization of Pussy Palace and SheDogs is one that consciously strives to be both 'sexual and social', where people can meet and enjoy personal exchanges as well as sex (Hammers 2009: 331).

As these brief examples indicate, there is a rich ethnography on the ways in which space and location are central to the negotiation and enactment of gay sex. In many places the extent to which gay sexual cultures are territorialized is striking, with location a central influence on the sexual possibilities and risks. In Glasgow in Scotland, for example, distinctive sexual cultures have developed around particular locales which directly affect sexual activity (Flowers et al. 2000). The 'bars, bogs, and bushes' of the city are each characterized by distinctive styles of sex shaped by the specific spatial and physical characteristics of the setting (and also by the temporal shift from night to day; on Marseilles, see Gaissad 2009). Gay bars provide the possibility of personal relationships and the prospect of romantic as well as sexual attachment, while public parks offer the excitement of what one man described as 'instant sex'. So too in public toilets, or 'bogs', sex is generally 'easy access', anonymous and fleeting, with a focus on physical sensation rather than personal engagement, even though those between whom the sex takes place recognize that they might have understood their encounter differently had it occurred in a different setting. In contrast to the clubs, in the bushes of the park there is 'no bullshit chit-chat' (Flowers et al. 2000: 76) and there is the possibility of multiple sexual partners, who are represented and referred to not by their names but purely in terms of sexual body parts. As one man described:

> I was just wanting to have sex there and then and not have the bother of actually taking someone back… I'm much more interested in the sexual act preferably with more than one person. And you don't know who is going to be joining you next and I'm not really particularly interested in who the people are. (Flowers et al. 2000: 77)

Flowers et al. (2000) provide explicit detail of gay men talking about the sexual practices that take place in each of three locales that some readers may think verges on the voyeuristic. Yet their account is hardly gratuitous and makes the critical point that in Glasgow (and presumably elsewhere) the gay sexual repertoire is influenced by location, which determines the probability and feasibility of certain acts in ways that must be understood if government campaigns for sexual health that mainly stress individual agency and responsibility are to be effective (Flowers et al. 2000: 79–83). In other words, campaigns for safer sex should not be directed only at the decision-making of individuals, since even for those not otherwise inclined to take risks location may shape the kind of sex in which they are at times prepared to engage.

Parker's (1999: 54) suggestion that gay sexual geographies are especially intricate and complex when compared to the spatial patterns of female prostitution and heterosexual dating seems to be borne out by these examples and by the attention they are given in the literature. Certainly much less consideration has been given to heterosexual geographies (Knopp 1995: 150), and spaces of prostitution are often discussed only in terms of a dichotomy between work and non-work (Hart 1995). Yet there are indications that gay sexual geographies have had an impact on the locations sought for some forms of heterosexual sex, particularly in relation to cruising and the emphasis on outdoor sex (although the appeal of outdoor sex may be less obvious for those born in the countryside, since this was sometimes their only option; see Bell and Holliday 2000: 134–5; Fox 1978: 160). As with the gay scene, these heterosexual spaces can be contested, shifting and complex. David Bell (2006) argues that the growth of 'dogging', a practice chiefly associated with the United Kingdom, has its antecedents in gay sexual practices. Dogging is characterized by a number of elements, in some or all of which participants may be involved, and combines multiple partners with public sex, voyeurism and exhibitionism. Bell's chief interest is in the technologies which enable dogging – such as private cars, mobile phones and the Internet that facilitate travel to secluded sites, planning assignations and developing networks – and which, he suggests, elide and blur the boundaries between the public and the private (for example, sex in the 'private' space of the car while parked in 'public' view). As a space for sex, cars offer unique opportunities for their liberating mobility to travel elsewhere – offset only by the limited sexual mobility feasible in their cramped interiors! – and a transport-related map of 'auto-erotic' zones (such as 'lovers' lanes') has grown up around cars in gay and heterosexual cultures alike (Bell 2006: 395–6).

In Japan, male–female dating (and even marital sex) can also demand quite complex reterritorializations, particularly given the spatial limitations on such activities at home. Sarah Chaplin (2007) describes how Japan's love hotels provide a short-term space for sexual intimacy in urban and domestic environments that limit sexual options. Often unmarked on city maps and concentrated around entertainment districts and railway stations, with rooms rentable by the hour, the very size of the rooms in love hotels is the inverse of domestic life, offering 'the largest possible space occupied for the shortest possible time' in contrast to the relatively condensed spaces in which the bulk of one's life is spent (Chaplin 2007: 95). The physical and spatial features of the rooms accentuate their function as a space for sex. Beds are large and centrally positioned, the first thing one sees on entering the room. This spatialization is itself both exotic and erotic, since, in contrast to their eroticization in the West, beds have not historically been sites of desire in Japan, where they were rolled out only to sleep on at night. Japanese love hotels have consequently played on and expanded beds as sexual technologies capable of arousing and shaping erotic desire, from the classic love hotel *dendō* bed with its circular form and ability to rotate (thereby transforming a bed from a place of sleep to a revolving erotic stage on which occupants can view themselves from every possible angle in the mirrors mounted on walls and the ceiling) to novelty beds shaped like space rockets or clam shells (Chaplin 2007: 91–4). Other spatial and physical features of the rooms – bathroom peepholes, mirrors, video recorders and the technology to stream one's activities to the occupants of other rooms so that they can watch your activities at the same time as you view theirs – similarly amplify their sexual function and stimulate the erotic imagination in ways that encourage occupants to realize sexual possibilities literally inconceivable in other areas of their lives. Japanese love hotels thus offer a 'third space' beyond the public and the private, one that interrupts the crowded flow of urban life and facilitates a productive and transgressive liminality, 'a space of loosening ... that gives [occupants] an agency that informs their actions and alters the nature of their relationships with others' (Chaplin 2007: 10).

These themes of transformation and transgression run through much of the literature on sex and space: transformation from heterosexual to homosexual space, and from public to private, invisible to visible, hegemonic to resistant; and the transgression of boundaries of morality, secrecy and the forbidden (see Donnan and Magowan 2009: 13–17). They are apparent, for example, in discussions of 'slumming', where middle-class whites patronized black nightclubs in the sexually transgressive bohemian neighbourhoods of mid-twentieth-century Chicago (see Chapter 6). And as we have seen, they are evident too in 'dogging' and in the gay sexual cultures in Glasgow and Brazil. Yet as Bell (2006: 402) has pointed out, these activities are not just re-appropriations of public space; nor do they simply represent 'counterpublic' or 'secret' sites 'carved out in the interstices of heteronormative geographies', as others have theorized. Rather, the relationship between public and private is much more fluid and complex, as indeed the comments of many of those involved in these activities attest. The thrill and excitement generated by the dangers of transgressing space are repeatedly mentioned as one of the main attractions of these practices as participants play with physical and social space, imagining it as neither public nor private but in ways that generate new identities and subjectivities.

INNOCENCE AND THE INTIMATE ANTHROPOLOGIST

The globalized spaces in which sex takes place, whether virtual or real, have exposed all kinds of people to new ways of behaving and experiencing sex, raising problems for both the analyst and the analyzed. On the one hand, they bring into question the kinds of status and intimacies those entering into new sexual arenas or becoming cultural adepts of new sexual understandings and practices may acquire. On the other hand, trying to uncover the subtleties of these shifts highlights the privileged position of the analyst, who is often located outside the sexual experiences and impacts which they critique, taking particular stances on advocacy, representation and ethical engagement in order to evaluate their influences.

Now that the disciplinary taboo has been lifted on sex in the field, the erotic subjectivity of researchers has also been brought to the fore as part of an explanation of the process and production of ethnography. Invariably, though, exposure creates vulnerability and it is notable that until recently relatively few publications existed on discourses around this taboo (see, for example, Kulick and Willson 1995). The revelations of erotic subjectivity entangled within the fieldwork method highlight the sexual predicament that all researchers face to varying degrees and in different ways as they negotiate their sexual subjectivity in the practice of anthropology. The nature of intimacy is no longer part of a secret domain as it is entailed in the construction of identities through reflexive analysis (Giddens 1991) and any discussion of sex reorganizes its meaning and intention.

For a long time it was unclear what role, if any, sexual involvement played in fieldwork, and most anthropologists maintained a wary silence in the face of sometimes intrusive probing or were forced by friends and colleagues to clarify the reasons for their interest in a particular topic (e.g. Shokeid 1995: 1). In the novel *Regeneration*, Pat Barker has one of the characters ask her semi-fictionalized W.H.R. Rivers: 'I did once think of asking you if you ever fucked any of your headhunters' (1992: 99). While Rivers fails to answer, we do know from Malinowski that anthropologists of his generation sequestered details of any erotic desires in the pages of their field journals, if they wrote them down at all. Malinowski pondered how he could tease out the synthesis of moods, feelings, thoughts and higher awareness that would, at one level, enable him to maintain 'absolute mental faithfulness' to E.R.M. [Ellie Masson], his future wife, when he struggled with thoughts that 'other women have bodies and that they copulate' (Malinowski 1967: 200, 201). For a while he was able to look through 'the slender agile bodies of little girls in the village' and not long for them but 'for her'. But his resolve weakened a few days later when he noted 'I was sorry I was not a savage and could not possess this pretty girl', and later that evening when he 'pawed a pretty girl' he suffered a guilty conscience (Malinowski 1967: 202, 203).

The publication of Malinowski's diary in 1967 is sometimes credited with opening up debate about sex and fieldwork but, as Ashkenazi and Markowitz (1999: 5) observe, it can just as easily be argued that its reception closed the conversation down by reiterating the risk of professional marginalization to those who choose to kiss and tell. Yet, as they point out, the growing centrality to the discipline of research on women, gender and sex roles, as well as the reflexive deconstruction of the positionalities of fieldworkers, did ultimately produce a shift in attitude and practice. By the mid-1990s Esther Newton's 'My Best Informant's Dress' (1993) and Don Kulick and Margaret Willson's *Taboo* (1995) had compellingly introduced 'the erotic equation in fieldwork' as a necessary and legitimate topic for reflection, at least as far as some were concerned. While Newton (1993: 4) was able to write in 1993 that 'rarely is the erotic subjectivity or experience of the anthropologist … written about for publication', this is no longer true, as the expanding volume of work on the sexual encounters of fieldworkers attests (see, for example, Blackwood 1998; Borneman 2007; Kristiansen 2009; Lewin and Leap 1996b;

Markowitz and Ashkenazi 1999; Parker 1999; Wekker 2006). And although most accounts are about sex between anthropologist and informant, some of them consider the issues that can arise when fieldwork is conducted by heterosexual or homosexual couples (Ariëns and Strijp 1989; Boellstorff 2007a; Seizer 1995).

Despite (or because of) all this work, some retain a squeamishness and scepticism about the value of being told about sex in the field that echoes critical reviews of Malinowski's diary as lacking social scientific value. Although some clearly believe the risks are worth taking, others are less convinced and consider the sexual revelations of fieldworkers to be a titillating distraction. Klaus Peter Köpping (1998), for example, questions the intellectual insights generated by sexual intimacy between ethnographer and native, rejecting such accounts as narcissistic and as diverting attention from those the fieldworker is supposedly there to study. He would therefore probably enjoy David Schneider's joke about the postmodern anthropologist to whom an informant responds: 'Okay, enough about you, now let's talk about me' (cited in Newton 1993: 3). But even though we might share some of Köpping's reservations, particularly where accounts verge uncomfortably on the confessional, recent work repeatedly shows how sex in the field has sharpened professional insight in ways that the traditional stress on fieldwork celibacy could never have done (Parker 1999: 11–14; Wekker 2006: 4).

What originally prompted some of these reflections (e.g. Markowitz and Ashkenazi 1999) was the absence of any systematic discussion of sex in manuals on field methods and the need for more frank consideration of what novice fieldworkers might expect and how they should deal with what could arise – literally so in one case while dancing with a local dignitary (see Huseby-Darvas 1999: 153)! These texts were thought to be generally less than clear about the ethics and appropriateness of engaging in sex with informants in the field. Such ambiguities often, and perhaps necessarily, persist and while some ethnographers remain uncompromisingly concerned about the ethics of research that even implicitly seems to entail sex as a research strategy, others emphasize the enhanced understanding and access to data that sexual involvement can entail. Thus Peter Wade (1993: 203) candidly admits that he 'actively sought a young, single, black woman … to transcend the separateness that [he] perceived as distancing [him] from the constructed otherness of black culture'. And while Gloria Wekker (2006: 18) worried for months that 'being sexually intimate with "an informant" was certainly not the thing to do' before beginning a relationship with a woman who became a key source of information, Wim Lunsing (1999) had no hesitation in exploiting sexual relationships to collect data on homosexuality in Japan (see also Murray 1996). Less provocatively, others have noted how local lovers during fieldwork have been neglected and silenced sources in teaching them things they would not otherwise have known (MacClancy 1988: 239). Sex has even been advocated as a metaphor for conducting good interviews, and Joseph Hermanowicz (2002) has developed Erving Goffman's alleged remark that 'you don't really know people until you have slept with them' to advance a research strategy modelled on getting someone 'into bed'. While some of this work has been criticized for privileging research over sexual intimacy, the lines between friends, lovers and informants can sometimes be very difficult to draw. This can be further complicated by the positionality of the researcher, particularly when the sexual engagements in the field of heterosexual male ethnographers are more likely to be seen as ethically transgressive or exploitative than those of their female and gay colleagues (Goode 2002: 502–3, 532; Newton 1993). Moreover, while there has been much discussion of the issues of identity management when gay and lesbian anthropologists work in a straight (and gay) environment (Lewin and Leap 1996a: 17), there has been rather less consideration of the reverse (though see Shokeid 1995). Such hierarchies can only be understood by breaking the disciplinary silence about sexual desire in the field, as Kulick (1995: 19) persuasively argues.

Where sex itself is the focus of fieldwork rather than some other topic, these questions become particularly acute and students and colleagues alike predictably speculate on the extent to which sexual participation was the main research strategy or crack lurid jokes about 'intimate immersion', 'cultural penetration' and 'going native'. 'Going native' has in fact been used effectively by a succession of ethnographers working as strippers to facilitate access and generate insight into the lives of dancers and their (mainly male) clients (e.g. Egan 2006; Frank 2002; Ronai 1992) and even in one controversial case when an ethnographer spent a day having sex with female clients of an Amsterdam brothel to better understand prostitution (Chapkis 1997). Indeed, some argue it is 'as absurd to study sex without sexual participation as to study dance without dancing' (Kutsche 1998: 496). Others researching the sex industry have drawn the line differently when deciding how far to go for field notes and have hesitated even to observe and watch. Teela Sanders (2006, 2008c: 21–7) outlines the ethical, emotional and other hurdles she had to overcome in researching the male clients of indoor sex workers in Britain, sensitively describing how she managed to ensure that her intentions in interviews could not be misconstrued. Elizabeth Bernstein (2007a: 189–201) similarly reflects at length on the degree to which she would or should participate in her study of San Francisco sex workers (see Chapter 4) and, while learning much from posing as a streetwalker, concluded that engaging in 'sex-for-pay' would have yielded no research advantage. Other topics, such as children's sexual experiences, remain almost uniquely difficult for ethnographers to research (Montgomery 2009b: 200).

However, as we have tried to show and as Bernstein and others carefully point out, considering erotic subjectivity in the field is not just about its role as a strategy of access; it is about alternative ways of reading and writing theoretically. Malinowski (1961 [1922]: 25) argued that we needed to grasp the (male) 'native point of view, his relation to life, to realize his vision of his world', but we were able to grasp much more about Malinowski's male subjectivity in the process. In our anthropological review of sexual accounts, we will see throughout this book that narrators of sexual cultures and anthropologists have ways of revealing and concealing their 'personal and ethnographic' selves (see Bruner 1993), and so we try to remain sensitive to the particularities of subjective experiences in order to bring the written accounts to life.

Where cross-cultural sex research was once a primary domain for anthropologists, it has since been appropriated by a wide intellectual field in which anthropologists have become increasingly invisible. When anthropologists have been vocal about such issues as sexual rights, the label anthropology is seldom identified and anthropological views become subsumed in the politics of the sexual subject, merged with the voices of activists, human rights organizations and other scholars. Thus, students are not always aware of the disciplinary background of the authors they are reading, and particular agendas, such as the global politics of sex, sex as citizenship or sex and nationalism, may be stressed over the anthropological analysis of cultural expressions of sex. One of the purposes of this book is to put anthropologists back in the centre of sex debates and to show how they have contributed to explaining localized expressions of sex and sexuality alongside sexual politics and strategies. By doing so, we seek to recognize the ways in which cultural expressions and anthropological interpretations of sex have been taken up by other scholars in debates about sex practices in a global world.

CONCLUSION

In this brief overview of historical developments and key issues, we have set up the background of sex research and given a sense of how anthropological studies of sex have changed. We are aware of the enormous task that trying to analyze change represents because of the scale and volume of writings on sexual practice and experience, and no single book can cover all of the issues within the area of sex research. However, we consider some of the theoretical shifts in anthropological scholarship over the past twenty years since Davis and Whitten's (1987) review of gender and sexuality. In particular, the anthropology of aesthetics, senses, performance, borders, emotions, transgression, rights and political economies are all represented here. Some of these areas are ones that we have published on in other guises and they are subject areas that students of the anthropology of sex might currently be expected to cover. The chapters, however, do not review all of the literature available on each of the subject areas as this would not be possible, but they take some of the key themes and ideas that have emerged and attempt to draw out their significance for an anthropology of sex. Overall the book shows that sex has no natural basis that is outside of culture and history. Rather, debates about what constitutes sex have evolved with the discipline of anthropology and other social sciences. What is clear is that, depending upon which aspects of anthropological and respondent multiplex subjectivities and cross-cutting identifications are chosen (Rosaldo 1989: 168–95), sex may be analyzed as a particular kind of processual and culturally conditioned relationship. Anthropologists, like other scholars of sex, are products of their culture, and so an anthropology of sex is also a history of anthropological perspectives upon sexual culture.

We hope that individuals speak from the pages through their sexual experiences as much as anthropologists also come to life in debates about how sexual feelings and practices have been analyzed cross-culturally. There is no doubt that discourses intersect and 'position' sexual subjects (Harding 1998: 20) and this book shows that discourses about sex and sexual experiences can fracture and multiply in contested expressions depending upon the pressures and influences exerted upon both anthropologists and sexual subjects.

The richness and complexity of the materials used in this volume suggest that there is a need for a comparative holistic social science discourse that can bring together the divergent faces of sex through the interrelationship of economic, political, ritual, social and performative lenses cross-culturally. Anthropology is well placed to do this, as is illustrated in the case studies outlined here. By addressing theoretical issues in detailed ethnographic case studies, rather than focusing, as other studies of sex and sexuality have done, on just one of these areas, we hope that the reader will better see the highly complex and multifaceted interconnections between these domains.

NOTES

1. That so few of the Malinowski Memorial Lectures hosted annually by the London School of Economics over the last fifty years have systematically developed Malinowski's work on sex suggests a continuing professional ambivalence about addressing the topic.
2. *Yoni* worship is based upon veneration of the female genitalia in India to ensure fertility in the land. The term *yoni* means vagina in Sanskrit.
3. In order for the warmth of opposite-sex relationships to persist with marriage partners, and not result in conflict, there had to be careful and slow attention to intercourse, a situation that Robin Fox (1980: 45) elaborates in relation to Wolf's (1966: 884) research in Taiwan, where young boys and girls lived together as siblings until they reached an age when they could become husband and wife.

2 BEAUTIFUL BODIES

Sex loses all its power and magic when it becomes explicit

(from a letter by Anaïs Nin, cited in Allende 1999: 99)

'MAKING' THE SEXUAL BODY

In Western societies, a desire for manufactured beauty has increasingly become part of the criteria of sexual attraction, thus rendering beauty virtually synonymous with 'sexiness'. With the expanding potential of cosmetic surgery to enhance breasts, lips, thighs and even genitals, sexy bodies are now being bought and fashioned, re-siting 'natural' beauty within the reconstructive domain. However, as a panoply of values persists as to what constitutes 'beauty', we might ask what is the role of beauty and physical attraction in cultural expectations of sex; what insights can be gleaned about the sexual body by comparing the relationship between sex and beauty cross-culturally; and are beauty and sexual desire necessarily dependent upon one another?

This chapter examines the meanings of the sexual body across different cultural systems in which concepts of the erotic are highly contested, variable and shifting. As we have seen in the previous chapter, ideas about what constitutes 'normal' sexual be-haviour have reflected dominant social ideas of intercourse in turn defining what are (and are not) commonly perceived as erogenous zones. Divergences between sex acts and sexualities are, to some extent, based upon the perception of particular body parts and their boundaries, which determine sexual identities. For example, breasts have always been eroticized and fetishized in the West (Harding 1998: 24), although they are often meant to be kept taboo for those who claim rights in ownership (rather than actual ownership) of them. This is because secrecy realigns body parts with degrees of sexual allure as well as sexual control and status. The greater the protection afforded to particular body parts, the more erotic they may become, in turn generating ideas about how they are owned by individuals, groups and the state.

While beauty and sex have moved closer to one another in Western thinking in the past fifty years, sex and reproduction have gradually drifted apart. Female sexuality was once tied in to reproductive potential and acceptance by a male husband, but today the possibilities for sexual experimentation through 'safe sex' have meant that reproduction has been cast away from sex for family purposes to allow for varieties of erotic experimentation. Instead of women being confined to the home and to the jobs that reflected assumed biological differences from men, enhanced sexiness could empower women's employment opportunities, affording social, economic and political advancement as well as increased choice over a sexual partner.[1] Yet, shaping the sexual body in terms of beauty could be repressive and reinforce gender stereotypes at the same time as it liberated men and women from certain social constraints. As we shall see, illusions of sexual attractiveness today are shackled by social control, and the potential for cosmetic surgery to enhance breast shape and size does not necessarily liberate contemporary women's bodies. While women in earlier times were deprived of this opportunity for sexual enhancement, it is not always the case that those who choose to increase their breast size are freeing themselves from the more strait-laced sexual expressions of the past. Rather, it might be argued that they are placing a different kind of sexual expectation and set of desires upon themselves that they aspire to fulfil. A tension then exists between the freedom to choose to 'improve' the sexual body in order to enhance sexual potential and at the same time being subject to the forces of social expectation and sexual discipline.

Beauty systems remake the body as a human canvas upon which public standards of decency or lasciviousness may be written and also provide commentary upon them. While the sexual body is of course much more than simply its sexual parts, we focus upon the comparative meanings of three body parts most commonly associated with sex – hair, breasts and the genitals – to demonstrate how beauty and 'sexiness' are differentially value-laden cross-culturally. By shaving, piercing, tattooing or cutting the body, sexual meanings are inscribed upon it in order to enhance, discipline, resist or accommodate social mores. We begin, however, by considering feminist arguments about male objectification of women's bodies, as historically this way of looking has come to shape contemporary perspectives about particular aspects of the nude and naked body.

THE 'LOOK' OF SEX

In Western societies, the male gaze has defined women's sexual status and desirability and in so doing subjected women to male ideals of feminine sexual beauty, although this has changed radically with women consuming masculinity in magazines and adverts that promote 'sexy' male models. The incongruity between beauty expectations as a system (largely based upon heterosexual desire with beauty implications for women) and the reality of sexual fulfilment has resulted in beauty and sexual desire being embroiled in feminist sexism debates. In her study of beauty and pornography, Lynn Chancer (1998) argues that beauty has become the ultimate form of sexual attraction through what she terms 'looks-ism'. Both male and female bodies are 'made' by processes of sexual enhancement and the objectification of perceived sexuality. By emphasizing looks as a determinant of sexual style and desire, Western societies have created a discriminatory gender system of ultimate bodily characteristics that promise love, sexual prowess and recognition, and yet this system is less about the bodies that have been changed than about the relationships between those who are evaluating them. But how have looks reached this apex of sexual significance in the West and how do they compare with other cultural ideals of sexual attraction? What kinds of sexual goals have been imposed upon Western women and men historically and how have they aspired to them?

THE SCIENCE OF THE EROTIC BODY

Perceptions of eroticism are culturally complex and the nature of an erotic look has shifted over time. The erotic objectification of women has been perpetuated through commoditization, media and advertising and by women participating in the beauty system that sustains it, as viewers buy into the seductive and illusive possibilities of the images' general sexual and erotic fulfilment (Chancer 1998: 112). Media images and their reproduced fashion counterparts have created impossible ideals of the ultimate female sexual body. In a study of Barbie dolls, Urla and Swedlund (1995) have demonstrated that the measurements of Barbie were far thinner than those of average American women in the 1990s. As young girls engage with the world of Barbie, so they are taught the middle-class sexual values created around her:

> Barbie dolls personified the good girl who was sexy, but didn't have sex and was willing to spend, spend, spend... In lieu of backseat sex and teenage angst, Barbie had pyjama parties, barbecues and her favourite pastime, shopping. (Urla and Swedlund 1995: 280)

Feminine sexual ideals, such as those applied to Barbie, have been developed and refined as an outcome of historical scientific debate. From the 1900s, science assumed that size and appearance determined social ability and value of the sexes. Physical anthropologists compared male and female body measurements and decided that women were inferior to men, lacking intelligence on the basis of smaller skull size. As a result, women were equated with non-Europeans and primates (Hrdlicka 1925). Alongside mental ability, the average statistics of American women have been a subject of controversy since Louis Dublin developed the Dublin Standard Table of Height and Weight in 1908, which in America was subsequently used by doctors as a guide to determine eligibility for insurance (Bennett and Gurin 1982: 130–8; Urla and Swedlund 1995: 290). These ideals were embodied in the 1945 models of 'Norm and Norma', who represented the average American male and female as determined from a study of the average statistics of thousands of young people in the 1940s (Urla and Swedlund 1995: 290). Norma was a true American heroine whose characteristics were those of maturity, modesty and virtuosity; she was also 'fit', 'strong-bodied' and at the peak of her reproductive potential (Urla and Swedlund 1995: 290). The emphasis on pre-war physical fitness and moral integrity was to be replaced by a focus on sex appeal from the 1950s onwards, which brought the 'tyranny of slenderness' into focus (Chernin 1981). However, by the 1990s it was no longer the skinniness epitomized in the 1960s icon Twiggy which symbolized sex appeal, but the sexy body had to be taut and firm and should not show excess flesh that wobbled, bounced or became flabby (Bordo 1993: 187ff.). The naked body was valued according to standards of sex appeal as well as moral propriety. In assessing degrees of fattiness or firmness, fashion changed correspondingly to show off more of the quality of the flesh and to celebrate nudity as a form of sexual power. Nudity came under scrutiny as being sexually attractive in itself rather than just an aspect of the shape and size of the body.

BODY BITS, NUDITY AND SELF-CONSCIOUS SEXUALITY

The experience of collective nudity as a context in which the naked body is exposed before others has been instrumental in shaping young people's senses of shame or pride about the sexual body. In her study of nudity as a social metaphor, Barcan (2004: 130) draws upon Goffman's idea of shame as an experiential mode rather than a moral quality in which dressing or undressing is a result of contextualized activities and cultural expectations arising from 'the *orientational* implications of exposure' (Goffman 1965: 50, original emphasis). Barcan notes that, according to secondary school teachers in Australia, children who go away on camps or to sporting fixtures are becoming less and less likely to undress or shower in front of each other. As ideal bodies are airbrushed over in advertising campaigns and magazines promote healthy lifestyles, sensible eating and hot tips for dating, so young people are becoming increasingly conscious of their bodies as sexual objects from an earlier age. Teenage angst about changing body shape and acquiring pubic hair has shifted to a general concern for younger children about the naked body as something essentially private and individual. In the case of teenage girls in Australia, Barcan found that the social values of nakedness as standing for immorality and sexual shame were still fairly strong. In her interviews with physical education teachers she was told that:

> If a girl was comfortable with her own nudity in the school changing-room, this would be negatively interpreted as a sign of 'sluttishness' rather than positively as a sign of confidence or unselfconsciousness. One of my students told our class that having large breasts was enough for her to be labelled both stupid and a 'slut' at her high school. (Barcan 2004: 115)

Equally, in her analysis of teenagers' views of female pop stars, Baker (2002) explains how breasts are a source of embarrassment for pre-pubescent girls as they present a problem of liminality and transition into a new state of reproductive capacity and signify their sexual womanhood. In trying to negotiate becoming a woman and coming to terms with breasts as marking heterosexual attraction, pre-teen girls resist conforming to an idealized bodily size that appears somehow unattainable. Baker reports how breasts in female pop stars were the hardest parts of their bodies for girl fans to negotiate. For example, much controversy raged around whether Britney Spears had breast implants. One nine-year-old, Rosa, felt they were artificial; she wrote on a piece of paper: 'I hate Britney Spears. She is a bitch and asswhole [sic]. She is a lezbion [sic] and takes drugs and she had a boob implantation!!!' Instead, Rosa tried to suppress her sexuality by mimicking dance moves of the boy band 5ive (Baker 2002: 25). Other girls also said they found Britney's breasts repulsive. In rejecting breasts as markers of sexual attraction and reproduction, the girls present a dilemma to adults as to how best to introduce sex education to them. For some young girls the breast signifies shame as it coincides with 'the twin "problems" of sexualization and "floppiness"' (Barcan 2004: 129). Yet breasts occupy an ambivalent cultural position in the West as organs of life and sustenance for a child as well as pleasure and erotic enjoyment for a partner. It is this dual accessibility that also makes the breast taboo, since the sensual experiences of breast feeding and breast play conflate the relationship between husband and offspring. It has been argued that:

> tiny, pretty breasts neatly packaged in Miss Northern Ireland's bikini as a sweet-treat commodity, safely categorized and controllably sexy are the only acceptable breasts to be seen in public but definitely not the voluptuous and fleshy breasts of a breast-feeding mother in a coffee shop. (Meredith 2003: 15).

Along with the fetishization of the breast as the locus of male sexual desire, so the taboo surrounding large breasts has gradually been lifted through pornography and increasingly raunchy and explicit sex programmes that celebrate large breasts as the epitome of female eroticism. For example, Channel Four's *Eurotrash* has featured Lolo, 'the woman with the largest breasts in the world' (Meredith 2003: 14). At size 54G Lolo Ferrari had taken the relationship between looks-ism, attractiveness and the desire to be loved by the opposite sex to its extreme. However, apart from having difficulty breathing and being unable to sleep on her stomach or back, 'she was terrified of flying in case her breasts – each of which contained three litres of surgical serum – exploded' (Meredith 2003: 14). Her voluptuous chest no longer resembled a reconstructive naturalness as she lamented, 'I've created a femininity that's entirely artificial' (Meredith 2003: 14), and thus, in exceeding the limits of desirability, she created a sexual spectacle of herself leading to depression and suicide.

Somewhat less dramatic are the aides to sexual attractiveness and performance on offer from Ann Summers Limited, a company selling sex toys, vibrators and other erotic accessories such as latex and lingerie, and which in Britain organizes 4,000 home-shopping parties a week at which women get together to inspect the company's products, play party games and chat about sex (Storr 2003: 2). At these homosocial gatherings women's bodies are explicitly and unambiguously represented as heterosexual, sexually receptive and penetrable, a representation and self-understanding that company reps promote among the party-goers and among whom any mention or suggestion of same-sex attraction is quickly stifled or politely overlooked. The sexual female body at these parties is principally organized around a small and select number of 'erogenous zones' focused on the breasts, mouth and genitals, with other potentially penetrable access points such as the anus being completely ignored because of the association with sex among gay men. The 'erogenous' female body has both a receptive *exterior*, such as clitoris, breasts and nipples (to which products such as stimulating gels, fruit-flavoured licks and vibrators can be applied), and a receptive *interior*, such as the vagina and the mouth (the products for which take phallic penetrability as paradigmatic). Attention to the vagina at these parties may seem obvious now, but we must remember that until 'recently the vagina was effectively "invisible" in public' in the West (Ardener 1987: 126). Some of these body parts mirror and 'repeat' each other in ways we elaborate below, so that clitoris and vagina are paired with or 'ghosted' by nose and armpit respectively, ambiguities and parallels that are emphasized in some products and are used as a focus for humour, party games and puns at the party itself (Storr 2003: 167). For the participants, Ann Summers parties are clearly occasions for fun, chat and female bonding as much as they are opportunities for marketing, and products are presented and distanced by joking: 'like the Banana Dick Lick... "Yes, don't use it on a dick, put it on ice cream!"' (cited in Storr 2003: 155). They involve no physical exposure of the body, and women modestly model the lingerie and other outfits over their own clothes or by retiring to the bathroom to change (unlike the politicized consciousness-raising feminist gatherings of the 1960s and 1970s at which women explored their own and other women's naked bodies). Thus, while these parties may 'liberate' suburban women to talk freely and explicitly about sex and even 'to learn a few things', in the end – much like Lolo's breast enhancement – they reproduce heterosexual practice and confirm the centrality of certain selected body parts to the sexed female body in middle and working-class Britain.

The moral worth and the aesthetic appeal of the sexual body can be enhanced or despoiled by changes in its shape or feel. In the townships of Cape Town a 'loose bum and big breasts ... communicate that a girl is sexually active' (Lindegaard and Henriksen 2009: 35) and though this may increase her attractiveness to potential partners, it damages the reputation of single girls. Spanish Gypsies (Gitanos) determine whether a woman has been sexually active by the physical condition of her genitals. Gitano women identify with great accuracy the kinds of sexual relationship in which young women have been engaged by distinguishing:

> whether a woman is *abierta* (open) as opposed to *entera* (whole), that is, whether full intercourse has taken place, or whether she is merely *rozada* (rubbed or jagged) or *picoteada* (pecked) because the couple have been 'playing around that area' (*jugando por esa zona*) without actual penetration. (Gay y Blasco 1999: 91)

The area around the vagina is said to become dark and hard through contact with a penis (or tampons) so that young girls strive to ensure it remains soft 'pink and glossy'. Gitano women are responsible for the prenuptial defloration of brides, when an examination of these physical signs precedes the bursting of the woman's *honra*, a small grape-like sack (*uva*) within the vagina which, on being squeezed, releases a yellowish fluid.[2] Here, then, the consequences of the spoiled body as revealed by the compromised beauty and moral valuation of its external and internal organs can only be averted by eloping with one's lover.

Women's bodies may also transgress male space and confound beauty norms when vulnerable female parts are clothed by male accoutrements and exposed to dangers that men cannot control, such as in the Spanish bullring. One writer notes: 'however hard I try, I can't see such sweet, succulent and upright breasts among [the] embroidered adornments [of bullfighters' clothing]' (Pink 1997: 157). Vaginas in the bullring are also a source of men's derision and unsettle their sense of protectiveness over women. Pink (1997: 158) tells how men worry about female bullfighters risking breast injuries, which elderly men consider a serious threat to the 'vocation' of motherhood. While breast injuries would not normally affect pregnancy, men's concerns over damage to reproductive organs do not extend to male genital injuries that would end the chances of fatherhood.

However, it is not just the forces of social oppression, repression and regulation that female sexuality is struggling against. As women become their own regulators of what constitutes sexiness, so they operate in a complex dialectic between what Foucault (1979) has described as 'self-surveillance' in the internalization of disciplinary power and the expectations of sexual display. The impact of increasing regulation of the self and bodily discipline is manifest in greater self-criticism and dissatisfaction with the 'docile' body, an attitude that demands yet more discipline and subjectification of the body to senses of shame and guilt. As cultural codes of shame fluctuate in context-dependent volatility, states of dress or undress must be suitable for the occasion and conform to the expectations of looks-ism. Just as 'nakedness is intersubjective; it could not exist without the gaze of the other' (Barcan 2004: 23), so sexual eroticism is created in the dialectic of the perspectival gaze. For example, swimwear is considered to be more sexually enticing and erotic than nakedness by nudists, who stress that the naked body is erotic only for those who wear clothes (see Bell and Holliday 2000), while in the strip show nudity is integral to the stripper's art and so nakedness is the expectation of a sexual norm rather than the titillation of anticipation (Barthes 1973: 92). By contrast, lingerie or traditional pasties (nipple caps) can fetishize and eroticize as much as conceal the stripper's nipples (Barcan 2004: 18). It is not always the ambiguity of being naked or clothed that engages sexual desire but rather the transition between states of dress and undress (Perniola 1989), and in other cultures sexy movements may be the ultimate mode of eroticizing the body rather than its state of attire (see Chapter 3). Whatever state of dress or undress the body is in, one natural attribute embodies a range of meanings relating to sexual availability, desire or control, and that is hair.

THE SEDUCTION OF HAIR

Hair carries diverse and conflicting social, religious and economic meanings. Colour, length, style and visibility, as well as techniques of plucking, shaving, waxing and cutting, can alter how head hair, underarm hair and pubic hair are perceived and act as indices of sexual difference. Hair can invite sexual advance or signify virginal or marriageable status. A change in its shape, length and style can alter a person's social and sexual status, where shaving the head may signify penitence or concealing the hair can indicate sexual modesty or chastity. Hair further embodies the paradox of being neither fully culture nor nature, dead nor alive, and yet it epitomizes the aesthetic as well as the abject and obscene (Barcan 2004: 25). Since it persists after death, it can be used to commemorate the deceased (Synnott 1993: 122). The social value of hair may change over time and with it the sexual connotations it holds. Speaking of blond hair, Pitman (2003: 4) has observed that:

> Blondeness became a prejudice in the Dark Ages, an obsession in the Renaissance, a mystique in Elizabethan England, a mythical fear in the nineteenth century, an ideology in the 1930s, a sexual invitation in the 1950s and a doctrine of faith by the end of the twentieth century.

Blond hair has played a key role in male sexual fantasy and female aspirations to sexual desire and power, originally embodied in Aphrodite for the Greeks and Venus for the Romans. The divine figure of Aphrodite of Knidos became an icon of erotic energy for prostitutes, who emulated her by 'singeing and then plucking their pubic hair and rubbing their skin with pumice stone until it glowed and ... stung' (Pitman 2003: 11). The pursuit of sexual allure entailed various painful treatments, although it was the transformation of head-hair colour by rubbing saffron into the scalp and using coloured powders to create blondness that ensured female desirability. Blondes came to be viewed as both beautiful and dangerous, a transgressive power that could be used to convey illicit sexuality. By the mid-fourteenth century, images of Eve depicted with flowing, golden locks had acquired all the sinful allure of Aphrodite, being 'both eternally desirable and for ever forbidden' (Pitman 2003: 43). And yet the arbitrariness of symbols has meant that long, flowing blond hair has stood for both promiscuity and virginity over time (Cooper 1971: 67, 77). In Elizabethan England, Elizabeth I signalled her virginal femininity by bleaching her hair blond, powdering her face white and wearing abundant pearls, thereby asserting control over her own sexuality and its public reading.

With the rise of Aryanism, blondness in the Nazi regime came to be an ideology of superior intellectual status indicating moral cleanliness. It was part of Goebbels' propaganda campaign to ensure the depiction of all German female film stars as blond (Pitman 2003: 184, 190). In 1930s racial adventure films about white explorers charting unknown territories in Africa and Asia, blondes came to exemplify animality and wildness in their roles as seducers and victims. In 1932 the poster for the film the *Blonde Captive* showed a bare-breasted blonde being dragged off by a simian aborigine, while in 1933 the film industry banned for forty years the showing of the biggest love scene of all time. In *King Kong*, the gorilla ripped off the skirt of his blond victim before sniffing it and drumming her chest with his fingers. As one film critic put it: 'A giant gorilla sniffing fingers, removing garments of clothing and tickling her fancy would be very, very dodgy these days.'³ By 1976 King Kong was depicted as giving Jessica Lange a blow job across her whole body. Commercial film depictions of the helpless blonde may have contributed to a trivializing of blondness where, far from constituting superiority of intellect, blondness began to become associated with 'the dumb blonde' or the American 'broad', a stereotype famously subverted by the flaxen-haired country-and-western star Dolly Parton, who quipped: 'I am not offended by all the dumb blonde jokes because I know I'm not dumb … and I'm also not blonde.' By the 1950s the epitome of sexual liberation and the erotic power of the blonde were personified by Marilyn Monroe, a product of male voyeurism who was aware that she could please her male audience through her sexual persona, signified by her radiant white hair. In these changing meanings of hair in Western culture, it is clear that hair and sexuality have become intimately entangled and reified as part of a male fantasy in which women are constructed in terms of masculine ideals of sexual attraction and erotic performance. Distinctions are made between the Madonna and the whore or virgins and sluts, whereby sex with the slut is attractive because 'she is expected to "want it" even where sex is built mostly around pleasing him, but in a mode in which it seems to be just as hotly craved by her' (Chancer 1998: 141).

In other societies, anthropologists have variously argued that hair can convey local meanings (Hershman 1974; Leach 1958), and that there are universal sexual differences embodied in oppositional meanings (Synnott 1993). In examining the local meanings of hair in Polynesia and Samoa, Mageo (1994: 407–8) cites reports by various missionaries present in Samoa in the 1830s and 1840s explaining how rules for the hairdos of young women in pre-contact Samoa paralleled rules surrounding sexual behaviour. Hair could be fashioned in seven different ways but one of these, the *tutagita* style, was worn only by young women to indicate their virgin status. The style involved shaving the crown of the head apart from a long lock hanging down the left side of the face. Today, if long hair is cut in Samoa, it is considered to be a waste of a girl's beauty. Bleaching was common for Samoans, just as for Westerners, with ideals of fertility and fecundity evoked in the light reddish-brown colour. The term for 'head' (*mana*) was associated with redness and, by association, with the vital energies of the natural world and fecundity (Handy [1927] 1978; Shore 1989). Long hair was indicative of pre-contact pregnant women and characteristic of twentieth-century narratives of female Samoan spirits whose skin and hair were also a reddish-brown (Mageo 1991: 360–81). By the early 1970s Samoan beauty pageants had arrived and the length of the contestants' hair was measured with a yardstick to determine who would become queen of the pageant, as the lock of long hair in the *tutagita* displayed a girl's sexuality (Mageo 1994: 411). Redness and length signified the power of the reproductive potential that was embodied in women's hair, a schema for fertility that was mirrored for men in the assumed power of chiefs who were known for their ruddy complexion and red hair, just as the long hair of female spirits was analogous to the long penises of Samoan chiefs. Male pride and status were enhanced by the size of male genitals, and Polynesian chiefs' genitals were taken as a sign of status and extolled (Shore 1989: 142).⁴ Like Marilyn Monroe's blond luminescent locks, which signalled her sexual availability and power over men to engage their desire, the display of Samoan bleached *tutagita* was an invitation to and confirmation of a virgin's sexual fertility.

Apart from hair, the display of Samoan sexual availability was enhanced at all-night dance parties (*poula*) that emphasized sex in the performance of humorous and lewd movements by *poula* girls, accompanied by men's *poula* songs that offered instructions in sexual performance:

> Loosen your kilt and throw it in the house
> Then do the slap dance in the nude.
> When the papaya is yellow on one side
> That is when it is sweet!
> It is splendid, the white ass;
> It is splendid, the white ass.
> The girl's kilt is in tatters.[5]

Rather than being embarrassed or ashamed of such sexual display, Samoan women and girls would tease the missionaries by dancing naked in front of them or would tell their wives:

> to tie a shaggy mat around their waist such that the left thigh was bare, to rub their skins with oils, to powder their breasts with turmeric, to adorn themselves with beads, 'and then … walk about to shew themselves' (*f]ā'alialia*), so that they might inspire longing in the *mānaia*, the sons of chiefs. (Williams 1984 [1830–2], cited in Mageo 1994: 413)

Revisiting Hallpike's (1969) argument that long hair symbolizes freedom from social regulation and short or bound hair subordination to social authority, Mageo poses the question: if the *tutagita* style includes a partially shaved head, should this not result in sexual restraint? If so, how can such lewd sexual display be so openly entertained? Mageo (1994: 414) notes that female sexuality was controlled through a girl's hair in pre-contact times because it was an embodiment of power (*mana*) and of fecundity. Pre-Christian Samoan villages sponsored various *taupou*, high-ranking girls who would be groomed 'as a lure' and a 'self-advertisement' to increase a family's standing (Mageo 1994: 415), and these girls could give the impression of availability without sexual transgression (Ortner 1981). Virginity was publicly proclaimed by their distinctive ringlets, sometimes dyed yellow, but these were shorn off once the girls were married (Gell 1993: 87). While the *tutagita* style could allow virgins to flaunt their virginity safely, promiscuous behaviour could lead to a girl being dragged home by her hair or having her whole head shaved, which would reduce her sexual desirability and thus forfeit her potential to entice wealthy suitors. For example, one girl, Laulii, who had committed a sexual indiscretion, had her head shaved except for a couple of locks (Mageo 1994: 414). In spite of girls' efforts to convert missionaries to endorse more licentious relationships, sexual displays were curtailed and women are now condemned if they flout their sexuality by their deliberately provocative behaviour. The comment that a woman is 'walking about suddenly swollen, and lastly fat' is used as a moral reprimand to suggest she is pregnant as a result of illicit trysts (Mageo 1994: 419). The ambiguous treatment of Samoan girls' hair alludes to the tension between the sexual freedoms of the pre-colonial past and the introduced values of sexual restraint.

While women such as those in Abu-Lughod's (1988) study of Awlad 'Alis Bedouins may submit themselves to codes of sexual modesty by covering their hair, other women may resist what they see as sexual repression by renegotiating the symbolic power that their hair may hold. Obeyesekere (1984) has argued that Sinhalese female celibate ascetics have achieved social empowerment by controlling their sexuality through adopting long matted hair and sexual abstinence, thereby liberating themselves from normative patterns of sexual duty, a choice that has gained them social prestige. As public symbols of sexuality change social practice, so they influence individual experience and perception. Thus, there is a personal price to be paid in contravening the meaning of a sexual sign which may have lasting effects on society and the individual, especially when 'body symbols become the markers of moral conflicts that are powerfully felt despite their commonality' (Mageo 1994: 426).

PUBIC HAIR

In some places, pubic hair may carry a heavy emotional load of sexual invitation but its ritual removal may constitute an integral transition of the neophyte from innocence to sexual awareness. The meanings of hair removal or other forms of marking such as tattooing and scarification are not universal, and daily practices around shaving have varied between cultures and within cultures over time. Although full female depilation has a long history, it has not always received positive acclaim in contemporary Western nude forms. While Ancient Greek statues displayed men with pubic hair and women fully shaved, the Ancient Egyptians were appalled by pubic hair as dirty and unattractive. However, in contemporary Western contexts it is often thought that pubic hair, like head hair, contains the power of sexual attraction. In a survey of 200 British men and women at a university, Cooper (1971: 88, 89, cited in Barcan 2004: 148) found that 65 per cent of men felt aroused by female pubic hair, while 80 per cent of women considered their pubic hair to be 'a powerful weapon of their sexual armory' and hair removal was at the request of male partners.

In Western society, pubic hair has wielded enough power to regulate imagery. Barcan (2004: 26) describes how one of her interviewees had worked as a model for an erotic photographer. The photographer refused to employ her when she shaved off her pubic hair, as this would mean his photographs would be considered pornographic. Thus, visible pubic hair may be thought to be shameful in some arenas, but it may also be considered an appropriate covering for the naked body because of its erotic power. In 1950s Australia, naturist magazines were required to retouch or airbrush photographs and pictures depicting pubic hair, as only medical books were permitted to illustrate it

(Barcan 2004: 26). Ron Ashworth, editor of the nudist magazine *Australian Sunbather*, remarked in 1951:

> [The law] quite definitely states that no publication, other than medical, can show hair on any part of a woman's body other than her head, nor can it show the organs of a male… [W]e in Australia have absolutely no need to break the law to popularise naturism. (quoted in Clarke 1982: 191)

It was not until 1972 that the magazine *Solar* broke the taboo by publishing a photograph of pubic hair without retouching. As Barcan (2004: 27) notes: 'Pubic hair is a highly labile cultural sign whose "obscenity" or "naturalness" is produced in relation to representations.' These signs have changed radically over time. What was once dirty has become clean, and cultural notions of cleanliness, fitness and even masculine sporting prowess are gaining strength in hairlessness. Where depilation was once the domain of women in controlling unwanted underarm odour, today the zenith of depilation coalesces for both men and women in 'Brazilian waxing', which was originally associated with porn. The undercurrent of moral disdain has meant that it has only increased in popularity since the late 1990s. Barcan (2004: 29) notes that to sell full-genital waxing one Australian beautician euphemistically renamed it the 'Down-Under wax'. Where a hairy male body once signified 'virility, power and sometimes nobility' (Barcan 2004: 144), hair removal from all over the body has become a more regular practice of sportsmen and sportswomen for a variety of reasons. Male bodybuilders, athletes and cyclists, for example, may begin by removing the hair on their calves and then progress to other parts of their body, including arms and chests, as they become accustomed to the look. The image of leanness and sleekness conveyed by hairlessness enhances sporting male projections of sexual prowess, fitness and attraction, even though there may be underlying concerns about the affirmation of masculinity in full depilation.

PHALLIC POWER

A conflation between the meanings of head hair and genital hair gives rise to ambiguities around hairiness and hairlessness and points back to the Freudian Oedipal complex of having a penis or being castrated. Rubin (1975) constructs a theory of female oppression from psychoanalysis and anthropology to show how erotic potential is repressed by girls as they become aware of the absence of a phallus. This approach, drawing upon Freud, Lacan and Lévi-Strauss, has two potential outcomes: the first is the internal seething of suppressed anger at a girl's recognition of her inability to escape oppression, and the second is the understanding that her father loves her because of her castration (Rubin 1975: 196–7). While Freudian psychoanalysis has been criticized by feminist scholars, it raises questions about how Western notions of oppression, gender anxiety and divergent sexual meanings may be interpreted through body parts. In other cultures, there is considerable evidence of psychologies of repeated body parts, some reflecting an aesthetics of shame or embarrassment potentially leading to sexual oppression and repression, others celebrating anatomical beauty, fertility and reproductive powers. Some of these cultures have long histories of advocating direct correlations between the erotic power of two different body parts and sexual desire. Footbinding, for example, was practised in China for a thousand years until it was outlawed,[6] fuelled by the belief that girls with bound feet had vaginas that were more tightly muscled and with greater sensitivity; Chinese men who had women with bound feet felt they were constantly having sex with a virgin (McGeoch 2007). The Chinese sexual foot fetish has been analysed as an obsession with female purity and male domination in which torture served to ritualize female sanctity. Footbinding controlled sexual availability, ensuring women's chastity and protecting the family honour (Mackie 1996: 999). Some scholars have compared the practice of footbinding to female genital circumcision despite the differences in bodily suffering involved.

The significance of repeated body parts does not just pertain to an individual body, but meanings may be transferred between men's and women's bodies. For example, in Papua New Guinea female genitalia can be signified by male genitals in order to align female menstrual capacity with male virility. Wogeo men hack at their penile glans in order to simulate menstruation (Hogbin 1970: 88–9), and as women are thought to have male genitalia they may also suffer symbolic castration (Mageo 1994: 423). Consequently, the gendered division of men and women in this society is not correspondent with the sexual symbolism implied by the transference of body parts as cultural fantasy.

Body parts may also be mirrored by plants in some cultures, with hair and genitals acquiring analogous relationships to trees, foliage and leaves. It has been argued that in Christian Europe the fig leaf came to stand for the genitals and pubic hair, because by covering them it 'repeat[s], in simplified contours, precisely those of the phallus, testicles, and pubes, which [it] ostensibly replace[s] and conceal[s]' (Howard 1986: 289). Hiding hair does not mean that its significance is necessarily concealed, but devices such as the fig leaf may symbolically highlight the reproductive powers of male and female bodies and deliberately seek to draw attention to them as sources of pride (see Langdon-Davies 1928: 50).

In Gell's (1971: 165) evocative study of penis sheathing among the Umeda in the West Sepik, he explains that nakedness is the 'permitted absence of any genital covering or container'. Nakedness was not considered to be shameful but was a state of permanent undress for old men and a choice for mature married men. Embarrassment rather than shame was intrinsic to nakedness, but only when it was invoked in relation to penis gourds belonging to young unmarried bachelors. Just as plant materials have been associated with the penis, so systems of phallic meaning have been signified by wooden objects. For Umeda, the decorated penis sheath (*peda*) conveys ideas of the sexual status of the wearer to society at large because:

> the word *peda* metonymically stands for the penis itself. *Peda* is equated with the phallus and corresponds with suggestive parts of plants and yet, paradoxically its function is to conceal the phallus itself. (Gell 1971: 173)

Amongst Umeda, the role of the penis gourd was to conceal the glans penis on which feelings of shame were centred rather than the organ as a whole (Ucko 1970: 51). Younger men would take off their penis gourd (*peda*) to wash and sleep despite the presence of women (Gell 1971: 167), or it could be relinquished temporarily during times of mourning or during ill health (Gell 1971: 172). However, the daily use of the penis sheath was not given up lightly, even in old age. Intermittent use by younger men only occurred in family settings, but when they met in the village the bachelors were more 'concerned about what they wore, trimming their hair, shaving, wearing beads and pig's teeth and perhaps the odd feather' (Gell 1971: 171). Since the *peda* is a decorative wooden gourd inscribed with designs, it acts in the manner of a fig leaf insofar as it draws attention to the genitals and can be worn with pride as an attitude of display. Some bachelors would go to great lengths to enhance their appearance, as the adornment of the *peda* signified their personality and attitude to social possibilities. In contrast to male nakedness, women did not give up wearing their sago skirts in old age and, adorned with armlets, shell necklaces and a net bag, remained clothed. Since bachelors occupy a liminal position between boyhood and manhood where their virility is not to be released, their sexuality must be controlled through the use of the penis sheath.

In addition to the *peda*, different ritual penis gourds regulate the sexual freedom of wearers, some highlighting the potency of senior men and others the neophyte status of bachelors, thereby mediating the display/shame dynamic of ritual activities. Sexual restraint and the potential for bachelors to be shamed is offset against the flamboyant and oversized ritual penis gourd (*pedasuh*) worn by male cassowary dancers along with a pig-belt (*oktet*). The *pedasuh* emphasizes full male sexual maturity and vitality, which is further expressed in bushy masks and exuberant dancing (Gell 1971: 175). It is only in ritual that sexual licence can be fully displayed through the *pedasuh*, and its ritual opposite is represented in one category of Umeda ritual characters: the *ipele* bowmen whose prepuces are fastened over the glans penes with white palm fronds (*nab*). In the ritual, old men show the *ipele* bowmen how to shoot their arrows with their powerful small black barbs, also bound by *nab*, thus affirming their bachelor status of restraint and sexual repression. The erotic value of repeated parts is created in the relationship between different penis sheaths, where large penis sheaths demonstrate flamboyant and unfettered sexuality whilst bindings around a penis are symbolic of celibacy. As we have seen, ritual modes of adorning or fashioning hair, breasts and the genitals are variously intended to show off or to conceal sexual status, availability and prowess. As the attention of the viewer is attracted to the outward appearance of the body, he or she is simultaneously distracted from the essences of reproduction - blood, semen and milk - that are often regarded negatively or ambivalently. Thus, a discussion of beautiful bodies must be balanced by a consideration of what is sexually repugnant or defiling of bodily attraction and sexiness.

SUBSTANCES AND STICKINESS

Bodily substances are seldom described within cultures as 'beautiful', but many ethnographies discuss how their power is celebrated as life-giving at the same time as they are feared as being threatening and polluting. The life-enhancing quality of semen, for example, is reported in China, where ancient bedchamber texts are both erotic manuals and medical texts that advise how sexual health can be achieved by managing an economy of bodily substances through *jing*, which refers to both semen and a fundamental substance of the living body (Farquhar 2002: 264). The release of *jing* requires regulation through sexual moderation that will afford balanced vitality (Farquhar 2002: 265–9). The deleterious effects of substances and their constitution of personhood, power and relationship have also been extensively documented by scholars around the world,[7] and thus we highlight only some examples to show the diversity of expressions elicited by the connections between semen, blood and breast milk. In South Africa, for instance, the flow of sexual substances has temporal and social dimensions as well as cosmological significance, and an understanding of local conceptions of purification, cleaning and contamination in these contexts offers hope of more culturally sensitive ways of dealing with the spread of HIV (Thornton 2008: 202–19). Semen is most often considered to be inherently despoiling. Amongst Muslims in the Middle East, the release of semen outside marriage through masturbation in IVF clinics or testicular surgery is a 'deeply threatening' and 'shameful act' that often leads to 'performance anxiety problems' (Inhorn 2007: 46).[8] Egyptian women also find semen repugnant, requiring internal washing of the vagina after the first half an hour of sex (Inhorn 2007: 42). For many South Asians, sexual fluids, but especially semen, are at the heart of all substances. In E. Valentine Daniel's (1987: 278) study of Tamil pilgrimage, a ghee-filled coconut is created by boiling down milk and pouring it into the centre of the coconut so that it contains the 'essence of all food substances' which 'corresponds to man's own essence'. The ritual of breaking the coconut over the statue of the deity of 'the universal soul' – the Lord Ayyappan – in his shrine (Daniel 1987: 278) binds the essence of sexual substance with that of the deity. This complex of essences is captured by the term *intiriam*, which refers to sexual fluids and is closely bound up with the five senses in general and with the essence of all the sensations which is the basis of the taboo against sexual intercourse for Brahmin pilgrims (Daniel 1987: 275).

Like semen, saliva is a substance of impurity in many cultures that can pollute the outside from within. In India, for example: 'If a Brahmin inadvertently touches his fingers to his lips, he should bathe or at least change his clothes' (Harper 1964: 156, cited in Douglas 1966: 33). Blood is also a powerful contaminant, particularly menstrual blood, a 'primordial symbol' whose political power was spectacularly demonstrated by the women prisoners who smeared it on their cell walls to protest against government denial of their political status as combatants in the Northern Ireland conflict (Aretxaga 1995: 137–42). Menstrual blood is often associated with sexual heat, as evocatively suggested in the following Tamil poem about a girl's first menstruation:

Tell me, my precious one;
Has the mist run away
Seeing the lotus-bud unfurl,
Or is it the sun's awakening
That has driven him into hiding?

(Daniel 1987: 188)

The significance of the Tamil perspective is the transformational properties of blood, milk and sexual fluids mixing and recombining with one another. This is quite a different understanding of the power of substances from that analysed by Marilyn Strathern in her influential account of Gimi maleness and femaleness in Highland New Guinea. Unlike Tamil notions of transformational efficacy, Gimi substances may be separated from the bodies in which they were produced, and it is their potential for exchange that determines the extent to which they enable bodies to be viewed as male or female. For example, Gimi male sex is made known through transaction with femaleness where 'women's capacity to give birth to the appropriate offspring is proof of male efficacy in the matter' (Strathern 1990: 123). It should not be surprising, then, that semen is androgynous and also constitutive of female milk which amongst the Sambia is rendered detachable from its female source through semen ingestion rituals of unequal homosexual relations (Strathern 1990: 213). In comparing Indian with Melanesian substances, Carsten (2004: 128) notes that the difference between the two cultures is due to substances being determined through relationships in Melanesia while persons are distinguished by substances in India.

Sometimes, however, the very possibility of symbolic or literal contamination by bodily fluids that repel some people is sexually sought after by others. In the gay subculture of barebacking, for example, men seek unprotected sex with HIV-infected men, actively 'chasing' the virus and creating new communities of kinship based on viral exchange as a result (Dean 2009). Scat sex and 'poop porn' also invite sexual exchange either as spectators or active participants through bodily substances normally thought of in the West as contaminating.

In other cultures, the defining quality of semen and saliva that makes them abhorrent to differing degrees is viscosity. To elucidate this essence Mary Douglas (1966: 38) quotes Jean-Paul Sartre's (1943) essay on stickiness in which he asserts 'stickiness is a trap, it clings like a leech; it attacks the boundary between myself and it'. Thus, the problem with semen and other sexual fluids is the fact that their slime does not let go. Sartre (1992: 776) pondered:

I open my hands … and it sticks to me, it draws me, it sucks at me. Its mode of being is neither the reassuring inertia of the solid nor a dynamism like that in water which is exhausted in fleeing from me. It is a soft, yielding action, a moist and feminine sucking, it lives obscurely under my fingers, and I sense it like a dizziness.

Corroborating this finding in her analysis of sex workers, Sophie Day (2007) shows how women do not just find semen repulsive but some also feel defiled by the slimy and potentially dangerous lubricant on Durex. One noted: 'I always wash inside, even with my boyfriend. With clients it is because Durex has something that takes off your nail varnish: with my boyfriend it's because I hate the smell. I use dilute Dettol [to wash] after sex, or soap and water' (Day 2007: 157). Elsewhere condoms may be avoided, not because of polluting lubricant but out of a preference for 'dry sex', which in Indonesia is said to enhance male pleasure and is facilitated by local medicines that advertise their ability 'to dry sexual organs that excrete fluids' (Lindquist 2002: 164).

Boundary separation of undesirable fluids is essential to the maintenance of the social order. Yet, substances speak to more than simply the control of their potential for bodily or sexual pollution. As we shall see in Chapter 8, the embodiment of different kinds of substances determines acceptable alliances between individuals, groups and the establishment of sexual rights to procreative capacities. Substances also are not the only essence that embodies ambivalent responses towards sexual intercourse. In the next section, we examine how skin piercing, tattooing and cosmetic transformations mark and mould sexual feelings of desire, restraint, eroticism, control and abhorrence.

SKIN, TATTOOS AND SEX

Skin facilitates connection with other people at the same time as providing distinction. It is therefore an ambivalent surface that may be used as a canvas upon which to attract, tempt or reject sexual encounter and engagement. As Turner (1980: 139) notes: 'The skin (and hair) are the concrete boundary between the self and the other, the individual and society.' Western treatments of the skin would suggest that it is regarded as separate from and discontinuous with the true essence of the person inside the body. Thus, whatever might be read from the skin in terms of moral and social responsibility is only partially true of what the bearer actually thinks or feels. In some cultures, this division between the essence of the inner person and the meaning of the skin is dissolved and the skin not only comes to stand for but actually is the very nature of the person. As Gell (1993: 39) has argued:

> Tattooing is thus the exteriorization of the interior which is simultaneously the interiorization of the exterior, i.e. making an inside of an outside and an outside of an inside, in effect double skin folded over on itself.

In cultures that use tattooing to mark the skin, they are not just emphasizing a transient or external state of belief or feeling, but rather tattoos display qualities of personhood. As Strathern (1979) notes, New Guinea Highlanders express their 'true selves in defiance of our prejudices concerning the basic mendaciousness of cosmetics and adornment'.

In his work on Polynesian tattooing, Gell (1993: 28–39) draws upon Didier Anzieu's theory of the 'skin ego', in which he explains how the skin is not a single entity but a system of interrelationships with the orifices and sensory organs of eyes, nose, mouth and genitalia. In tattooing there is an integral relationship of the tattoo design with the intersensorial effects it evokes from the body. Thus, through what Anzieu (1989: ch. 7, cited in Gell 1993: 31) calls 'the support of sexual excitation' and 'libidinal recharging', it is possible for the skin to be marked out into areas of localized erogenous significance, which 'registers the steady accumulation or sudden depletion of libidinal desire'. But why should tattoos provoke sexual excitement if cultural markings and understandings of sexual morality and desire differ?

Although it is impossible to do justice here to the full complexity of Gell's rich ethnographic work on Polynesian tattooing, we draw upon some examples to give a sense of the distinction between Western notions of tattooing and Polynesian relationships between tattooing and sex. Within tattooing's role of 'libidinal recharging' Gell suggests that tattoos allow the eye of the beholder to get beneath the skin because, unlike other kinds of cosmetics, tattoos penetrate and reside under its surface, thereby transgressing the boundary between inside and outside and inviting the viewer into the tattooed body, especially when tattoo designs include images of erotic seduction. Furthermore, the process of tattooing is an analogue for sexual intercourse as its completion involves 'sexual subjection, piercing, and flux', suggestive of conquest and defloration that reinforces 'a sexualized looking' applicable to either sex (Gell 1993: 36). In Polynesia, instead of tattoos offering seductive protection against sexual invitation, as some colonizers erroneously believed, missionaries and Polynesians viewed tattooing as a catalyst of depravity and coarse behaviour. Since eroticism was a fundamental element of tattooing and tattooing was a mode of eroticism, tattoo ceremonies involved sexually arousing displays of dancing (Gell 1993: 35). Yet not all tattooing invited sexual advance. Rather than opening the body up to the outside world, some modes of tattooing closed it off and acted as strong barriers against would-be conquerors, sexual or otherwise. Thus, Marquesan men 'wrapped themselves in images' (*pahu tiki*) in a whole-body suit of tattooing armour (Gell 1993: 38).

Gell compares tattooing practices in Fiji and Samoa and highlights sexual and gender differences between the two cultures, even though both places use tattooing for sexual desire and control. On the Fijian island of Viti, virgins were tattooed in a hut called a 'black bottom' where incisions were imaged in their buttocks, thighs and genitals which could only be viewed by women or a girl's husband or lover, the latter only for an instant. Tattoos were also incised on the upper lip. The analogy of repeated parts ensured that tattooing on the girl's hands and mouth spoke of tattooing under her fringed skirt (*liku*) that made her irresistibly sexual (Thomson 1908: 219). Tattooing not only evoked sexual invitation but also established political rank. In Fiji and Samoa it was the lower ranking sex that were tattooed, i.e. girls in Fiji and men in Samoa. Thus, although Samoan women were considered to be objects of sexual desire, daughters of chiefs, as well as *taupou* (high ranking girls who were sponsored by the village for marriage), epitomized the political power and status of the village in beauty and adornment, and were not tattooed on the hands or genitals because this would have amounted to defloration and their virginity was sacrosanct. Instead, they were tattooed behind the knee in the area known as the popliteal space that emulates a vulva but is impenetrable and permanently closed, as well as on the front and back of the thigh.[9] While traditional tattooing practices are inevitably subject to reinterpretation and modification in post-colonial times, it is interesting to note that the undercurrent of sexual significance remains despite clothing changes. In post-European Samoa, the popliteal space was only just covered by a skirt, thereby engaging and focusing erotic interest, since partial concealment of an erogenous body part was just as, if not more, enticing than its full exposure, as has been demonstrated elsewhere with the changing fashions of see-through tops or crotch-hugging shorts in the West.

Gell (1993: 85) notes that Vitian marking 'signals the potential eroticism of the *taupou* yet places it permanently beyond reach'. This is not to say that Fijian women who were tattooed were not prized for their virginity; they were, but rather that tattooing denoted opposing sanctions in the different cultures. In Viti the libidinous regions of women were protected whilst being made desirable by the tattoo. In Samoa, the tattooing of repeated parts analogous with the genitals meant that virgins were not sexually spoiled by tattooing their genitals prior to the ritual manual defloration performed upon marriage either by the groom or, if he was too high in status, by one of his *tulafale* or assistants. Samoan defloration was a mirror image of Vitian chastity and desire as the blood from the hymen was smeared on the bride's lip, just as the Vitian girl was tattooed on the lip during her genital tattooing. In these two rituals of tattooing and defloration the skin is a deliberately teasing surface upon which the future status of the girls is written and from which they cannot escape. On the one hand, the girls demonstrate their chastity and virginity in undergoing the rite and, on the other hand, they are ritually and physically defiled, thereby delineating a permanent change of status. Various repetitions of sexual exchange and interchange are indicated in these events. Firstly, the skin of Vitian and Samoan girls becomes the expression of property rights and exchange between chiefs and villages, and secondly an analogy exists between puncturing the hymen in Samoan exchange and Vitian genital tattooing since both signal marital status (Gell 1993: 84).

Tattooing was not just a way of engaging men with their sexual desires for women but also of assuring men of their fitness and attraction to women. On the French Polynesian island of Moahi, male genital and anal tattooing was not a means of covering the naked body, but rather of drawing attention to it. Far from erasing nakedness, tattooing highlighted the elegance, desirability and display of the male physique. Whilst Vitian tattoos may indicate sexual protection and availability, Moahi tattoos were essential for sexual relationships since without them people were potentially polluting. Mariner (1827: ii, app. 2, p. 105) and Vason (1810: 179) argued that 'male tattooing resembled tight underclothes and that it was adopted from a sense of decency'. But these early missionaries did not fully appreciate the significance of this tattooing and attributed modesty to Polynesians that was not part of indigenous thinking. Undergarments did not serve to cover shame as the missionaries thought.

FAT FANTASIES AND SURGICAL SEXINESS

As with many aspects of sexual display and desire, erotic potential does not reside in one part of the body, even if a complex set of sexual meanings is primarily located there. Instead, various sexual markings and nuances combine to reinforce the message. As we learned previously, Samoan hair is powerful when it is dyed a reddish-brown colour, yet in Mangareva – one of the Gambier Islands in French Polynesia – skin colour and body shape combined to create sexual meanings where a red skin signified wealth, plenty and fatness. While young Mangarevan chiefs were tattooed, they were admired for their stoutness and growth (Gell 1993: 234). The ability to provide both reproductively and nutritionally for a family further determined the relationship between tattooing and fattening regimes in central and eastern Polynesian and the intrinsic nature of eroticism and sexual sustainability. Due to chronic food shortages on Mangareva, the greatest wealth a man could have was not his wife's virginity, represented in her tattoo or defloration ritual, but rather her body fat, a measure of her aristocracy and insurance for her future as a wife and mother. The accumulation of fat was considered to be a permanent symbol of wealth. While tattooing was no longer a major element of attraction for Mangarevan female sexuality, males would add more tattoos as they got older in order to protect themselves from increasing dangers presented by an accretion of enemies over time (Gell 1993: 234).

Force-feeding to fatten women as marriageable propositions has been practised in various countries around the world where thinness is considered a sign of poverty. A 'fat farm' manager in Mauritania, Fatematou, starts with seven-year-olds, who are forced to eat dates, couscous and other fattening foods so that when they grow up they will be 'proud and show off their good size to make men dribble' (Harter 2004). According to Fatematou, girls experience the fat farm as a place of control where parents will punish girls if they refuse to eat and where they have no choice as they are forced to eat. However, the practice is dying out in Mauritania, where the Ministry of Health has reported that 11 per cent of girls are now force-fed, as attitudes are changing and girls consider controlling their weight in order to appeal to European men's tastes of thinness as much as Mauritanian tastes for fatness.

If we consider the cultural associations between force-feeding and wealth in Polynesia and Africa and compare them with the control of body shape and aspirations to wealth in the West, we might ask whether Western women are really any freer to choose their body shape than women in countries that apply other kinds of regimes to effect certain body types. After all, some women in the West also practise tattooing and force-feeding in addition to modifying their body shape and size in other equally painful and potentially life-threatening ways. But why would women want to risk becoming one of the casualties widely reported as resulting from complications of liposuction or breast implants (Morgan 1991: 328)? Who are these bodies being constructed for and is this preference or perversion, liberation or oppression, or both?

Where 'natural' body parts were once sites upon which libidinous desires were inscribed, advancing technologies have meant that bodies have become bio-technical engineering experiments in which subjection to physical danger is perceived as necessary to guarantee sexual desirability. Scholars have examined how cosmetic alteration is a consequence of the medicalization of the female body that disciplines and normalizes it (Bordo 1993; Chernin 1981; Jeffreys 2005). In her analysis of the complexities of cosmetic surgery, Morgan (1991) draws upon Foucault's (1979: 136–7) theory of the 'docile body' to question whether choice is not in fact simply a matter of conformity. In producing a docile body, women who elect to have cosmetic surgery may appear to be free and treated individually, although they are submitting themselves to others' control of their bodies. In order to do this, they must be constantly coerced by social expectation and convinced of the liberating potential that disciplining their bodies within the cosmetic regime will bring to their lifestyles. Where such cutting and deformity of the body through surgical change would once have been considered deviant or pathological, Morgan (1991: 327, 336) argues that, instead, not to choose to submit to 'magic knives' and buy a new body is increasingly being seen as deviant or narrow-minded. And it is not only the publicly visible parts that are being altered to improve the chances of the sexual body, but also the hidden parts. Vulvas may undergo makeovers for a partner's enjoyment, while penile implants, performance-enhancing drugs, patches or penile extensions that promise up to fourfold growth in length in just weeks mean that male bodies are also becoming technologically enhanced machines.

In Brazil 'plastica', as cosmetic surgery is termed, is seen as the panacea for counteracting the effects of everything from puberty to menopause amongst women. Where motherhood is blamed for 'thickened waists, "dead flesh", Caesarean scars, and bellies and breasts that are "fallen", "flaccid", or "shrivelled like an old passion fruit"' (Edmonds 2007: 374), surgeons are viewed as the saviours of improved health. The growth in *plastica* has been fuelled by curiosity about new technologies that offer an escape through bodily fantasy, especially for the socially deprived. As one shanty-town resident commented: 'If a girl from Ipanema can have a $5000 breast job . . . then I have the right too' (Edmonds 2007: 371).

Rather than fatness, plumpness or curviness raising the stakes for marital potential, the technologically perfected body is usurping the place of the 'normal' or 'average' sexual body and will come to forfeit and perhaps permanently destabilize senses of femininity and masculinity, as well as altering the possibilities of marital choice and standards of sexual desire. By raising the beauty stakes to new heights, the average body may be considered sexually unattractive or perhaps even ugly, in turn undermining the potential for economic and social success.

It is not only Caucasian women who opt for surgery; black men and women use toxic bleaching agents to alter the colour of their skin and in China fashion is changing. Although state-owned television cannot show female flesh between chest height and just above the knee, Chinese magazines now feature scantily clad Western models who have set new standards in Beijing, where some Chinese women flout cultural norms by shockingly exposing their belly buttons or not wearing underwear in apparent emulation of these models. Nowhere perhaps is the illusion of choice about sexual presentation more evident than in beauty pageants where contestants are expected to conform to social expectations that may uphold a local beauty aesthetic, whilst at the same time being influenced by international (Western) beauty standards. In these kinds of contexts, it is often not simply sexiness that is at stake but the reputation of the nation, as Haller (2000) shows in his analysis of beauty contests in Gibraltar. Among the plethora of beauty competitions, which include 'Miss Computec', 'Miss Security Express' and 'Miss Platter', young women's bodies are moulded to classical feminine heteronormative ideals in line with Gibraltarian fashion, which is more subdued than the Spanish and more flamboyant than the English. The persistence of these contests for beautiful women fourteen years after the opening of the border is a statement of national identification and resistance to Spanish claims over Gibraltar (Haller 2000: 68–9).

FLAUNTING IT

So far the analysis has concentrated upon the dominant framework of heterosexual sex and beauty, but the objectification of female bodies has since been matched by the objectification of the male body, especially in meeting homosexual or transgendered desires. Transgender beauty pageants are potentially arenas for resisting and parody-ing heterosexual erotic ideals since 'gay masculinity is subversive (in that it challenges orthodox masculinity) and reactionary (in that it reinforces gender stereotypes – a crucial factor in the oppression of gay sexuality)' (Forrest 1993: 105). In Tonga, Besnier (2002: 540) describes how the 'Miss Galaxy' beauty pageant held at the end of the month-long Heilala Festival provides an opportunity for transgendered 'Miss Galaxy' contestants to create their own version of Tonganness that stands in opposition to that displayed by the 'Miss Heilala' contestants. These *leiti* or 'ladies', 'men who act like women' (Besnier 2002: 534), are consumed by preening and body image. Somewhat ironically, in their efforts to resist Tongan male sexuality they present themselves in the manner of a Western colonial lady with 'highly elaborated sensitivities … [and] in constant need of cosmetics whose desires are insatiable (gin and handsome 'native' men complete the picture)' (Besnier 1997: 19). They enhance the feminine qualities of 'a swishy gait, an animated face, a highly emotional comportment, a fast speaking tempo and a tendency to be verbose in contrast to the masculine impassiveness and *sang froid* that mainstream Tonga men cultivate' (Besnier 1997: 10). Their aim is to attract straight, young men in their twenties who serve their erotic desires until they may later marry as a heterosexual and, as long as their trysts are not discovered, straight men do not compromise their own sexuality.

The ideals of the beauty pageant include contestants with lighter skin tones who are elegant and competent in dancing solo the *tau'olunga*, which embodies Tongan virginal femininity (Kaeppler 1985). Tongan *leiti* are controlled by the expectations of the Tongan beauty system, but some contestants who have lived overseas may assist their looks with cosmetic surgery and hormone treatments that result in 'a self-contained, self-referential reality, the terms of which are determined in local standards of aesthetics and social action' (Besnier 2002: 554; cf. Johnson 1997: 193–210). Contestants who are based outside Tonga may have difficulty performing in a sufficiently Tongan style. They may compromise their masculinity and symbolically reveal 'visible crotch bulges in otherwise glamorous evening gowns' (Besnier 2002: 559). Drunken men and women in the audience may attempt to reveal their true identity by ripping their dresses and pulling off their bras, to the hilarity of the onlookers (Besnier 2002: 552). Rather than being sexual predators, *leiti* are more often harassed by drunken 'straight' men (Besnier 1994: 300–1) who are exploitative towards them, and so some *leiti* are at pains to display their innocence and virginity even if this is not the reality. Straight men, however, expect *leiti* to make sex attractive with alcohol, gifts, entertainment and payment (Besnier 2004: 318).

In contrast to the Tongan stereotype of *leiti* as promiscuous, *leiti* beauty queens assert the normative ideal of female virginity, which is closely supervised by brothers and male cousins in order to ensure family protection and reputation (Besnier 1997: 14). Although they behave literally 'in the fashion of a lady' (*fakaleiti*), the virginal ideal explains why they prefer the shortened version *leiti*, since 'the prefix *faka* sounds too much like the English word "fuck"' (Besnier 1997: 19) and reinforces the image of wild sexual abandon and uninhibited sexual desire. The Miss Galaxy stage is a platform not only for competition between *leiti* in demonstrating sexual desirability but also in competing for the attentions of the straight male audience. Thus, the competition interview can include sexual double entendres and contestants' performances may be highly sexual and provocative, inverting the proper behaviour expected of Tongan women. In pushing normative sexuality to its limits in subversive sexual play, the event has become extremely popular for Tongan audiences (Besnier 2004: 11). Cultures like that of Tonga have responded to the global circulation of sexual values and beauty techniques most visible in Miss World and Mr Universe competitions by integrating, adapting or in some cases resisting their effects. Although cosmetic surgery is only possible for Tongan *leiti* living overseas, they are also subjecting themselves to the artifice. Greater freedom for bodily change has raised both the tolerance and the risk of self-harm without any guarantee that the changes made to enhance sexiness may not in fact destroy or disfigure. The chimera that beauty will increase sexiness has gained an allure born out of the trend towards 'plastic sexuality' (Giddens 1993), where a sexy body has become an end in itself rather than a means to generating sustainable social outcomes.

Bodily aesthetics and their performance may combine with sex acts to define sexual beauty. In performing particular sex acts, masculine and feminine bodies are made in the relationship between 'passive' and 'active', giver and recipient. The Samoan *fa'afafine*[10] define their femininity by the way that sex is enacted (Schmidt 2003). In adopting the passive 'feminine position *fa'afafine* do not compromise their partner's heterosexuality' (Shore 1981: 210). They also parade their style in beauty pageants to promote identity politics as well as to entertain. Cosmetic surgery, female dress and homosexual preferences also underscore the transgendered prostitute life of the Brazilian *travestis*. However, unlike *fa'afafine*, in modifying their bodies to be essentially feminine they do not consider themselves to be women. The *travesti* life is not a pretty choice but one in which violence and abuse are rife (Kulick 1996), as we explore in Chapter 7. In these and other examples – such as the *waria* of Indonesia (Boellstorff 2005), *kathoey* of Thailand (Jackson and Sullivan 1999; Totman 2003), *'yan daudu* of Nigeria (Gaudio 1994) and *hijra* of India (Nanda 1990) – which all have categories of biological males who dress and act as women and who are attracted to straight men, notions of beauty and the ways in which attraction is performed cannot be thought of as equivalent to those of Western homosexuals. They are quite distinct from the Western notion of drag queens, who, although they may perform sexual acts with a man, do not view themselves as women and therefore portray a particular kind of femininity (see Moore 2005). In addition, some of these transgendered people emphatically distinguish themselves from other kinds of homosexuals within their own cultures.

CONCLUSION

In contrast to the West, in which individual freedom of choice underpins body modifications for sexual enhancement, strict controls characterize some cultures that depend upon body modifications for reproductive or marital success, while other cultures defy any singular correlation between beauty, cosmetic surgery and sex acts. As we have seen in indigenous societies, such as those of Tonga and Samoa, body rituals of shaving, piercing, hair cutting and tattooing control cultural perceptions of sexual chastity and promiscuity. Ritual displays of penis sheathing in West Sepik which stands for body parts may enable men to assert their masculinity and rights to a wife. However, as we have shown, where one body part 'repeats' or stands for other parts, sexual connotations may be ambiguous or contradictory when viewed in cross-cultural contexts. For example, Leach (1958) argues that cross-culturally the head represents the penis and head hair semen, while Obeyesekere (1984: 35) has equated head hair with penises since Sri Lankans characterize the matted locks of Sinhalese female ascetics as penis-like 'buds of flesh' and 'tender fleshy growths'. As advances in cosmetic surgery occur and global ideals of 'sexiness' expand, they continue to impact upon indigenous orthodoxies that mediate how sex is displayed and valued on the body, further challenging what constitutes beauty and sex in these cultures.

NOTES

1. While biological arguments about sexual differences in the workplace have long been refuted in feminist scholarship, beauty seems to have replaced biology in debates about how status and sexual difference are marked.

2. Gay y Blasco (1999: 99) identifies the *honra* with the Bartholin's Glands and suggests that because these glands have no role in the popular (as opposed to scientific) Western representations of female biology on which anthropological models so heavily rely, they are not part of these models. While the *honra* defines a Gitano woman as a woman, this is not the case popularly in English or among the non-Gypsy Spanish.

3. Comment from *Sex on Film*, BBC2, October 2006.

4. Similarly, in Hawaiian *mele* (songs) the genitals were eulogized for members of the aristocracy (Sahlins 1985: 15–17).

5. Mageo (1994: 428) notes that as Samoans consider white skin to be beautiful, this is praised in the song through the term *mulipaepae* referring to 'white ass', although the spelling of the word actually translates as 'dispersed ass', or other nonsensical phrases.

6. Footbinding is said to have started in the upper classes in the palaces and courts, fanning downwards to the middle and lower classes and giving daughters greater marital capital.

7. For an overview of some key theories on substance relations, see Carsten (2004: 109–35).

8. A view long shared by some in the West and based on biblical accounts of Onan's fate when he failed to fulfil his leviratic responsibilities. However, Mars (1984: 435–6) argues that Onan's 'crime' was not masturbation, nor indeed *coitus interruptus* as Pitt-Rivers (1977: 169) suggested, but murder.

9. Similarly, on the French Polynesian island of Moahi, female tattooing in the popliteal space on the inner part of the elbow (*amo'a*) mirrors the tattooing of female Samoan popliteal areas (*malu*) behind the knee. Gell (1993: 141) argues that both are analogous to the genital area and its sacred status.

10. *Fa'afafine* are men who take on women's roles; although they traditionally married women, they no longer do so and are considered by Samoans to be feminine boys seeking intercourse with masculine men.

3 DANCING DESIRES

Whatever else can be said about sex, it cannot be called a dignified performance

(Helen Lawrenson 1904–82)

This chapter examines the relationship of sex to desire as expressed in various kinds of bodily display and sex acts. We ask what kinds of experiences are sexual desires, passionate love and eroticism and how are they evoked, represented, enacted and interpreted around the world. We take the notion of performance to incorporate theatrical, staged and ritual contexts as well as the everyday and consider how sex acts embody meaning and desire in cultural performance. Analyzing how desire is related to sex in the history of the 'sensual revolution' (Howes 2005: 4), we illustrate how the senses and emotions are mutually constitutive of social, political and religious processes that circumscribe sexual practices and sexual relationships. We reflect upon why sex is more than just *one* thing and more than simply *one* aspect of a single body. Instead of a single body, we view sex and its expressions as part of 'a multiple body' that involves 'the social and the physical' (Douglas 1973) and 'the body politic' (Scheper-Hughes and Lock 1987), encompassed by individual desires and social, political and ritual constraints. The chapter begins by exploring how sound, music and dance variously shape sexual meanings and emotions in ritual display. These modes of performativity are then shown to be related to everyday sexual behaviours, raising questions about how intimacy, passion and desire are embodied and experienced cross-culturally.

SEX AND MOVEMENT

Since the 1960s symbolic approaches to sex and its substances have preoccupied anthropologists, many of whom emphasized physical and spiritual dichotomies between purity and pollution. However, understanding erotically sensuous experiences intersubjectively is a more recent approach, stemming partly from the reflexive turn in anthropology that made gazing at our own navels, as much as those of others, analytically acceptable and partly from the 'sensual revolution' in the humanities and social sciences (Howes 2005: 4). Sexual aesthetics were not only written on the body through scarification and tattooing amongst other means, as we have seen, but also expressed in sexual performance. Scholars have long recognized the relationship between sex, movement and display in ritual and other kinds of performance, initially in studies of kinesics and proxsemics (see Reed 1998 for an overview). For example, Birdwhistell (1970: 184, cited in Harrigan 2008: 153) stressed the need for 'context analysis' of the structures of body kinemes and kinemorphs, and he identified 'courtship readiness' by 'high muscle tonus' and 'preening actions'. Anthropologists went on to explore how seductive and erotic powers could be understood through symbolic movement systems (Blacking 1977; Spencer 1985). John Blacking analyzed the body as a complex nexus of biology, involving the brain and nervous system, cognition and emotion. For him, sex was 'a learnt activity of the mind' and terms like 'falling in love' referred to a higher plane of consciousness that entailed more than physiological attraction. He noted:

> Love is most rapturous when it transcends the obviously sexual, when genital arousal subsides and gives way to a more general awareness of the whole body, and bodies are carried away in a counterpoint of movement, of which actual coitus is but one phase. (Blacking 1977: 7)

Blacking considered music and dance to be fundamental vehicles for this transcendence, but his recognition of the connection between sex, music and movement had been pre-empted fifty years earlier by Havelock Ellis (1923: 43–4), who noted the relationship between kissing and dancing in *The Dance of Life*: '[Dancing] has an equally intimate association with love… It is a process of courtship and, even more than that, it is a novitiate for love, and a novitiate which was found to be an admirable training for love.' The French avant-garde poet Philippe Soupault (1928: 93–4) made a similar point in 1928 when he remarked that: 'There is no reason to deny the fact that dance, in many cases, exerts a sexual influence, if we dare to express it this way. Said differently, the art of dance is the most erotic of all arts.' These two early writers speak as if the body is natural and its performance inevitably stirs a sensual or sexual response in the viewer. Indeed, sex and sexuality are intimately bound up in movement and dance and thus it is very difficult to separate sexuality from moving (Adair 1992). This fusion is further reflected in a broader problem of the relationship between language, dance and desire (Archetti 1999; Blacking 1985; Hanna 1987; Polhemus 1993).

Other scholars have approached the analysis of desire by asking how sexual desire differs from passionate love or romantic love; what the fundamentals of universal and biological intimacy are (Jankowiak 1995, 2008); and how socio-cultural factors influence distinctions of intimacy (Lindholm 2001). Deconstructing passionate love as separate from sexual desire has involved teasing out their psychophysiological characteristics; passionate love has been defined as intense, erotic, lasting sexual attraction, whilst sexual desire entails the fulfilment of sexual gratification with heightened physical pleasure (Jankowiak 2008: 11, 13). Various terminologies have been employed to capture their different cultural manifestations, such as 'deerotic', where public sexual expressions are frowned upon, 'the polyerotic', where men and women deliberately use sexual teasing and joking but must suppress physical shows of affection, and the 'uniromantic', where an aesthetics of love is promoted as the highest ideal (Jankowiak 2008: 25). However, desire and passionate love are mutually enhancing urges and all forms and performances of sexual display are rooted in and related to the need to control these potential expressions of eroticism appropriately. The possibility of unregulated sexual urges being unleashed poses a threat to various levels of social order. As we shall see, the focus of anthropologists analyzing music, dance, ritual, carnival and other contexts for sexual display has changed to take account of the interpersonal and emotional dynamics of communicating sexual desires in sounds, rhythms and movements cross-culturally. Patterns of social interaction and their performance in music and dance, along with extra-musical factors such as social expectation, institutional pressure, the sexual politics of ritual, the carnivalesque and fantasies of sexual repression, all play a part in determining what constitutes sexual desire, passion and romance.

SENSING SEX

In order to understand the theoretical perspectives on passion and desire in performance, we offer an overview of how the senses have been viewed in relation to sex and emotion. The legacy of the European hierarchy of the senses has been influenced by the Cartesian dualism of mind and body, often framed in male/female terms that related to contrasting poles of rationalism and emotionality. This dichotomizing of intellect and emotion has been viewed as being largely responsible for why men and women adopted their particular sex-segregated roles. Classen (2005: 70) explains how men's sensibilities were thought to be superior to women's as they were based on sight and hearing, while women's were associated with touch, taste and smell, and being essentially feminine in nature these were placed at the lower end of the sensory spectrum. 'The hegemony of the visual' (Levin 1993) in European societies meant that men could be empowered by God and nature to see and oversee the world in a masculinization of the senses that allowed them to justify their place in the workforce, while women were firmly relegated to the domestic tasks of cooking, cleaning, sewing and nurturing. Whilst men controlled the rational order of things through the male gaze and to a lesser extent hearing, women had the potential to disrupt that order by the power of touch that could entice men to sin. 'So fearful were the Christian monks of the corrupting powers of female sensuality that they even fled the touch of their mothers' (Classen 2005: 72). According to Suzanne Frayser (1985: 194), touch is central to foreplay in most human societies and features in all ten of the top ten methods of stimulating a sexual partner, while vision, hearing and smell show greater cross-cultural variability in their use, functioning as secondary stimulants that 'add spice' to the proceedings.

The European sensual hierarchy is only one form of ordering sexual difference and contemporary theorists now recognize that different senses may be highlighted within particular cultural logics (Sacks 2005); that intersensoriality permits the elements of sensory awareness to be interconnected in different ways (Kondo 2005); and that the correlation of the senses with elements of the social order may reveal religious, political and gendered preferences (Classen 2005; Drobnick 2005; Mazzio 2005). In many cultures tasting and smelling are systems of knowing that involve sexual connotations, as both are conduits of the intimacy of shared substance (Corbin 2006; Pinard 1991; Schechner 2001; Stoller 1989). For example, Tuzin (2006: 65) describes how, after an Ilahitan Arapesh honeymoon period, a groom cuts his penis and the blood is eaten by the bride so that she will be faithful and the scent will be recognized by her husband's ancestral yams. The art of seduction through the nose and taste buds is often closely related to sexual performance, although references to sexual pleasures or distastes raised by smell and flavour are cited infrequently in music and dance studies.[1] Perhaps because smell is 'pervasive, invisible, capable of threatening and a vehicle of contagion' (Millar 2005: 342), smells have tended to be relatively overlooked in performance analysis in comparison with visual and tactile aspects that are identifiable, localizable and relatively direct. Anthropologists, however, have examined how cooking and sex bring together the sensuousness of taste, smell and lovemaking in which competence and capability are reflected back upon each domain, influencing male and female sexual power in different ways (Arnfred 2007; for a classic statement on the linguistic correspondence between sex and eating, see Leach 1972: 212–15). In many cultures the taste and smell of eating are associated with sex; the nose is associated with the penis and the mouth is symbolic of the vagina, making essential bodily activities such as eating and preparing food sexual and erotic pleasures of the palate and bodily desire. In Amazonia, the Mehinaku say that the act of grinding manioc is a performance of sexual intercourse: as the 'woman grinds manioc, she is having sex with the manioc tubers. The tuber is a symbol for the penis, and the thorn board is a symbol for the vagina. She is scraping the penis against her vagina' (Gregor 1985: 82). In the act of preparing manioc, the sounds of a woman's breathing, her seated position and the rhythm of the scraping are all performative gestures associated with sexual intercourse. References to women who are sexually desirable are often phrased along a scale of taste or edibility, for example from the flavourless (*mana*) to the delicious (*awarintya*) (Gregor 1985: 84), or, as a Brazilian would say: 'You analyze sexual pleasure like you analyze a good *feijoada* (black bean stew) (José)' (Parker 1991: 116). Elsewhere, erotic performance in same-sex relations has also been mediated by food. Evans-Pritchard (1970: 1432) tells how wives of Azande kings used to take female lovers who would pleasure one another using manioc, banana or sweet potato fashioned as a circumcised penis.

SOUNDS OF SEXUAL DESIRE AND THEIR INSTRUMENTS

Of course, taste and smell along with the other senses can be disruptive, threatening, destabilizing or polluting, and their effects are often controlled through ritual. Ritual serves to bridge the relationship between the biological individual and the social collectivity (Bloch and Parry 1982) and ritual performance balances male and female sexual aspects of life by containing pollution and shaping the sensory effects of menstruation, pregnancy, sexual intercourse and childbirth. The sensory evocation of sexual action and reproduction is embodied in onomatopoeic metaphors, patterns and processes of ritual music and dance. There are numerous examples around the world of the ways in which instruments carry sexual meanings due to their symbolic shapes, the processes of musical production and the way they are played (see Doubleday 2008 for an extensive review); just a few are explored here. Instruments are variously associated with male and female sexual powers, but these are not universal as gender roles of instrumentalists may be inverted in some cultures. For example, in Albania one 'sworn virgin' (biological females who are recognized socially as men and adopt male gender roles, but abstain from sex), Selman, has the status of a man because she upholds the law, which allows her to play two instruments reserved for men, the *fyell* (a kind of flute) and the *lahutë* (stringed instrument) (Young 2000: 86).

The sexual connotations of instruments operate in many different and ambiguous ways. Flutes or long conically shaped drone instruments are amongst the instruments that most visibly suggest phallic imagery. These and others, such as mouth resonators, may be attributed magical sonic properties that arouse desire or relate to sexual inter-course and reproduction. When played in rituals and accompanied by dance, they may reveal sexual meanings to neophytes. Speaking of the Domba dance in which Venda girls 'learnt the laws' (*uguda milayo*) of childbirth, marriage and motherhood, Blacking (1985: 75) tells how the circling movements of dancers around a fire enclosed a space akin to the womb and, when combined with music, they 'symbolized an act of love. The ashes of the fire symbolized the semen that was said to build up the foetus in the womb and the bass drum represented [the heartbeat] of the unborn baby' (Blacking 1985: 75). Through repeating the dance and moving to the sound of a drum a baby would be symbolically created and born in the initiation.

Musical sounds may be combined with instrumental shapes to embody masculine or feminine sexual traits. James Leach (2002: 711) explains that the Nekgini-speaking people of the Rai Coast of Papua New Guinea refer to the *garamut* or slit-gong as a man because it has a face and sexual organs when it is decorated. The drum has a hole bored at one end, where a rounded protuberance has been carved. A rope is pushed through the hole in order to pull it along. Above the hole a design is carved into the 'nose of the drum' which is shaped like 'the end of a man's torso, and the fruit hanging beneath it are likened to genitalia' (Leach 2002: 724). In the perception of the instrument as sexually male, it becomes not just an instrument of status and male pride but also an item of commodity exchange in one direction for women in cross-cousin marriage exchange and as wealth in the other direction.

Since permission for men and women to play instruments depends upon the impact of the sound in relation to the instruments' ritual and social significance, the right to play and the right to hear certain music may be restricted for women and children. One of the most widely used instruments around the world is a mouth harp, and in Papua New Guinea the *susap* mouth harp is played by plucking a flexible tongue that is cut into a frame to produce a twangy timbre. The distinctive metallic 'boing' is similar to a person speaking through an electronic voice modulator. The steady plucking creates a vibration whose sound is altered by changing the size and shape of the vocal tract and oral cavity. Whilst being an instrument of entertainment, it is also used in traditional courting rituals to seduce women, as the sound is said to be magical and the instrument itself possesses 'love-controlling magic' (Miller and Shahriari 2006: 83). In some parts of Papua New Guinea, the magical effects of instrumental sounds in procuring women and increasing male fertility and power have meant that secret cults have grown up around the sounds and shapes of particular instruments, based upon their sexual meanings. For example, fringe Angan peoples in the southern Eastern Highlands, who include the Baruya and the Sambia, use a secret ensemble of end-blown flutes with the far end closed. Men play them in pairs as they rarely produce more than one note, and they are associated with male–male sexual activity (Herdt 1981). The taboo on women and children viewing Sambian homosexual activity extends to the flutes, which embody the phallic activities of the men.

While flutes may be played by men and women in secular contexts in some parts of Papua New Guinea, those attributed male or female sexual characteristics are subject to both visual and aural control. The dangers of seeing, hearing and touching the instruments are enough to bring strict sanctions and punishments for those who breach the rules. Sexuality is integral to the performance of flutes in Sepik societies. Nancy Lutkehaus (1998: 245) reports how the Manam, who live along the mouth of the Sepik River, used to have secret male rituals around the performance of flutes that were between 1.5 and 1.8 metres long. While these practices no longer exist, they still play flutes in pairs, with one being a decimeter shorter than the other. The shorter flute is considered to be female and the longer one male, producing a lower pitch. Musical performance with the flutes involves the imitation of sexual engagement as the male flute takes the lead and the female flute (as men enjoy saying) follows. Men describe the behaviour of the performers as being like sexual intercourse as they stand facing one another, their bodies moving with the rhythm of heavy breathing (Lutkehaus 1995).

The performative associations of the flutes with sexuality are derived from myths that describe why men have control over them. Amongst the Manam, women were said to have discovered the flutes, which only they could play. However, they became so distracted by them that they began to neglect their domestic tasks and their husbands became suspicious of their activities. When the men found out the reason for their wives' neglect, they stole the flutes and, as punishment, women decreed that men would have to undergo painful initiation to learn to play them (Lutkehaus 1998: 246). The symbolic association of the flutes with the pain of childbirth is indicated here, as the men of Wogeo, who share the same flute-origin myth as the Manam, say: 'men play flutes, women make babies' (Hogbin 1970, cited in Lutkehaus 1998: 246). In these sex-segregated social roles, it becomes evident how dichotomous correlations of men as bearers of culture and women as nurturers of children have been derived. Yet, the sexual connotations of the same instruments do not correspond across cultures. In

Vanuatu, bamboo aerophones are ubiquitous and include 'a two-node centrally blown instrument' that men joke about as a 'bamboo to satisfy two women at once' (Crowe 1998: 693). Ritual performance is key to the mediation of sex acts and desires that would be considered otherwise inappropriate in daily life.

MASKING EROTICISM IN DANCE AND MUSIC

Ritual disguise and masquerade allow sexual expression to be flaunted whilst providing cover for the dancer, and these expressions are about displaying sexual prowess at the same time as referring to the natural world and to transitional periods. Speaking of the *ida* ritual in the Umeda village in Papua New Guinea, Alfred Gell (1975: 232–4) explains that certain organic processes are ritually emphasized through sexual innuendo and expression, especially in the explicit or evocative use of the genitals in dance. As we saw in the last chapter, all of the male dancers draw attention to their genitalia via a penis gourd. This makes a sharp clicking sound as it strikes a belt strung with seeds that hangs around the dancers' abdomens as they leap about and the penis gourd flies through the air. This 'orgiastic style' is adopted by the Cassowary, Sago and, to a lesser extent, the Fish dancers, in which there is an interplay between personal and social growth and the cosmic order to create a 'labour' of cosmic rebirth (Gell 1975: *passim*).

In his reanalysis of Gell's ethnography, Richard Werbner (1989: 150) describes how the first act images delivery, 'with a novice passing through his mother's brothers' legs', and then the sequence of reproduction takes place in three acts of copulation, gestation and finally parturition. Through the masks, sexual ambiguities and plays upon categories are made possible. Anatomical regions of the dancers' bodies – head, arms, penis/pelvis and torso – are broken down into experiential modes and characters that each relate to eating, shooting, copulating and killing in the dances of the Fish, Arrows, Cassowaries and Mud-Men respectively. Ambiguities of meaning are captured in these actions, as a single portmanteau-verb, *tadv*, refers to the entire range of sexual, aggressive and gutatory experience (Gell 1975: 116). The Cassowary dancers begin their erotic displays of copulation in front of women followed by a senior male Sago dancer, who is the epitome of release and must undergo ordeals that relate to the ejaculation of jelly/semen. Gell regards the Cassowary as a threat to the boundaries between nature and culture, because it embodies both male and female qualities in the dance and in the mask:

> Cassowary is a hunted hero; he dances at the opening of the festival's masquerade, and is its most prestigious character. Simulating copulation for as much as eight hours at a time, with an elongated penis gourd, Cassowary is a figure of enormous, sustained virility and erotic fulfilment; he lets himself go and come, with orgiastic abandonment. His heavy mask, a tree, is female and 'pregnant'. (Gell 1975: 296)

However, Werbner (1984, 1989) argues that Gell overlooked a significant aspect of the *ida* ritual by dismissing the Mud-Men clowns as no more than 'comic relief' (Gell 1975: 281) and ignoring the fact that the clowns conceal the truth about sexuality that is hidden from women. He argues that the clowns are 'anti-types' representing the perverse, taboo and boundary-crossing elements of sexuality that threaten the cosmic order. One of the characters of the Mud-Men clowns, the father's sister, is subversive, 'a copulator who is still a hunter, a patrikinswoman not yet a matrikinswoman' (Werbner 1984: 283, 284). This ambiguity is embodied in the dance where the penis is bound and therefore cannot become potent. Another character among the Mud-Men, the Ogre, represents this lack of reproductive capacity, in contrast to the Cassowary who is the 'sexually fulfilled mature hero' (Werbner 1984: 284).

In many cultures, masking the clown or the fool allows performers to confound sexual norms by emphasizing sexually erotic movements through hip rotations and pelvic thrusts. In the first *mukanda* institution of boys' initiation and circumcision, which occurs throughout Central Africa, boys learn basic dance movements that will serve them in later *mukanda* masked rituals. The masks are associated with particular dance patterns and behaviour. Kubik (1977: 272) notes that in 'the dance of the comic mask called Chileya (the fool), *mutenya* is a rotating pelvis motion with sexual meaning, and *kátonda* the name for jerky hip thrusts' that parody the pelvic motion of female dancing in boys' attempts to be deliberately sexually provocative. This masked dance context allows boys to parody women, while elsewhere women make fun of their own forms of erotic movement. In Senegal, women's provocative dancing may enable them to gain confidence through the juxtaposition and transformation of emotions. Analyzing the women's *sabar* dance in Dakar, Hélène Neveu-Kringelbach (2007: 260–3) argues that dancing enables women to be less restrained and express sexual emotions such as 'strength', 'sexual confidence' and 'togetherness', along with 'jealousy', 'fear of gossip' and 'social exclusion', more freely. Some women 'playfully lift their skirt, revealing their underwear and, in a few cases, the full extent of their female anatomy', which, a friend explained to her, went with the Senegalese saying 'the bigger the better'! Similar teasing was reported in Ribáuè, Mozambique, on the eve of a wedding, where two women danced naked in a circle, grabbing each other with sexual movements and feigning intercourse from front and back whilst dancing, as others rolled around on the floor naked (Arnfred 2007: 155). The power of sex to invert the moral order has long been a catalyst for its ritual containment. In other parts of the world, such as among the Yap of Micronesia, songs that tell of the sexual inadequacies of the opposite sex are accompanied by erotic dances, *kuziol* (women's version) and *gasalaew* (men's version), which suggest coital positions and techniques (Marshall-Dean 1998: 733).

Where masks are not used, sex in performance can be confrontational – a means of challenging the status quo, demonstrating aggressive displays to outsiders and provoking an invitation to war. Traditionally in Māori *haka*, men would have challenged one another through vigorous war dances in an effort to boost morale and frighten enemies, and the *haka* is still used as a ceremonial dance of confrontation and challenge. Bolwell and Kaa (1998: 948–9) note that some of the gestures are obscene, such as the action of a fist, which is usually to do with the phallus:

When you wave that at people you're making a statement about the anger and the bitterness you feel. In many dances where people are making this angry kind of statement, they frequently gesture, talking about the males to the genital area, and you know, the pelvis sort of does a rotation, and they hoist their hips up.

As some *haka* hold sexually explicit references to intercourse, their composition is supposedly taboo for women, although there are exceptions. One *haka* about the penis in motion is thought to have been written by a woman because she understood its movement as the recipient of it (Bolwell and Kaa 1998: 950). With the rise of new public arenas for *haka* performances, sexually provocative gestures and references that would have caused offence were reinterpreted rather than altering the actual movements.

In other cultures, ambiguities of interpretation are key to understanding sexual meanings in display, which operate along a continuum of restriction to openness (Morphy 1990). At one end, sexual display is confined to private ceremonial access and at the other sexual meanings may be ambiguously encoded through metaphor. For example, in some male-only rituals in Aboriginal Australia, sexually suggestive movements accentuating the hips, buttocks and genitalia may be accompanied by phallic objects to affirm the fertility of the physical and cosmic order. Where restrictions are placed upon sexual referents in public, they may be encoded in metaphor in song or alluded to by pushing the boundaries of dance. Amongst Yolngu of north-east Arnhem Land, 'movement motifs' performed in song and dance suggest sexual intercourse, birth, marriage and death through waters bubbling, mixing and swirling, sung in specialized esoteric ritual language, naming people and clans coming together (Magowan 2007: 136–9). Dancers who are able to perform with great energy, vigour and sharpness of movement often receive acclaim as well as whoops of laughter and delight at the suggestiveness of the underlying sexual connotations of the dance.

Globalization has provided a catalyst for young people to reposition sexual suggestion in traditional performance contexts, often challenging traditional norms. In Keramas, Indonesia, teenagers have incorporated a sensual movement of the hips known as *goyan Inul* into styled disco dancing after the Dangdut star Daratista. Jonathan McIntosh (2006: 234, 237) tells how young people challenge the boundaries of what is sexually acceptable, as 'the dancers raised their arms above their heads and gyrated their hips while also corkscrewing up and down'. Although such routines were acceptable on stage, these movements would not have been performed freestyle in a village disco.

In what might be termed 'deerotic' cultures (Jankowiak 2008: 25), where the performance of sexual desire and intimacy in public is forbidden, romance is not completely absent. Songs can carry double entendres that may only be understood by people of a certain age or status, and they provide the medium through which romantic and sexual desires are expressed. Amongst the Lahu of the Tibetan Highlands, any sexual contact in public is prohibited, divorce is restricted and severe punishments exist for extramarital or illicit relationships (Du 2008: 108). Love songs offer a bitter-sweet respite from erotic suppression. On the one hand, they are sung by a young man and woman to each other in front of friends as a prelude to marital intimacy, while, on the other hand, lovers in illicit relationships choose to sing love-suicide songs as a pact prior to dying for love, when they will be married in the world of the dead in the highest ideal of intimacy (Du 2008: 109). In many cultures the singing of sensual songs has to be regulated for the threat of moral and social disintegration. As Koskoff (1997: 154–5) has argued in the context of Orthodox and Hasidic Judaism, women's singing is especially dangerous because the voice has illicit sexual qualities that can entice and damage group cohesion. Singing may therefore lead a woman into promiscuity since the voice joins body and sexuality. It is considered that in Lubavitcher society those who perform are engaging degrees of excess beyond their control with the potential to create social harmony or destruction through their music. Similarly, Christian missionary ideals insisted upon sexual propriety and the restraint and eradication of erotic words and movements, the latter being concealed beneath layers of morality, fabric and suppressed emotional display.

SEX AND THE CHURCH: NO 'MONK'EY BUSINESS

Colonial and Christian religious authorities banned songs and dances that referenced sexuality as part of ritual episodes. The dangers of visual and aural sensuality had to be contained so that they did not give rise to lewd and unholy sexual desires and acts. When the American Board of Commissioners for Foreign Missions arrived in the Marshall Islands in 1857 along with whalers, traders and administrators, they banned indigenous attire, dances, drumming and singing and introduced hymn singing along with new, less ebullient songs and dances with mixed choral singing and dances in a circle (Lawson-Burke 1998: 752). Some traditional dances persisted into the late 1800s, such as the one described by the German ethnographer Otto Finsch: 'The girls participating wore a mat ... but in the course of the performance they let this covering fall, and then appeared completely naked. Besides the ... accompaniment of singing and clapping by the women's chorus, [their dancing] ... consisted principally of a vibrating motion of the lower belly and wiggling the buttocks, thus an imitation of coitus in which the motions of the man were also represented' (Finsch 1961 [1893]: 389–90, cited in Lawson-Burke 1998: 752–3). Elsewhere in east Micronesia, the colonial administration banned the parties to which young, unmarried men of one Nauran district would invite Nauran women from another district, and Christian hymns replaced party songs which the youth would start to sing, women facing the men in two rows. Eventually, the women crossed over to the men's row and each woman sat in the lap of the man opposite her; he then placed his arms across her breasts in order to hold her firmly while she swung her arms in accompaniment to the song. Missionaries considered these rituals of sexual affirmation posed a threat to Nauran spiritual well-being. Instead, holy bodies were to be silent, untouched and unseen, in opposition to sensual bodies which were highly visible, audible and available to the touch (Smith 1998: 756).

Similarly, in European societies, religious, patriarchal ideals of chastity and virginity dominated as a result of bourgeois concepts of respectability and purity that sought to protect female sexuality from unwanted advances or encounters with the opposite sex. Where dance practices were regulated, they generally reflected responses to the sexual moralities of the culture. In discussing characterizations of Irish sexuality, Wilson and Donnan (2006: 47) note that conservative and repressive attitudes towards the sexual body were a result of a pervasive religiosity of the rural Irish that endorsed the Catholic Church hierarchy, allowing it to frame both institutional and personal control of sexual mores. As the Catholic Church attempted to exert state-sanctioned ideals to ensure sexual propriety, modes of resistance and subversion were inevitable. Deviations from the ideal led to some religious authorities demonizing dance. In Ireland a priest in West Cork wrote in 1670: 'Women dancers are the cause of many evils because ... the devil compels them to gather on holidays for dancing, a thing which leads them to bad thoughts and evil actions' (Whelan 2000: 15). Dances that involved physical contact would come under the closest scrutiny. Waltzes and polkas were condemned by Pope Pius IX in 1864 because of the intimacy, entertainment and gaiety involved, leading bishops of Ireland to decree in 1875 that foreign dances in particular were 'occasions of sin' (Whelan 2000: 15). As Reed (1998: 517) notes, 'dance opponents cast women as either "pure and pious" – in need of protection from dance – or "fallen and sinful", and therefore either victims or perpetrators of the evils of dance'.

When movement combined with touch, it was seen to heighten the potential for lewdness to occur. As sexual energy could be conveyed by touch, the Church felt it was a threat to purity and the protection of people's morals. Yet, Helena Wulff (2007) notes that in some cases it was not the *act* of touching in dance that was problematic but the very possibility that dance might permit touch to occur, which caused objectors to voice their disapproval. Citing a statement issued to all Free Presbyterian churches in Northern Ireland in April 2001, the Reverend Ian Paisley, leader of the Democratic Unionist Party, remarked: 'Line dancing is as sinful as any other type of dancing, with its sexual gestures and touching' – despite the fact that line dancing is virtually devoid of body contact with other dancers (Wulff 2007: 131). In an explanation of this sensual panic, choreographer Michael Keegan-Dolan told Wulff that the Irish had a 'fear of touch' and a 'lack of sexuality' that comes across in how Irish people move, which he associates with the Catholic Church (Wulff 2007: 47). So as formality and precision marked the nature of Irish dance, they also served to build up the moral character of the nation (Wulff 2003: 180) and act as markers for the negotiation of sexuality and regulation of eroticism.

REPRESSING AND PROVOKING SEXUAL DESIRE

Unlike Irish Catholicism, the Eastern Orthodox Church did not teach that dancing was essentially sinful, although there were holy days and times of mourning when people would refrain from dancing. Regulating dance and movement was a means of controlling sexual desire and promoting sexual purity, but in practice such regulation could lead to illicit or ambiguous expressions of sexuality. For example, in nineteenth-century ballet the paradox between the virgin and the temptress was embodied in the titillating idea of an unattainable sylph being danced by a real woman who might agree to a sexual liaison, and it has since been a common theme in dance forms in the West (Adair 1992: 96). This relationship between pure and wanton female sexuality is danced out in various parts of Europe. Within the masculine-dominated world of Greek officialdom, feminine practices were subjugated to masculine national discourses. Dance was frowned upon only if it was performed with the intention of causing someone to sin (Shand 1998: 129). Angela Shand (1998) argues that the dualistic nature of Greek identity has been partially responsible for sexual ambiguities in dance. Following the rise of Hellenism in Western Europe, modern Greeks were termed 'ancestral Europeans and this was a period during which anything to do with the East was viewed as corrupt' (Herzfeld 1987: 20; Shand 1998: 130). Eastern elements of folk songs, dances and language within Greek traditions had to be reinterpreted in Western Hellenic terms, for example 'Turkish coffee' became 'Greek coffee' (Shand 1998: 130), yet cross-overs persisted. One of these, the Greek dance *tsifte-teli* with its characteristic rhythms, was derived from Turkish belly dance. Shand (1998: 127–30) has argued that the dance is problematic for its unrestrained celebration of the female form, its frivolity, expressions of enjoyment and potential invitation to sin, causing consternation about its role within Greek national discourse. Characteristics of the East primarily associated with frivolity, the female body and enticing sexuality contrasted with the serious, virtuous public male (Western) intellect (Kazantzakis 1965: 167) and threatened the social order. This sexual dichotomy endured in spite of the fact that male displays of unrestrained physicality and sexuality, including gyrations of the pelvis in folk and *rebetika* dances, were acceptable modes of display for Greek men (Cowan 1990).

However, dancing for women can be a dangerous business. In her research in the northern Greek provincial town of Sohos, Cowan explains how the concept of the virgin, as part of male rights over women, is central to the mediation of social relations. Even though premarital sexual relations were not uncommon for Sohoian girls, they did not confess this to their fiancés as they were afraid of generating an angry response. The need for a woman to conceal the truth about her sexual past requires the covering up of emotions in order to gain acceptance. Yet, such sexual subversion rests uneasily in some contexts where women are encouraged to 'make a spectacle' of themselves in dance (Cowan 1990: 190). In dance-events, the female individual 'as celebrant and dancer is invited to act in ways she would not in public contexts of everyday life and is encouraged to make a display of her beauty, energy, skill, sensuality and even seductiveness' (see Caraveli 1982: 142–3). In doing so, Sohoian women put themselves in a vulnerable position, for their virginity becomes threatened by the potential sexuality of the temptress and the wanton woman. If they go too far in the dance, they may be criticized and looked upon with suspicion, since the female sexual body offers a fine line between 'good or bad sexuality' (Cowan 1990: 190). Ironically, flirtation, energy, the display of beauty and even subtle seduction are acknowledged and valued aspects of female performance in these events, especially so for unmarried girls to be noticed by potential husbands (Cowan 1990: 228). Female sexuality, then, teeters on the boundary between acceptable and unacceptable behaviour, defining who a woman is and how she is perceived.

The language used to describe such dance movements is pregnant with ambiguous overtones of possible scorn or reprimand as much as praise and adulation. The term *aerata*, meaning 'confidence', can also mean 'effrontery', impudence and a kind of erotic boldness, while *tharros*, meaning courage, can euphemistically suggest brazenness, as can a girl who is *petathi*, leaping or lively, which also alludes to her being sexually uncontrollable (Cowan 1990: 200). Women who are able to improvise in the dance understand how to draw attention to themselves by 'embellishing' or 'tricking' (*kolpa*) in movement, a term that also refers to 'seductive tricks' (Cowan 1990: 200). Such ambivalence in language and behaviour means that the nature of female personhood is fused with female form as a potentially threatening sexual entity. Thus, the physicality of Sohoian female sexuality extends outwards from the body to influence the social world impacting upon her identity and how others come to value and respect her. Movement is therefore significant because it impacts upon the values of society; it creates a space for sexuality as being potentially harmful and yet, paradoxically, it contains the potential to transform social relations for the enhancement of social well-being. Dance is not merely a pastime of sexually entertaining advance and retreat; it challenges patriarchal traditions and requires men to act and react in relation to how female sexuality comes to reflect upon the performer and how its meaning is controlled. Even when Sohoian men dance, whether or not with explicit sexual movements either sincerely, in parody or in irony, they are negotiating power and prestige amongst themselves, no matter 'whether they demonstrate bodily control or the stylized performance of its absence (as in somatic representations of intoxication)' (Cowan 1990: 189).

Sexual exoticism has taken many forms, being especially prevalent in dances of Eastern origin analyzed in discourses of Orientalism and imperialism (Koritz 1997; Strong 1998). In Saudi Arabia, belly dancing is used as a competitive forum in which women display their wealth, social status and sexual desirability to each other (Deaver 1978) and, thus, women can use the ambivalences of the dance to their own ends. Similarly in Iran, Shay (1995) has shown how *bazi-ha-ye nameyeshi*, a women's theatrical dance-play, is a site of erotic and coarse display for other women but also encapsulates a social critique of male domination of a patriarchal system in which women gain value and status primarily through their husbands. Elsewhere, Boddy (1988: 6, 22) illustrates how women become entranced through possession spirits that manifest in various roles such as those of kings, slaves, male homosexuals or prostitutes, displaying wanton behaviours and making the women dance about wildly. This behaviour is the antithesis of the sexually pure dance of the unmarried women at wedding parties who perform the 'pigeon dance'. Flaunting sexuality through spirit possession allows women the freedom to resist normative expressions of sexuality, test the limits of female sexuality and affirm their autonomy amongst themselves, albeit only temporarily.

In Jharkhand, India, *nacnīs* (sexually active women whose behaviour is beyond the control of near kin) are allowed to flaunt their sexuality in public by dancing a celebration of sexual freedom and romantic devotion that reveres the divine relationship between the god and goddess Radha and Krishna (Babiracki 2004: 38, 39). Embodying the mother goddess, the *nacnīs'* sexually alluring dances are intended to bless their recipients. Babiracki (2004: 39) explains how *nacnīs* may be viewed as prostitutes since their sexual availability is paraded before men, as it is in the case of temple servants such as the *devadāsīs* in other areas. In performance, these dancers merge 'human and divine, mother goddess and sex goddess and male and female into a singular essence of sentiment', creating ambiguous illusions about sexuality that place these women both at the centre of ritual fertility and at the margins of socially acceptable sexuality (Babiracki 2004: 42).

PASSIONS OF SOCIAL DANCING

The threat of unrestrained sexuality is a problem not only in traditional dance contexts but equally for mainstream religions. As we have seen, in some parts of Europe social dancing has been constrained by the Christian church, although it was unable to prevent it taking on independent forms within secular domains. Its arrival in permitted contexts did not necessarily mean social dancing left behind the conservative attitudes that had fashioned earlier taboos. 'Even the waltz, which came to symbolize the very essence of nineteenth century gentility, was denounced by many when it became popular in the first decade of the nineteenth century because of its closed partnering hold' (Cook 1998: 134). Social dances such as ragtime were condemned by critics as 'tough' or 'rough' dancing that was '"indecent" and "vulgar" for the kind of wiggling, shaking, swaying and pivoting motions it permitted and even legitimated as these movements were read as explicitly sexual if not imitative of intercourse' (Cook 1998: 137). Social dancing had the power to induce female passion because of its relationship to courtship, and when senses of touch combined with acts of looking they were considered to arouse intimacy, passion and desire. In contrast, for men, dancing brought with it problems of potential effeminacy and emasculation (Cook 1998: 134), which required a masculinization of dance through the displacement of female sexuality.

One folk dance form in which masculinization was prevalent and which captured the European imagination was flamenco. Emerging from the impoverished social conditions of southern Spain in Andalusia in the mid-1800s, its influence spread across Europe so that by 1860–1900 flamenco was part of a golden age of passion. In fiestas and carnivals, the vibrant and provocative dresses of female dancers have always attracted attention, vying with the power of the men who strive to retain control of the event. Comparing these interactions to bullfighting, William Washabaugh (1998: 15) tells how the dancer

> is the provocateuse, the temptress whose appearance and movements, so obviously
> but crassly reliant on the power of 'nature,' threaten to throw the 'cultured' man off

balance. In the face of such dance, the singer and guitarist (*cantoaro* and *toacaor*) – like the bullfighter facing a bull – reassert their cultural composure by taming the feminine animal force that they confront.

Masculine domination of the woman by 'taming' (*trastear*) her links the parallel spheres of the guitarist's control of song and taming a bull, in each case allowing the man to demonstrate hypermasculinity, but the display does not heighten her status; rather, it increases approval of the male singers in the eyes of male spectators. 'In all these domains, the man becomes the centre of attention and the heroic main-event' (Washabaugh 1998: 16).

Alongside flamenco in Spain, in Britain and America the term 'tango' became a catch-all term for dances such as ragtime that for some suggested questionable morals. Just as flamenco displaced the sexuality of the woman in favour of masculine domination, a similar ambivalence was evident within tango. Jeffrey Tobin (1998: 79, 96) notes that there were two faces of desire in tango: one in which men danced tango with each other in virtuoso displays of steps on street corners and the other where 'male johns and female prostitutes transgressed marital, class and racial boundaries to the rhythm of tango' in Buenos Aires brothels. Sexuality is essentially masculine in the dance, represented by the display of women who mediate masculinity as the 'exhibited signifiers' (Savigliano 1995: 46). Tobin (1998: 91) notes that in 'Lacanian terms, the male lead in tango *has* the phallus while the female follower *is* the phallus'. Women's sexuality is thus displaced onto his desire for her as a phallic representation. Instead, homosociality commands the success of the male dancers in terms of how a woman (*la tanguera*) will submit herself to him on the dance floor, raising his status in the eyes of other men. Tobin (1998: 84, 90) argues that the tango is not about heterosexual love between a woman and her dance partner but rather about the forbidden desires of men watching other men dancing with women which suggest the possibility of repressed homosexuality, since *tangueros* always operate 'across a leaky border that separates the straight and the gay'.

TUTUS AND 'TUT-TUTS': GUARDING SEX IN STAGED AND SOCIAL DANCING

The proliferation of different kinds of social dancing offered new potentialities for dangerous liaisons through which the boundaries between 'good and bad' sexuality could be stretched to the limits. The tights and tutus of ballet that displayed the crotch and legs, with low-cut tops emphasizing the woman's 'to be looked-at-ness' (Mulvey 1975: 418; see also Kaplan 1983), meant that voyeurism became an acceptable part of movement consumerism where displays of kinesthetic pleasure and elegance were deliberately intended for a paying audience. This alternative outlet for eroticism meant that the sexual body was relocated as a site of consumer desire that could encode 'cultures of pleasure' (Featherstone 1982). The consumer body was an essentially passive object of gaze and exchange, objectified in its relations with others (Featherstone 1982: 52).

In ballet, the audience expect to be entertained as voyeurs of the dance. Hanna (1988: 124) explains how the 'ballet girl' was synonymous with prostitution, the term harbouring pejorative overtones until the mid-twentieth century as a ballet dancer was a slave to the stage until a wealthy man fell in love with her and she became his mistress. Women were moulded by men into their image of an aesthetic ideal of beauty, grace and excessive thinness (Gordon 1983: 177) that fulfilled the male fantasy of 'pert-breasted, narrow-hipped virgins being deflowered' (Hanna 1988: 128). In the svelte bodies of the dancers an ideal of female submission was created around suppression of sexuality.

The 'natural' representation of ballerinas as delicate, light, slim and graceful reinforced a stereotypical heterosexual hierarchy of sexual difference, according to which men chased and attempted to conquer and win over women until they were handled like, and became part of, the male anatomy. English (1980: 18, cited in Adair 1992: 78) comments that:

> The ballerina rises from the man's waist, from his crotch, above his shoulder, across his legs. He carries her erect, though her arms may soften the line, her legs remain stiff… He handles her as he would his own penis. Fondly he holds the phallus in his arms, longingly, he looks into his princess' eyes, ecstatically he lifts her, his hands around her long, stiff tube of a body.

English (1980: 19) interprets the male lift of the ballerina as representing orgasm after the masturbatory preparation, and he is not alone. These culturally determined sexual meanings have been discussed in a number of ways. Jill Johnston (1971: 199–200) has argued that the dancer soaring is a soaring phallus that, once erected, must fall (ejaculate), while the ballet 'stretch' or leg extension is 'an unrelieved exercise in phallic erected exhibitionism'. Similarly, it has been argued that the openness of the female crotch in ballet positions indicates a willingness to engage with the dancer rather than being his prey (Siegel 1984: 219). But were female dancers to remain powerless sex objects in the hands and gaze of a male fetish?

With a growing critique of nineteenth-century subjugation of women in the spheres of economics, politics and education, women's voices became increasingly prominent in the workplace, making waves in all areas, including the birth of modern dance. This time women asserted themselves as agents rather than recipients of male desire by 'breaking the rules of the rigidly codified traditional ballet' (Hanna 1988: 132). While the ballet corset had enabled a male dancer to lift his partner, it had prevented him from feeling her flesh (Kunzle 1982: 84). In the new era of women's suffrage and greater sexual freedom in the 1920s, American modern dancers went braless, corsetless and barefoot, enabling 'spectators to see the body – crotches, asses, thighs and breasts – from every possible angle' (Hanna 1988: 133). Thus, the taboos of sexuality on the body were gradually broken down and, far from projecting an image of the sexually passive, virginal sylph, modern dancers fought to gain control of sexual perceptions of female bodies, inviting sexual tension, unbridled passion and open eroticism in their works. By the 1960s the sexual revolution allowed 'stark naked dancers with dangling penises, bobbing breasts and visible pubic hair' (Hanna 1988: 191). On the one hand, Mick Jagger epitomized an era of aggressive sexuality in gyrating, thrusting phallocentric performances with excessive sexual drive, expressed in lyrics such as 'I Can't Get No Satisfaction'. On the other hand, it has been argued that the expression of male power that demanded sexual return from women evidenced in Jagger's performances was in fact tempered by allusions to his own sexual ambivalence. Rock stars and other figures of popular culture thus contributed to a shifting focus in sex debates in the 1970s (Whiteley 1997: 95). From rock musicals such as *Hair* in 1967, with its nude duet to 'Elvis the pelvis', also known for his gyrating pelvic movements, the acts of stage performers soon translated into activities on the dance floor as a means of leisure pursuit rather than as elements of consumerist sexual ideals or moral degeneration.

However, unlike the excesses of dance for public consumption in which sexual openness is carefully staged, some forms of social dancing occupy an ambivalent and liminal space whilst giving the appearance of being tightly controlled. Sex, like gender as Butler (1991: 24) argues, is thus performative rather than a performance 'in the sense that it constitutes as an effect the very subject it appears to express'. In his analysis of ceroc classes, Jonathan Skinner (2003: 16) describes how the grammar, tone and movements of the lessons have clear structure to their teaching which allows a safety valve for the expression of erotic play and sexual desires; as one dancer commented, these were 'nights to act out and act up, to perform, feign illicit passions and create romantic impersonations within a carefully controlled and contrived social matrix'. Yet, an unspoken tension and pleasure seem to remain between the dancers as they 'play to each other' without necessarily revealing the truth of their relationships. The possibilities for flirtation and seduction increase in the bodily intimacies of the salsa context, where 'notions of *being and desire* and *feeling "with demure"* behaviour come into play', although this too is a calculated risk but one which cannot be wholly controlled (Skinner 2008: 69, emphasis in original). Some dancers find the intimacy 'too close and suggestive, too exotic and alien/foreign' (Skinner 2008: 71). As Skinner (2008: 73) notes: 'For Annabel, the salsa is safe sex, whereas for Debbie the salsa could be a prelude to sex.' In comparing ceroc and salsa, it seems sexual desire and passion can only be partially regulated in both contexts, although dancers have a belief in how the conditions of dancing mediate the safety of sexual boundaries whilst offering a potentially seductive and tantalizing mix to participants through opportunities to dance out their desires.

Social dancing may also provide a cover for engaging in erotic relationships within a predefined group. As Kirtsoglou (2004: 2, 7, 14, 153) shows in her work on same-sex dancing, a network of women known as the *parea* drink and dance at a nightspot with live Greek music as a cover for expressing their sexual desires in 'a constant politics of "concealment and display"' (cf. Herzfeld 1987). Their sexual encounters are not intended to be long term and the deliberate shroud of secrecy around their activities, as well as their wish to confound sexual categories, ensures that their engagements do not challenge Greek sexual politics. As the women flirt with one another, they and the community assess performativity on the basis of 'complexity, originality and surprise', which is strengthened and legitimized by the presence of an audience watching a stylized performance (Kirtsoglou 2004: 76; see also Herzfeld 1985). The blurring of public display and private sentiment in this context is a bitter-sweet game that facilitates the empowerment of women at the same time as it recognizes the suffering of being on the margins of culture as a gay woman.

As different forms of popular dancing have gained a foothold through discos and nightclubs, facilitating the sweat and grind of unfamiliar bodies, they have repositioned concepts of public and private space, sexual interaction and sociability, as well as adding to the release of sexual desire and eroticism as disconnected from passionate love. In his analysis of the clubbing scene, Phil Jackson (2004: 123) argues that 'clubs exist at the edge of both the civilizing process and the habitus' in that they are based on 'a desire to be together with people' but with a licence to 'occupy an "uncivilised" body for a night: to grin like a fool; to laugh too loud; to sweat it out on the dance floor; to flirt outrageously; talk well-meaning shite to strangers; feel sexual, carnal and exhilarated'. Here the sexual gaze rules male and female interaction and allows sexual power games to take place. Seeing dance as sex is at its zenith in these hyper-eroticized zones, as fantasy is given permission to have free rein. As one informant told Jackson (2004: 36):

> I love watching women and men dance; I love watching sexy people doing sexy things, I mean actual sex shows are damn boring. I've seen girls dancing and they're turning me on… I'm sitting there thinking… Oh fuck, the things I want to do to your body.

The experience of sex through dancing can be as viscerally intense for some participants as the actual sexual act. Music combines with dance in the club scene to be a sensuously seductive power that has the potential 'to rearrange your internal organs', as one of Jackson's (2004: 27) female informants put it. Thus, Jackson (2004: 126) argues that the attraction of music and dance in clubbing is about how sexual and sensual pleasures are unconsciously stored in emotional memory and are carried as part of the person's response to past and future clubbing experiences. Rather than sex being linked to a moral framework of social expectation, sex in clubbing is about sensual adventures for their own sake. It enables people to experiment sexually in different ways through the intensification of the senses. Jackson (2004: 151–2) cites one informant who told him:

> My man and I sat down and wrote out a list of all the things we'd like to do sexually and included some things we weren't sure about… Having a list and just trusting one another and being really honest about our experiences opens up a whole world… It's like giving myself permission to experiment and I'm finding I'm pushing myself further sexually, just to see how far I can go, how much I can feel. (Female, 28, nine years' experience of clubbing)

As clubbers do not view people or their morality as possessions, so their sexual relationships should be free from the cultural constraints of sexual monogamy and its marital expectations. The rules of sex and dancing in the club scene are those of a hypersocial freedom; they allow clubbers to fulfil socio-sensual experiences through sexual licence as long as no one gets hurt (Jackson 2004: 165). This is also true of the 'circuit parties' in the USA, rave-like events attended principally by gay men and where the dance floor explicitly facilitates sexual play, empowering the homosocial body through open displays of sex and sensuality (Westhaver 2006).

EVERYDAY ENTICEMENTS

Submission and emotional entrapment do not of course have to be played out through dance steps per se, but other more ritualized interactions involving domination and resistance take place in the everyday contexts of sexual or seductive displays at work, on the street and in the home (on sex and power at work, see Hearn and Parkin 1987). In these arenas, flirting – or 'sex without sex' as Zeldin (1995: 103) calls it – is a kind of performance that demands that power is exercised, contained and resisted in an atmosphere of risk-taking that can unsettle either the flirt or the recipient depending on how or whether the flirt is reciprocated. It is possible to distinguish various types of flirting, each with its own rules and contexts, and it can be 'with intent', 'recreational' or 'courtesy flirting' (Fox 2004: 331–4). Flirting can involve a range of seemingly contradictory elements, including the exchange of compliments or mock insults, aggression or tenderness, and humour or teasing. As Kevin Yelvington (1996: 315) shows for a Trinidadian factory, flirting entails 'rhyming performances in licentious play and joking', some of which engage a certain degree of mock aggression in order to establish masculinity and sexual prowess. Young women may be sexually objectified even as they play up to the men and resist their innuendos. Symbolic violence is integral to flirting in this part of the world and may be aligned with the Jamaican dance hall, where 'verbal and sexual skills are often indistinguishable' (Cooper 1993: 142). In India, as in Trinidad, dexterity and confidence with language in flirting are also key to the progression from 'harassment to *tuning* and then to getting a *line*' as young boys and girls in Kerala flirt at 'weddings, festivals, bus-stops, temples, choir practice or college' (Osella and Osella 1998: 193). Boys may try to harass girls verbally and physically by groping or pinching them in crowded public spaces and then initiate contact with an abrupt, aggressive question or demand as a way of '*tuning*', i.e. starting a tentative exchange (Osella and Osella 1998: 193). After flirting with demure glances and verbal duelling, a successful interaction may lead to having a *line* (Osella and Osella 1998: 195). Keralan boys and girls boast about the number of lines they can get, unlike Trinidadian men who only seek fame through multiple flirts (Yelvington 1996: 317; Osella and Osella 1998: 198).

Beyond the factory, carnival time in Trinidad offers unrivalled opportunity for men and women to spar in flirting as well as to show themselves off as sexually available, with images of revellers depicted in sexually provocative poses and dances gyrating their hips (Yelvington 1996: 318), or by engaging in 'wining', a dance that comments upon sexual relations, in which couples rub genitals with one partner pinned against a wall (Miller 1991: 326). This atmosphere of unrestrained revelry contrasts with that of Brazilian carnival, where flirting is juxtaposed with 'hard dancing' by young men who careen off one another in a frenzied aggression that can lead to other kinds of violence, from sexual touching to assault (Lewis 2000: 539). Such excess is constrained within the art of *capoeira*, in which 'singing, drumming and dancing skills are said to make a man a good lover … and tales of virility and sexual conquest are endemic in the *capoeira* world' (Lewis 2000: 546). The ambiguous dynamics of teasing, flirting, sexual play and aggression come together in the Brazilian Portuguese term *sacanagem*, which can refer to either positive or negative transgression, a notion of erotic sensuality that pervades carnival and comes to stand for Brazilianness (Parker 1991: 103).

Whether sexual desire is expressed in the formal arena of traditional ritual or the theatrical stage or the informality of carnival and nightclubs, erotic scripts and degrees of erotic licence encapsulate who is or who wishes to take possession of the object of desire. 'Sexual scripts' are learned and understood as part of everyday life and expressions of desire may be deemed proper, risky or transgressive (see Simon and Gagnon 1999: 37). As we have seen in this chapter, changes in patterns of sexual behaviour have an effect upon how senses of desire are understood and how sexual meanings pertain to the life cycle. Changes in the presentation and patterning of sexual behaviours can impact upon emotional intimacy. Holly Wardlow (2008: 199–200) notes how changing forms of sexual intercourse amongst Huli were considered to pose a threat to fertility, health and marital and emotional well-being. Huli men explained that spouses should only have sex on days 11–14 of the menstrual cycle. Marital sex is a ritual display of force with the man on top, raised on his hands or elbows to minimize contact with his wife's body in a 'dance of conquered resistance' (Wardlow 2008: 197, 206). However, those men who had been influenced by blue movies and magazines and had tried other positions were concerned that they had become weaker physically while their wives became increasingly disrespectful to them. Other men saved sexual experimentation for extramarital relations in what they termed 'style-style' sex (Wardlow 2008: 213). In a society in which desire or pleasure should not be publicly expressed, the main problem with changing traditional sex acts was the danger of encouraging displays of intimacy and emotional intensity that could upset conjugal relations of power. As Jankowiak and Mixson (2008) show, the equilibrium of marital intimacy is also integral to the success of swingers' relationships in American spouse exchange. There are limits to performing sex acts for another person who is outside of the conjugal bond, as one twenty-nine-year-old woman noted: 'We keep our emotions at home and save intimacy for our bedroom. Swinging is strictly sexual gratification' (Jankowiak and Mixson 2008: 253). Standard rules operate in order to maintain emotional distance from exchange partners, as a forty-eight-year-old swinger explained: 'Swinging is sex without a heart.' As in the case of Huli, the marital bond is upheld over the eroticism of the sex acts to avoid emotional disintegration, which happens in other contexts, such as in some open marriages, where sexual desire is uncoupled from passionate love.

CONCLUSION

In considering the relationship between sex and sensual experience as a means of everyday and ritualized performance, it becomes evident that sex is more than simply one aspect of the body circumscribed by signifying systems. Sexual desires may be sounded in the design and form of musical instruments, songs and dances at the same time as they reflect back to participants the boundaries of sensory transgression. In all of the performance contexts examined, the threat of the seducer is recognized as being antithetical to the maintenance of social cohesion. Sexual performance is, however, difficult to control, as we have seen, because of its enticement to sensuality, intimacy and eroticism with the capacity for provocative behaviour and virtuoso display. In each case, we see an ambivalence towards the possibility for a merger between sexual desire and love that must be guided, regulated and appropriately located. Both everyday and ritual performances allow alternative sexual expressions, desires and intimacies to be presented in anti-structure, anti-culture modes of subversion and taboo in order to reaffirm normative sexuality or to challenge the status quo. Thus, the regulation of sexual performance and the performativity of sex in part prevent unwelcome love bonds or sexual matches from developing and at the same time affirm intimacy as the foundation of social connectedness.

NOTES

1. One example from the Pacific discusses the power of smell as a factor in intensifying sexual excitement in dance, where the most potent odour is the musky aromatic leaf worn only by male dancers (Beach 1965: 183–4).

4 EROTIC ECONOMIES

Sex does not like to question itself about what it desires

(Theodore Zeldin 1995: 99)

Sex has always had financial pulling power beyond the marital sheets. The attraction of money for sex means that such encounters have come to be seen as having erotic capital in which profit variously rules over emotion, moral values and productive relationships. Stripped of the relationally binding powers of social obligation and reciprocity, commercial sex invites a Pandora's box of value judgements around autonomy, exploitation and entrapment with regard to human rights as well as individual and national well-being. The state has often been blamed for its heavy-handed regulation of sex industries and censorship, believed by some to deprive people of their freedom of choice in sexual practice and vocation. This kind of regulation assumes a natural dichotomy exists between sex outside of marriage and proper moral conduct confined to marital relationships. This chapter considers why these boundaries are not so clear cut and how the furry lines between sex at home and sex at work merge.

What constitutes 'sex work' is uncovered from the perspective of what men and women believe they are doing when they engage in monetized sexual exchanges. The chapter focuses primarily on three domains in which sex is for sale, local prostitution, the global sex tourism industry and lap and table dancing, and reveals how terms that denote sexual activity in these arenas are highly contested and fought over for their moral, legal and social capital. Sex at home and abroad raises debates around the value of the polluted or pure body as well as the nature of commoditized sexual exchange. Key works on the relationship between sex and tourism have emerged since the 1980s. Prior to this period, the few studies in which tourism-related prostitution is mentioned were particularly uninformative, as 'respectable' students of tourism studies were perhaps unwilling to engage the issue (Cohen 1982). Since then there has been a proliferation of research on both sex tourism and prostitution.

Bauer and McKercher (2003a) argue that tourism is a temporary, transitory phase in which freedom from social, moral and familial constraints allows normative boundaries to be explored and at times transgressed. Tourism is a liminal state that permits and condones erotic exploration, and in some countries it has become synonymous with it. The tourism industry, then, encourages, nurtures and endorses sexual experimentation; some motels offer more than hot chocolate for a good night's sleep, with 'vibrating beds, ceiling mirrors above the bed, X-rated movies, and spa units' (Bauer and McKercher 2003a: xv).

These images of erotic enticement have led some writers to speak of prostitution as a vocation in which sex is an erotic art and prostitutes are mistresses of that art (Truong 1990: 54). They are sex educators and social workers whose roles ensure that prostitution is integral to society even if it is denied. Others speak of prostitution as an effect of being in a patriarchal society in which no distinction can be made between prostitution and other forms of sexual relationships, where the housewife is depicted as oppressed and downtrodden, a victim of male patriarchy and a slave to her husband's sexual and domestic needs as well as being economically dependent upon him (Truong 1990: 13, 54). Yet, natural categories such as wife and prostitute cannot be taken at face value. At one end of the spectrum, diverse relationships exist within marriage, which may include open relationships or forced sex for the assurance of ongoing financial support. At the other end, where women receive money or gifts for sex even outside marriage, such as in Zaire, this does not mean that women are classified as sex workers (Schoepf 1992, 1993). Keith Hart recounts the story of a Ghanaian student who told him that in Ghana it is customary for a boy to leave a girl some money as a gift after sleeping with her at a party. When the Ghanaian tried this with a visiting American student, the response was explosive: 'Do you imagine that I am a prostitute?' (Hart 2005: 26). Hart goes on to ask why in Euro-America we think of money as so impersonal that its exchange transforms the meaning of even the most personal and intimate act. Anthropologists have repeatedly shown that there is wide variation in the meanings and symbolism culturally associated with monetary transactions (see Parry and Bloch 1989). As we shall also see in this chapter, the transient, momentary and traceless character of paid sex is challenged by women who exchange sex for money not out of economic need, but as a social commentary and an expression of resistance and anger against male domination and patriarchy.

In addition, where the literature tends to dichotomize marital and other sexual relationships, there may be a tendency to overdetermine the elements that comprise these kinds of sexual relationships and thus miss the nuances of how politics, economics, erotics and sociability interact in complex and highly variable ways. What is seldom highlighted is how the historical and cultural circumstances of sexual economies may differ cross-culturally. By exploring sexual economies in historical and cross-cultural perspective, this chapter considers the varieties of exchange and emotion involved in so-called 'sex-work'.

PROBLEMATIZING SEX FOR PROFIT

In Western societies some have argued that the sexual economy is characterized by three elements: financial remuneration, sex and psychological effects. Others have suggested it includes 'barter, promiscuity and emotional indifference' (Lemert 1951: 238) or 'payment ... for a specific, sexual performance ... distinguishing the prostitute from the mistress or females who accept a range of gifts while having sexual contact with a male' (Gagnon 1968: 592–3). But these elements are common to many sexual liaisons, so what makes a prostitute or prostitution different? Some authors argue that payment is the most fundamental criterion of the definition of prostitution and see the power of money to objectify and depersonalize, as reflected in the act of prostitution itself. Thus for Georg Simmel (1971: 121) when 'one pays money one is completely quits, just as one is through with the prostitute after satisfaction is attained', a formulation in which prostitution becomes a metaphor for the immorality of capitalism itself. However, monetary exchange may also be found in social arrangements such as marriage and courtship (Davis 1937), which has led other theorists to rethink the parameters of financial remuneration as a defining factor. Writing of prostitution in Thailand, Truong (1990) has considered that promiscuity is essential to definitions of prostitution, since it distinguishes these sexual acts from other types of sexual relationships, but in whose eyes are women seen as promiscuous? Some women may engage in indiscriminate sexual intercourse, but they are not necessarily to be considered promiscuous by officials or the public (Polsky 1967). Identifying prostitutes on the basis of economic reward, emotion and promiscuity has never been straightforward. In India and ancient Babylon the oldest form of prostitution was connected with fertility rites to honour the sexual power of the goddess. Visitors to temples would have sexual intercourse with women of the temple and give a donation in return, an erotic economy where proxy sex 'with God' ensured reproduction of the deity – a case where sex really was divine. Temple prostitutes or *devadasis* were able to elevate themselves to higher social standing through the status afforded by artistic and sexual prowess dedicated to the temple deity (Truong 1990: 14). Thus, a sexual economy based upon religious fecundity meant women came to be highly valued and acquired status and land in return (Lerner 1986). Elsewhere in East Asia sex has historically been viewed as an aesthetic art in which sexuality and sexual intercourse were highly esteemed. Women of all classes were recruited as either geishas or Ky Nu in China, Japan and Vietnam to serve courtiers and members of the aristocracy (Truong 1990: 14). A similar role was played by courtesans in Western Europe prior to capitalism. These high-class prostitutes were paralleled in Europe by those who served the lower classes and who had their own guilds until the fourteenth century, along with their own patron saint, Saint Magdalena (Mies 1986: 81). They were distinguished by their manner of dress and were stigmatized by respectable society (Truong 1990: 14). Ironically, the sexual prowess of prostitutes protected them from the witch hunts of the twelfth and seventeenth centuries, while clever women were targeted because of their perceived intelligence.

Broad-minded social thinking around prostitution in pre-industrial Europe was further reflected in its legal status and in the idea that brothels provided an outlet for socially isolated men and for homeless or dislocated women. Brothels offered an additional service by funding religious institutions and bringing financial incentives to towns (Perry 1985: 144–5). However, with the rise in sex-related illnesses prostitutes came to be viewed as polluting, not only to the medical health of others but also to the moral health of society, and prostitution gradually acquired a negative image, with the brothel becoming a site of contamination and containment. The pollution of prostitution was reflected in legal clampdowns on sex for sale as being deviant and, more damningly, as a psychologically disturbed activity. By the eighteenth century women accused of moral derangement in licentious sexual behaviours were arrested and deemed to be afflicted by moral degeneracy as a hereditary flaw (Kemp 1936). In the mid- to late-nineteenth century the Contagious Diseases Acts made women responsible for transmitting venereal diseases, a 'crime' for which they could be locked away in hospital for up to nine months. Prostitution was nonetheless viewed as a necessary evil for the military men whom they principally served, as homosexuality was criminal and these servicemen were discouraged from engaging in permanent marital relations. Women were:

> forced to attend examinations during the day... The domiciliary visitation by the police and the central location of the examination house made it impossible for a subject woman to keep her private and public worlds apart. This is what destroyed her 'self-respect'. (Walkowitz 1980: 202)

While soldiers were not tested for diseases, the medical surveillance of prostitutes meant that the relationship between 'the unrespectable and respectable poor' was made visible and 'forced prostitutes to accept their status as public women by destroying their private associations with the poor working-class community' (Walkowitz 1980: 192).

THEORIZING SEX AND PROSTITUTION

With the coalescence of the medicalization of sex and evolutionary theory, Truong (1990: 17) explains how socio-biological explanations of prostitution came to regard the sale of sex either as 'a moral crime of the individual and the act of prostituting oneself as a result of moral idiocy' or as a consequence of the forces of the market that served an excessive male sex drive. This theory was based on: 1) the reduction of the complex social and biological relationship between male and female to the male sex drive, 2) a static conception of the human body, and 3) the assumption that the female was both the seducer and the exploiter of the male (Truong 1990: 19). The evolutionary theory of atavism held that humans retained recessive elements of antisocial behaviour from a distant ancestral past, leading them into deviant practices such as prostitution, which was seen to reflect a lack of moral judgement. Instead of treating sex as a biological necessity, functionalism repositioned it as an instrument of social control, suggesting that it operated as a:

> means to an end, the end being the biological well-being of the individual, the procreation of the species and also the spiritual development of the personality and the establishment of a give and take in social co-operation. (Malinowski 1932: xxxvi)

Functionalism did not address how institutional control impinged on the emotional effects of sex. However, Marx (1973: 611) posited that sex in prostitution could not yield emotional satisfaction, since the provider is never free of the circumstances of exploitation that define the activity. In his view, sex in prostitution is alienated from the conditions of its production, allowing the degradation of prostitutes and their intellect as they become just one element within a much larger system. But such denial of agency suggests the prostitute is a sexual automaton whose emotional capacity is wholly subservient to the mode of production in which the person is caught. However, as we shall see in some of the case studies in this chapter, the power of emotion in sexual exchange is instrumental to changing the conditions of production as well as to ensuring the continuation of certain financially rewarding relationships.

WHAT PRICE SEX?

As a commercial enterprise, the sale of sex entails several key agents in addition to the prostitute: the procurer of sexual services, the regulator, the sex industries and the suppliers. In the West, working sex has a price, a workplace and codes of separation from other sexual relationships and intimacies. Good whores are those who maintain a code of fair work, ask for money in advance, leave their clients feeling satisfied, use healthy practices in maintaining bodily and emotional boundaries, never provide services that have not been agreed, keep off alcohol and other drugs when working, and warn other women about dangerous or unreliable clients (Scambler 1997: 109). However, rather than sex being the seductive and titillating activity depicted in media representations, many women in the sex industry find their work dull. Graham Scambler (1997: 114) quotes one working girl as saying: 'Whoring is boring, but lucrative.' In research spanning more than twenty years in a London genito-urinary clinic in Paddington's Praed Street, Sophie Day (2007: 37–8) reports that some sex workers enjoyed sex at work but, 'in general, pleasure was avoided' or described with 'embarrassment'. What they valued more than the possibility of sexual pleasure was the independence that their job afforded them. This sense of independence increased, the longer the sex worker's career. In the context of the entrepreneurial individualism of 1980s Thatcherite Britain, many London sex workers used their imagination and ingenuity to take charge of their lives and to create new markets free from state regulation and interference. 'Building on mainstream values of enterprise, sex workers valued the expanded individuality they could achieve in the market', which they saw as commercially enabling in contrast to an economically disabling state (Day 2007: 99). Sex work was thus a choice for many women, a way out of poverty rather than a mark of economic and social exclusion, and many operated as 'self-made businesswomen' (Day 1996: 86; Ward and Day 2006: 417).

Yet in spite of the financial rewards and the potential for developing an independent, entrepreneurial self, for some sex workers there is a high price to pay in the physical and emotional management of the commercially sexed body. Many London prostitutes try to minimize the dangers of physical and psychological contamination by adopting practices that restore agency and by transforming risk into safety (Day 2000). One woman had three towels to separate her sex work from her sex life, with one over the pillow, one on the bed and one for the client to wash with, while another sex worker explained how protection from the anonymity of casual sex must be managed with condoms and in conjunction with other contraceptive devices such as the coil and pill: 'I don't want strangers' semen inside. I only drop the barrier with someone I really love' (Day 1994: 174). Any breach of distance in working relationships allows contamination to seep not only between the sheets but also between the emotional ties of personal relationships, causing them to become more like working ones. One informant told Day:

> Last night, I had a twit. There was two hundred on the go for it and the twit doesn't want to wear a condom. I say the usual, 'it's not worth my while', so, in the end, he puts it on. Somehow or other it came off… They are crafty. Thing is, you could be doing the business and you check every so often, but, keeping your hand there, you can't do it. It came off inside. You're tired, all you want to do is get home and then there's this. (Day 1994: 178)

Thus a critical relationship with degrees of alienation or intimacy exists between working and personal sex, with many women striving to maintain 'two bodies', one public and the other private (Day 2007: 43–6). However, as Kulick (1997) points out, studies of prostitution are skewed towards the former and we learn little about the role of partners and sex in prostitutes' private relationships.

The clinically calculated mode of sex work in some domains of Western prostitution means that intimacy is necessarily distanced and another's body, substances, emotions and physicality must be kept at arm's length. We shall see later how this boundary is sometimes threatened, particularly by regular clients, who confound 'all those carefully drawn lines between one activity, time, identity or place and another' (Day 2007: 172). First, though, we examine how emotional distance from the client does not necessarily characterize paid sexual activities in other cultural settings, where indeed some of these relationships may not be termed 'sex work' at all.

TRICKS OF THE TRADE: WOMEN ON TOP

In her study of Huli *pasinja meri* (literally, passenger women) in Papua New Guinea, Wardlow (2004: 1081) argues that the term 'sex worker' suggests an income generator rather than an all-encompassing label. It implies rights for safety, legality and has remunerative potential as a livelihood. *Pasinja meri* is an ambivalent term, one that stigmatizes women at the same time as it signals their rights and independence. Its sense of denoting 'bad' women affords them sexual licence in terms of speech, action and movement. It gives these women additional buying power because their behaviour is understood as antithetical to normative social relations where 'good' women would not seek self-enhancement financially or move at will around the country, as this would challenge the authority of kin and be perceived as selfish (Wardlow 2002). As Wardlow demonstrates, *pasinja meri* do not engage in prostitution because they desire to earn money, but rather because they wish to make a social statement against male members of their families whom they feel have wronged them. In the case of one woman, Ogai, Wardlow explains how her husband and brothers did not seek justice for her after she had been raped and then belittled by her assailant, who sneered, '*Yu ting samting bilong yu em gutpela samting? Mi save repim wait meri, olsem na yu, mi no save kautnim yu*' (You think your 'thing' (i.e. vagina) is a good thing? I've had sex with/raped white women, so you, I don't even count you). This insult was not simply a violation of Ogai's marital status; the fact that her male kin did not consider it worth avenging meant it was a devastating denial of her female sexuality because she didn't 'count'. As a non-entity, who did not even figure in the rapist's score of victims or in her husband's sense of justice and masculine possession, she was rendered '"unrapeable" in the very act of rape' (Wardlow 2004: 1020).

For Ogai, becoming a passenger woman was an act of defiance and revenge. Wardlow tells how Ogai sneaked off to 'bush discos' (late-night dance parties), where she would dance with men and have sex in the undergrowth for a few dollars. While the majority of Western sex work is frequently portrayed as entailing isolated encounters one-on-one, passenger women cooperated in creating opportunities by pooling contacts and organizing group liaisons. Inevitably there are consequences for the women, who are rejected by their communities and become vulnerable to rape and the possibility of attack from other women who suspect them of having sex with their husbands.

Rather than being young and single, passenger women tend to be mainly older women who have been subjected to 'violence, loss or humiliation: rape, the murder of female kin and public shaming, adultery or abandonment by a husband (twelve out of eighteen interviewees)' (Wardlow 2004: 1034). They were not motivated by money but, having escaped from a relationship or family issue, they find other men to satisfy their emotional need and remuneration is a kind of recompense.

In comparing cultural notions of eroticism, Wardlow (2004: 1023) argues that Euro-American gender ideals situate women as sexual objects, so they become the 'natural' objects of desire, but, in contrast, Huli boys are the 'epitome of beauty and that which is desired'. Indeed, as Huli women's vaginas are *ngubi* (smelly), why should men pay for sex with them, especially when sex is not regarded as useful work and passenger women are not cooking, caring for men, raising the pigs or doing other domestic tasks? Wardlow poses the question: if Huli men do pay, what are they paying for? The possibilities of sexual experimentation introduced by modernization mean that Huli men know there are other kinds of non-traditional sexual practices available outside the marital home. Paid sex is thus a means of broadening experience, gaining status and demonstrating manhood in a 'conquest orientation toward women' (Wardlow 2004: 1029). Their sexual engagements are not taken hostage by notions of love and emotional entanglement, but paid sex still reflects badly upon proper social relations because it negates kinship obligations and enables women to accrue independent personal advantage. Passenger women are stealing kin resources from others, since their sexuality belongs to their families to be exchanged, and Huli contemptuously remark of a woman who accepts payment for sex that she is 'eating her own vagina' (Wardlow 2006: 167). One might think, then, that if women degrade themselves by relinquishing their family ties and the sexual values accompanying them, they have become oppressed by male desire, but Wardlow argues, to the contrary, that as men give in to dangerous and smelly vaginas, so women also conquer men and destroy their integrity. Thus, Ogai was finally vindicated from her rape by turning to paid sex in which she symbolically consumed other men and her attacker. In this complex set of encounters, sex as revenge should not be termed prostitution.

ILLUSIONS OF MEN IN CONTROL

Today, sex work entails many activities that may be grouped under the term 'commercial sex industry', and these range from performances in clubs and high-class hotels with strip shows or exotic dancing to escort services, Internet and telephone sex, pornography, gay video, massage parlours, sex shops and peep shows (see Weitzer 2000b). Although historically many of these activities have taken place face to face, increasingly this is not the case and 'intimacy' may be paradoxically 'distanced' via electronic media, available at the click of a button and payment in plastic, a point we return to later in the book. Face-to-face sex work usually entails a negotiation of price and the services to be offered and, even where customers are able to choose from a 'menu' listing the erotic fare to be had, an element of 'bargaining' may be involved, as we shall see below. Sometimes this has been described as a 'buyers' market', where men operate within a field of power in which they have the upper hand (Ronai and Ellis 1989: 294). Elsewhere some female sex workers retain a sense of agency by representing the market as in their control, believing that *they* select the client and fix the price and maintaining that they 'supply' (sex) in an economic sphere of unlimited (male) 'demand', a belief that effects an 'ideological transformation by representing a site of dependency as one of freedom' (Day 1996: 87).

What constitutes prostitution and who is seen as in control have many permutations between cultures and thus elude a fixed and stable definition that can transcend cultural boundaries. For example, in Japanese nightclubs the mother–child relationship is critical to the construction of masculinity and perceptions of adult heterosexual relations (Allison 1994: 171). Japanese men look to club hostesses as mother figures and are to some extent infantilized in this relationship as the women indulge their male fantasies as childish whims. Thus, it could be argued that men are passive recipients of their mothers'/hostesses' milk, nurture and care-giving. Typical patriarchal qualities are reversed here and, rather than the sex worker being the passive recipient of frequently dominant male desire, men allow themselves to be attended to and become recipients of female services. Like Huli passenger women, the *mizu shobai* woman is an enigma to female sexuality, but not because of her denial of kinship ties and desire to demonstrate maturity and independence; rather, on the contrary, it is her demeanour of motherly concern and voluptuous body that invite reproach (see Chapter 2). Hostesses serve their 'juvenile' charges with respect and acceptance of their comments and desires. Yet, rather than being passive recipients of childish male fantasy, these women are trained to put on performances that bolster their clients' confidence, reassuring them of their manhood (Allison 1994: 178). Sex is virtual insofar as it is more about teasing, flirting and fantasizing than intercourse. While it might be thought that Japanese men are emasculated through the passivity they display towards the women who control them, Allison argues that the unequal relationship in which women must pander to male lust is a form of violence. While sex does not take place between hostesses and their clients, it is enacted through talk-about-sexuality which strokes their male egos. The paradox in this situation is that although women are fully in control of their actions and seduce men by their services, they are in fact dominated by men because of the sex-talk that ultimately violates their respectability and degrades their sexuality. While women appear to be the powerful agent in this mothering relationship, Japanese men are not interested in the women themselves but only in the act of sex-talk received in return for money. Where Huli passenger women bolster their self-esteem by inverting familial ties and denying male kin the potentialities of their motherhood roles, Japanese hostesses are expected to engage in role plays of motherhood that facilitate the erasure of female personhood, in turn strengthening male bonding as clients collectively demean hostesses as 'animals' (Allison 1994: 187). Similarly, in another context, the idea that male strip shows in America are a 'liberating' experience for women because they invert the power structures of female striptease has been debunked. Rather, it has been demonstrated that they replicate the deeply embedded gender hierarchies of the wider society (Margolis and Arnold 1993: 347). Nevertheless, watching male strippers – and participating in house parties that market sex toys (see Chapter 2) – are among some of the ways that Western women participate as consumers in the erotic economy.

CAPTURING CONSUMERS

Stripping female sexuality of womanhood or personhood is not restricted to Japan or the West and can take various forms, from denial to the objectification of sexual body parts and their essentialization. New forms of moral personhood have also emerged in Kathmandu, where interpersonal ties based on caste and kinship have progressively given way to social relations based on the impersonality of class, facilitating a 'carnal economy' in which culinary and sexual services are increasingly commodified by the city's 'Restaurants with Dance', which cater for the 'modern' tastes of local men and South Asian tourists (Liechty 2005). A denial of female personhood is inscribed in Thai constructions of country, people and sexuality, as Thai hostesses become *the sex* (Manderson 1995: 311). For example, in Patpong women perform a variety of lewd sexual acts, including single 'trick acts using the vagina to explore two interrelated themes: female sex and power, and exploration of the unknown/fear of castration' (Manderson 1995: 312). The vagina is representative of female animality but, unlike Japanese clients, it is not men who construct Thai vaginas in this way. Rather, as Thai hostesses perform acts that re-create the vagina as a cavity that is dangerous and potentially a threat to the penis in its amputation, they play on a fear of male castration. Such acts include inserting a snake tail into the vagina and extracting metres of ribbon with razor blades threaded on a string with small bells (Manderson 1995: 313).

The influx of tourists to Thailand created a niche in the market for a new product, the 'sex package tour' sold by companies such as Jet Sex of Zurich and Euro-Tours of Amsterdam to European (especially German) and Japanese tourists who travel for sex. Thus, a critical aspect of commercialization is the marketing, commodification and representation of sex, not just its purchasing power (Manderson 1995: 307). The packaging of sex as display for consumers is integral to its powers of seduction and the language of the flyers distributed to tourists leaves little room for doubt about the nature of what is on offer – 'fire stick in the pussy show', 'egg cracking show', 'pussy smoke cigarette show' (e.g. O'Merry 1990: 168; see also Manderson 1992), where the vagina is constructed as an independent organ capable of performing feats such as popping ping-pong balls, blowing darts, bursting balloons, blowing out candles, opening soft drinks, using chopsticks and writing messages, as if having a separate and autonomous personality.

Other essentialized images of Thai sex are sold by tour operators and advertisers on the basis of pictures of scantily clad Thai women in G-strings or dancers wrapping themselves around poles in acts of sexual contortion. The message conveyed is that sex is free, easy and immediate in 'the land of smiles', 'the brothel of the East' (an accolade previously held by Shanghai until 1949; Broinowksi 1992: 39) and 'the world's largest sex resort' (Manderson 1995: 309). However, there is little that is new here. What is being sold is the same as that which early nineteenth-century explorers sought in the allure of the Orient, now succeeded by the sex shop of Asia in some 'festishized, imagined Other' in 'Thai sex' and Thai women as products (Manderson 1995: 309). The notion that it is possible to 'possess' the ideal Oriental woman who will prove to be not only the ultimate domestic help and the perfect submissive partner but also the ultimate sexual athlete is integral to the imagination of the Thai sexual nation. However, Thai sexual woman does not exist outside the minds of tourists/clients, any more than Oriental woman existed outside the minds of the European colonizers. Rather, relationships between tourists and sex partners take on the specificities of historical conditions, time and place. But, in the representation of Thailand, marketers have managed to pull off a sexual coup by taking captive the minds of the consumers, as if operating in a sexual void with the promise of barely imaginable sexual adventures and hitherto untold sexual zeniths that continue to shape the myths of Thai liberalism. Tourists come expecting what is offered, Thai and Filipina women being at the higher end of the imaginary sexual market and depicted as alluring, pretty and nice, in contrast with Chinese women in 'girlie bars' in Hong Kong who have been depicted as 'sexless ("flea bite" breasts), unintelligent, "sluts", "conniving, manipulative, wicked and deviant"' (Manderson 1995: 311).

Sexual representations of women's bodies do not simply sell sex to the West; they also market Thai products for Thai consumers through the secluded or hidden vagina (Manderson 1992: 321). Where Thai cultural attitudes protect women's virginity, Thai prostitution operates as an inversion of Thai sexuality in which women, 'genitals displayed, literally perform over the heads of men' (Manderson 1995: 314). Thus, Manderson (1995: 313) argues that, instead of Thailand being marketed as the romantic and seductive land of smiles through the mouth, face and eyes, it is now presented as the land of the vagina that rules supreme in an equation that reads: Thailand : Other :: vagina : penis.

COMMERCIAL SEX INDUSTRIES: MIXED MESSAGES

Ironically, what has sold Thailand abroad has also posed a major threat to its national image as a morally upright country with central values of filial piety that require children to pay respect and behave courteously in all areas of their lives to their parents. When prostitution was outlawed in Thailand in 1960, its prohibition coincided with significant foreign demand. When the American military arrived in 1962, they took mistresses or 'hired wives' or 'rented wives' (Smith 1971: 129). Bars and clubs grew up to accommodate the soldiers in 'rest and relaxation', with sex being available on tap as it were. The influx of *farang*, i.e. white foreigners, grew to around 40,000 American GIs (Cohen 1982: 407). This explosion in sexual engagements was nothing compared with the surge of tourist interest in Thailand in the 1970s, following the departure of the troops when men outnumbered women by two to one. In the 1980s the total number of women in the sex industry stood at between half a million and one million (Cohen 1982: 407). In trying to root out the 'moral' problem of a nation with a reputation as a 'whorehouse', police sought to punish the women rather than the financiers of the tourist businesses who brought the customers (Cohen 1982).

With the rise of international travel, it has been argued that tourism causes pro-stitution (Krawenkel 1981). However, as Cohen points out, '[p]rostitution, concubinage and sex-for-sale have ... long been familiar and accepted elements of Thai society', prior to the tourist industry. Tourism, though, encourages a broader audience by servicing an international mass market. Cohen has identified four types of exchange between Thai girls and *farang*: 1) mercenary: a pure economic exchange where the nature of the relationship is neutral; 2) staged: a form of economic exchange camouflaged as social exchange or love with the aim of gaining maximum financial remuneration; 3) mixed: social exchange with economic exchange, a very unstable form because of conflicting interests; 4) emotional: where the stability of the relationship depends on the strength of the bond between the two partners. These ideal types have blurred edges as some forms include elements of another. Most relationships between Thai girls and *farang* men belong to either the staged or the mixed forms of relationships. Cohen (1979: 27–28) argues that *farangs* suffer from 'staging suspicion' when the girl feigns attachment to get money. *Farang* suspicions are not wholly unfounded, as Cohen notes cases where Thai girls are not necessarily turned on by their partners and they may fake the heights of sexual arousal to create an illusion of erotic involvement in a special kind of 'staged authenticity' (MacCannell 1973). This staged authenticity depends on 'personalised service' (MacCannell 1973), where relationships based upon economic exchange are camouflaged to appear as if they were based on social exchange (Cohen 1982). When girls pass themselves off professionally in a continuing relationship over time in this manner, they may become confused about their commitment to their partner. Rather than Thai prostitution being characterized by a specific transaction with neutral exchange between sex worker and clientele, remuneration is not demanded as a fixed price but is left to the generosity of the customer; there is no requirement to behave sexually in a specific way or to carry out particular sexual acts – the Thai tourist girl can choose her partner and emotional involvement does occur between the tourist and the Thai girl. Furthermore, from the male tourist's perspective, there is an expectation that the Thai girl should be involved with him and be turned on by him. These actual encounters move our understanding of the complexity of sex worker relationships far beyond prostitution as being the strict sale of sex as defined by Gagnon (1968) or Lemert (1951), a point elaborated below. What is evident is that it is not particular social, sexual, moral and emotional responses that characterize prostitution per se, but how they are shaped, performed, received and managed in different cultural settings.

FINDING A PROSTITUTE: HIDDEN HUSTLING AND MALE SEX WORK

It should not be surprising, then, that it is difficult to identify what counts as prostitution or who counts as a prostitute. In some countries, heterosexual prostitution is intimately related to other forms of prostitution such as male-to-male, male-to-female, transgendered or transsexual. Where sexual passivity in male-to-male sex has a specific local cultural meaning, paid sexual encounters with other men must be delicately negotiated and clear boundaries set or one's involvement hidden. In Pakistan, for instance, professional masseurs in urban Punjab may perform sexual services for men including anal intercourse, but these are carefully solicited through suggestive sexual gestures that test 'the boundaries of shame' in a context where even the most innocent massage is considered morally ambiguous (Frembgen 2008: 18–19). So too in urban Brazil, subjective identities can be at stake for men who engage in homosexual relations where heterosexuality and masculinity are highly prized, and certain kinds of male sex hustler (*michê*) may strive to keep secret their involvement in paid sex work with other men. Although they may work the streets, many *michês* continue to live with their parents and to participate in conventional social networks, 'engaging in heterosexual

interactions with partners who know nothing of their involvement in male prostitution'
(Parker 1999: 68). At the same time, male prostitution and the gay economy in Brazil
have created novel spaces in which homosexuality can be constructed and expressed
in other highly public ways. Brazil's 'gay market' has become big business, spawning a
proliferating entertainment industry at the intersection between the international tourist
market and local notions of homoeroticism and resulting in commercial ventures that
are as much about life style and cultural performance as about sexual adventuring. As
Richard Parker shows (1999: 84–7), many of the features that characterize this sector –
such as gay nightclubs, travel agencies and film festivals – echo those of the gay economy
in Euro-America and have become extremely lucrative. Adapted to the Brazilian setting,
which in turn influences the gay economy beyond, Brazil's gay market participates in
a wider local–global dynamic that is shaping contemporary sexuality both inside and
outside the country.

In Barbados, hustling may refer to either female heterosexual or male homosexual
prostitution, and in the latter instance it is a marker of male socio-sexual identities
embodied in the beach boy or hustler syndrome (Press 1978). These hustlers are gigolos
– men who receive material compensation for the social or sexual services they render to
women. Hustling is further complicated by the existence of 'hidden hustlers'. Employed
in respectable jobs such as taxi-driving, these men deliberately hustle female tourists
but they are distinct from hustlers since they do not earn their living from hustling and
earn greater respect because 'hidden hustling' is merely an aside to their primary job.
Tourist women who enter into sexual relationships with local men have sometimes been
seen in terms of 'romance tourism' rather than as 'sex tourists' (Dahles and Bras 1999).
However, this distinction risks essentializing male and female sexuality, and evidence
from Jamaica shows how some women are themselves sexually predatory, procuring 'men
or boys of a particular age, penis size, skin tone, body type and even smell' (Sánchez
Taylor 2001: 759). Kempadoo (2001: 57) summarizes these differences in definitions
and experiences of male and female sex workers and male and female sex tourists in the
Caribbean, and suggests that variations in ideas about sex work coalesce not just around
differences of gender, but also around those of ethnicity, race and class.

Elsewhere in the Caribbean, Cabezas (2004) describes how Cuban hustlers referred
to as *jineteros* and *jineteras* emerged in the 1990s, along with *pingueros* and sanky pankies
in the Dominican Republic (both categories of men who engage in heterosexual and gay
sex), as a result of international mass tourism.[1] Sex activities encapsulated within these
terms are much broader than simply remuneration for sex. According to Fidel Castro,
they refer to sex for pleasure and indicate other kinds of activities involved in seducing
the tourist, including being street sellers and pedlars as well as 'tourist guides, escorts,
brokers for sexual services and romantic companions' (Cabezas 2004: 4). The terms are
racially defined, identifying black Cubans as distinct from white, light-skinned Cubans.
Race, class and gender are integral to the identification of sex workers in these areas.
Sex worker is a category some people belong to because it is worn on the skin, derived
from one's location and confirmed by the company one keeps regardless of the activities

in which they do or do not engage. While there are no laws in Cuba or the Dominican Republic that prohibit a person from selling his or her sexual services, the law comes down harder on black women in public spaces whose demeanour suggests they are 'dangerous' and potentially immoral, with the intent of harassing tourists.

As with Huli passenger women in Papua New Guinea and Thai hostesses, *jineteras* who become entertainers or tour guides do not work solely for money as their circumstances, often as single mothers, mean they may be looking for longer-term relationships. The possibility of sex work leading to romance and the prospect of financial support within a permanent relationship are incentives for those who take up jobs in this sector. Thus, rather than the emotionally indifferent, dispassionate act of sex without intimacy, connection, obligation or reciprocity, these *jineteras* are involved in 'an emotional economy' that confounds any simple separation between money, emotional indifference and sex. Gifts are rated more highly than money, because they create an ongoing relational tie in that they carry sentiments that can be invoked and ascribed with particular meaning. In contrast, money suggests a closure of relational debt, a paying off of the act. So, in both Cuba and the Dominican Republic the mercenary relationship between sex and money is avoided for a more subtle approach to love and the expectation of future economic exchange (see Chapter 5); 'tactical sex' with visiting foreigners may alleviate economic hardship, but exchanging money does not preclude durable, companionable and affective ties (Cabezas 2009: 120). As in Barbados, hidden hustling occurs here too in other forms. The hospitality industry is complicit in promoting sex tourism by allowing employees to make additional earnings from sexual liaisons with customers whilst they are carrying out their hotel or other hospitality tasks. Thus, the tourism industry encourages extramarital sexual relations because of the requirement to please guests and attend to them in whatever way they wish; as one tourist noted when propositioned by a Cuban chambermaid, 'and I used to settle for a mint on my pillow' (cited in Cabezas 2004: 1).

'PUTTING GREENERY ON THE SCENERY'

Ethnographies such as those outlined above shed light on the question long debated by academics and popular commentators about exactly what it is that is being bought and sold between prostitute and client. As we noted earlier, empirical studies of sexual commerce complicate an understanding of prostitution as a simple exchange of cash for sex. Although some scholars continue to argue that the prostitute–client relationship is predicated on the straightforward purchase of pleasure or domination, a growing body of material from a range of commercial sexual practices suggests that what the purchase means and how it is experienced by those who are party to it are more varied, interesting and complex than these arguments imply. It is misleading to reduce commercial sex to simple dichotomies between sex objects and sex workers or victims and agents (Weitzer 2000a: 3). When the DJ exhorts customers to 'put their greenery on the scenery' by tucking dollar bills into the garters of the pole dancers to encourage them to remove their clothes, it is not just the sight of their naked bodies that is being transacted, as the views of the dancers and their clients repeatedly show. Watching may be a singular pleasure, but as Slavoj Žižek (1991: 107–11) has argued, the gaze objectifies the spectator rather than the sexual actors on the stage.

Despite occasional claims to the contrary, strip clubs that offer personalized lap, pole and table dances as well as exotic dancing on a central stage have been extensively studied by social researchers (for a critical overview, see Frank 2007). While employment conditions and wage agreements vary widely for those who work in these clubs, and while they sometimes involve a retainer or nightly 'attendance' fee, the main source of earnings for most dancers comes from the tips and payments given directly to them by clients. These depend on a dancer's 'bargaining strategies' and reflect the nature of commercial service exchange in the wider society (Ronai and Ellis 1989). To be successful, therefore, a dancer can never be just the powerless, passive, objectified body consumed by a paying clientele that popular accounts sometimes evoke; she must engage the audience in a warm and personal way, something that must be learned by observing other dancers and by exchanging ideas or copying their tactics. The opportunity to connect is when she is on the central stage, from where a good dancer can not only excite her audience but also make eye contact with those who look most affluent and most likely to pay later for a personalized dance. Since many clubs (though by no means all) prohibit dancers from selling sex on or off the premises (even if they cannot always prevent it), maximizing income for dancers depends on successful strategies for selling a series of titillating table dances like the following:

> She swayed from side to side above him, her hands on his shoulders, her knee brushing gently against the bulge in his pants. He looked up at the bottom of her breasts, close enough to touch, but subtly forbidden. (Cited in Ronai and Ellis 1989: 271)

Connecting with the audience while on stage is such a lucrative opportunity that one dancer researched men's clothing stores so that she could tell at a glance which men were dressed expensively and so were worth engaging in this way (Murphy 2003: 316).

Critically, however, success resides in being able to convince a customer that the transaction in which they are engaged is meaningful and sincere, a construction of a 'counterfeit intimacy' (Enck and Preston 1988) that recalls the 'staged authenticity' of the tourist encounter that we mentioned earlier. As one table dancer explained:

> When you talk to a guy you have to make them believe you are totally into them. You lean forward and say, 'That is *so* interesting'. Or, when they tell you about their job you say, 'You must be *so* responsible'. (Cited in Murphy 2003: 317, emphases in original)

Clients are delighted when they feel they have been given the real name and phone number of a dancer, even though these may be part of the dancer's stage persona (Frank 2002). In contrast to the foreigners seeking commercial sex abroad who remain wary of sex workers proclaiming reciprocal erotic desire, as we noted above, the table dancers studied by Murphy (2003: 318) seem remarkably successful at establishing this sense of sexual interest in their clients:

> 'One time there was this guy who really thought I was going to go out with him.' [Annie] had been playacting an intimate role with him and was incredulous when he 'really' believed her. 'He said, "You mean you aren't really going to go out with me?" I couldn't believe he really believed me. I felt so sorry for him.'

Strippers are very aware of the tensions and contradictions that constitute the economic context in which they work. While they are dependent on the management to maintain the premises where they dance, they are there to make money for themselves rather than for the club, with whose organizational goals and values they do not identify and which they often subvert. In contrast to the work-oriented discourse of prostitution with its strict boundaries between public and private that we have considered so far, strippers seem more ambivalent about characterizing what they do as 'work'. While at one level they are clear that they seek to maximize their income, at another level they deny that what they do constitutes a 'job', thinking of it instead as just another aspect of their social life (Murphy 2003: 321). This creates conflict with management, who see it as unprofessional when dancers do not turn up for 'work', while the dancers themselves see their failure to show up as simply a case of not 'going out that night'. These divergent understandings of erotic work suggest again that the economic and social become blurred within the context of an erotic economy.

This blurring encourages us to interrogate more fully the ideas of counterfeit intimacy and staged authenticity. There are clearly many types of intimacy and these are not always easy to specify, even in everyday life (Berlant 1998b), but they are perhaps particularly difficult to distinguish in the context of sex work (Sanders 2008c: 88–91). Such concepts seem to depend on an assumption that if sex is paid for it cannot be authentic, and that only non-commodified desire can be genuine. Moreover, both terms presuppose that it is possible to identify a 'real' authenticity and 'genuine' intimacy against which the counterfeit can be judged. Yet there are likely to be many different views on whether or to what extent a particular emotion or response is counterfeit or authentic, so that it becomes more meaningful to ask why, when and by whom an emotion (object or act) is classified as one thing or the other. It is not that particular acts cannot be identified as staged or not staged, but a focus instead on the process of 'authentification', and on who makes claims for authenticity and the interests such claims serve, seems likely to be more fruitful (Peter Jackson 1999: 101). The 'mutuality' of intimacy is thus likely to be more complex than arguments about deluded clients allow, and Sanders (2008c: 98–103) identifies three possibilities: the 'authentic' delusion of mutuality; the 'authentic-fake' delusion of mutuality; and the 'genuine' mutuality. Which of these applies is usually in the control of the sex worker and may be just as much a part of 'performing the couple game' in romantic attachments as they are of other (commercial) forms of sexual contract.

Evidence from recent ethnography suggests that erotic arousal in commercial sexual encounters is not always considered to be staged. Certainly there are customers who believe that they have experienced the real thing and cite physical evidence of the sex worker's desire to prove their point, as in the following description of a visit to a sex club: 'We began with the usual touchy-feely… I could feel she was just soaking, an indication her moans were not faked' (cited in Bernstein 2001: 402). And though one might expect some male clients of sex clubs to boast about their ability to arouse those they encounter, and even to be self-delusional or to exaggerate, evidence of sexual arousal is not confined to them but is mentioned by some sex workers too.

The stereotypical view of commercial sex, especially where someone has been employed as a sex worker for long periods of their life, is that it is emotionally desensitizing, a disposition towards clients that is regarded as almost a prerequisite of continued involvement in the job. However, the opposite is sometimes also true. Exotic dancers who develop a stage persona specifically to distance their social from their working lives have found that the longer they perform, the more the boundary between these worlds is likely to blur. 'Multiple identities' can intrude upon the 'self', requiring a long hot shower each night to wash away (Ronai 1992). What starts out as staged intimacy can become 'real', at least for the performer, as candidly explained by one dancer-turned-researcher who describes how she became aroused when dancing for a beer-bellied, sour-smelling man in a dirty t-shirt:

> Dancing for Lenny was a powerful sensual experience. Without the distraction of conversation, I got lost in my own bodily sensation, moving in ways that turned me on. Lenny did not seem to care what I did and kept on buying. Every time I looked at his face, however, I got confused. How could I find someone that looks like this so erotic? How could he turn me on? … Not grabby or rude, he seemed more interested in viewing my pleasure than in 'getting his', and in so doing opened up a space where I explored a different kind of eroticism – mine. (Egan 2006: 29–30, cited in Barton 2007: 590)

Commoditized sex can clearly result in inauthentic intimacies and desires that are faked as a way of maximizing profit, but if such interpretations are applied universally we may misread the exchange and the meanings the parties ascribe to their transaction. Elizabeth Bernstein (2001, 2007b) has argued that in order to understand erotic economies we need not only to look more closely at clients' motives, an ethnography of which has only recently developed (e.g. Frank 2002; Hart 1994), but also to situate these in historical context, something that earlier work on clients has usually failed to do; according to Prasad (1999), fewer than ten of the hundreds of sociological publications on prostitution in the preceding thirty years dealt with clients. There is frequently an assumption, Bernstein suggests, that, like everything else related to capitalism, sex is somehow diminished by being 'commodified', and consequently compares unfavourably with the intimacies established within romantic and lasting attachments. Yet far from being diluted by commercial exchange, erotic expression may actually be facilitated by the culture of the market place, which promotes a variety of possibilities for realizing interpersonal connections in a world where public and private, intimacy and commerce have been mutually transformed by the ways in which they increasingly intersect and overlap (Bernstein 2001: 398).

It is not only sexual release that men are after, but a sexual experience within an emotional engagement and momentary emotional immersion that they feel they can believe in but that does not leak into or shape the other aspects of their lives as well. Men are looking for women who become briefly 'theirs', much in the manner they would expect of a girlfriend, and some explicitly describe their relationships in this way (see Day 2007: 173). However, it is an experience and involvement they wish to contain through payment. This was repeatedly stressed by the men Bernstein spoke to, as well as by the sex workers they patronized, one of whom explained the merits of the paid sexual encounter as far as the men were concerned: 'If you offer them anything but sex for money they flee... The men want an emotional connection, but they don't want any obligations. They don't believe they can have no-strings-attached sex, which is why they pay. They'd rather pay than get it for free' (cited in Bernstein 2001: 403–4). Sex workers in the United States increasingly market themselves through websites such as 'Temporarily Yours', offering the 'true girlfriend experience without the headache' (Bernstein 2007a: 129). Even in brief encounters like those in the strip club, clients stressed that they sought a 'real and reciprocal erotic connection, but a precisely limited one' (Bernstein 2007a: 127). As far as the clients of these services are concerned, therefore, what they are purchasing is not just sexual release – which is anyway not on offer in many strip clubs – but a genuine emotional attachment (however fleeting) characterized by a 'real', culturally authentic and mutual erotic arousal. In Britain, Sanders (2008c: 91–95) also found that 'deep' intimate relationships mirroring 'heterosexual male romantic scripts' developed between indoor sex workers and their clients in moments of 'suspended commercialism'. Elsewhere what is transacted may also not involve sex (or not just sex) but an elaborate, hybridized cultural performance, as in Pakistan, where expensive call girls combine stylistic elements from past and present, West and East, in a fusion of Bollywood, burlesque and classical courtesan (Brown 2007).

Bernstein (2001: 402) refers to these commercial sexual exchanges as a desire for 'bounded authenticity'. But they do not stem from a 'fear of intimacy', as some psychoanalysts and sex therapists might argue. Rather, Bernstein sees bounded authenticity as reflecting the broader social and economic transformations of late capitalism and the acceleration of the consumer age. Demographic changes such as the decline in marriage rates, increase in the number of divorces and dramatic rise in single-person households have resulted in a reorganization of social life whereby the male individual is disembedded from 'the sex–romance nexus of the privatized nuclear family' (Bernstein 2001: 399). For many, living alone has become a lifestyle choice, and they seek a sex life compatible with this, one in which sex is recreational rather than relational and where sexual encounters can be contained as a 'bounded authenticity' that is a 'real' experience without determining all other aspects of their practice and being. The market has responded to these changes and now offers many opportunities to purchase these services, with the exchange of money for emotion ensuring they are kept 'bounded' in this way. The men in Bernstein's study are thus neither seeking something they would prefer to find elsewhere – for example, within a romantic and loving relationship – nor making do with some commodified and emotionally inferior substitute. Far from being opposed to intimacy, the market can in fact provide it, and it is only a misleading insistence on privileging the analytical centrality of romantic and companionate relationships that makes us see it otherwise.

For Bernstein (2007a: 170), then, the commerce of sex has shifted from an emotionally contained sexual release characteristic of modern prostitution to an emerging post-industrial erotic economy where what is bought and sold increasingly requires emotional engagement as well as sexual labour. No longer is the economy the antithesis of intimacy, as is still sometimes popularly claimed; rather, economy and intimacy are mutually facilitating, with the market servicing a growing demand for the erotic connection of 'the neatly-bounded commodity over the messy diffuseness of non-market exchange' (Bernstein 2001: 409; 2007b). In other words, intimacy and commerce not only coexist and interconnect in complex and multivalent ways, as others have argued (Cabezas 2009: 119), but they are also reciprocally enabling and may even be a 'stabilising' factor in contemporary society (Sanders 2008c: 111).

Others too have suggested that the mass-market consumerism of late capitalism facilitates erotic desire by separating it from romantic love. According to Monica Prasad (1999), the prostitute-client encounter provides a particularly good example of the morality of market exchange. The clients she spoke too insisted that, in contrast to the hypocrisy and deception that often characterize romantic attachments in contemporary North America, the 'commodified' exchange of sex between prostitute and client is clearly unambiguous. The 'commodity' exchange of sex is consequently seen by many of them as morally superior to the 'gift' exchange of sex in romantic relationships, since unlike the latter it does not mask dishonesties and deceitfulness:

> I think they [participants in marriages where sex is exchanged for economic support] are no more or less moral than the prostitutes who are walking up and down the street. (Cited in Prasad 1999: 204)

> What's the difference between a person who will marry for money and security and a prostitute? You could say some women frequent men who will take care of them. I knew a woman from New York who went to the Detroit Medical Center and hung out in the bar until she met someone about to be a doctor. (Cited in Prasad 1999: 201)

These comments from male patrons of female sexual services indicate more than just the self-justification and rationalization we might expect. For Prasad, analysis of the erotic economy can reveal a morality in market exchange that she suggests was understated by Marshall Sahlins and Karl Polanyi when contrasting the socially embedded moralities of pre-market economies with the disembedded, self-regulating nature of the market.

Such conclusions compel us to rethink the erotic economy and to query received dichotomies that have sought to separate commercial sex from other forms of social and sexual engagement. It is not just that sexual arousal may be faked to maximize profit, as MacCannell has pointed out, even though this may often be true, but rather – as Bernstein, Prasad and others show – that new forms of intimacy are emerging in response to wider economic and social transformations in which erotic intimacy is facilitated rather than subordinated by market exchange.

CONCLUSION

This chapter has argued that prostitution and other kinds of commercial sex only constitute a proportion of possible sex work relations ranging from beneficial and positive ones to those that are exploitative and negative, making the identification of prostitution especially tricky. The full spectrum of sex work includes purely pecuniary, short duration commercial encounters, as well as ongoing and long-lasting romantic or loving relationships (Bauer and McKercher 2003b: 8). Yet, commercial exchange is only one aspect of the sexual economy. Where anthropologists have emphasized the structural implications of sex for profit, they have tended to be blind to the role of romance, love and lust that shape the nature of the erotic encounter and hence determine the manner in which pecuniary exchange takes place. Cultural notions of reward and the expectation of return from a longer-lasting relationship may often take precedence over financial gain, making sex tourism not just about money but about social advancement for locals with tourists, increased wage incentives, leisure, migration and marriage opportunities (Cabezas 2004, 2009). As we examine in more detail in the next chapter, sex work in Cuba and the Dominican Republic, for example, may include a hidden economy with informal sex work, but this is not necessarily to be viewed as subversive or criminal as many of the activities engaged in by sex tourists may be socially accepted. Elsewhere, the highly visible and ubiquitous nature of sex work means that some countries have come to be defined *as sex*, where 'fingers and vaginas are the synecdoche of both Thai woman and nation' (Manderson 1995: 323; see Montgomery [2009a: 207–8] on child prostitutes as symbols of Thailand). The moral indignation expressed by countries over sex tourism is understandable but then again if sex is an integral part of human daily life, it should not be surprising that visitors do not abstain from sexual participation when away from home. Some might argue that sex at home has no more moral claim than sex in a foreign country, at least when the sex is consensual, mutually supportive, edifying and gratifying in a relational context.

As we have seen, anthropologists and others increasingly question the value of a distinction that separates commercial from non-commercial sex. The many examples reviewed in this chapter suggest that this boundary is difficult to sustain and that the relationship between the market and sexual intimacy is neither straightforwardly contradictory nor deterministic. Failure to grasp this not only has consequences for our academic understanding of sexual commerce, but also has public policy and legal consequences that can be detrimental to the health, practical circumstances and safety of those who work in this sector and to the rights they enjoy (Day 2009; Day and Ward 2004; Sanders 2008a, 2008b). The ethnographic record repeatedly shows that sexual engagements within loving and romantic attachments have characteristics that are commercial, while the reverse is also true. The claim that sex is increasingly commodified is consequently too blunt to capture the diversity of the relationships between money and sex. Insisting that the intersection of sexual intimacy and the economy is complex in this way does not deny that sex and commerce have a seedy underbelly of sexual prejudice, exploitation and entrapment, nor that engagement in the sex industries can involve great physical and personal risk. But it does seek to recognize the diverse ways in which sex is embedded in the economy without being wholly subsumed by it and to understand the influence which this has on sexual agency and subjectivity.

NOTES

1. The terms *jinetero/a* derive from the verb *jinetear* (meaning to ride and break a horse) and evoke the image of riding the tourist, where, for example, the *jinetera* is on top and in charge (Fernández 1999: 4). *Pinga* is slang for penis. *Pingueros* engage in gay sex for greater pecuniary return and thus view themselves as self-employed with their own business. Contrary to sex for pleasure, this is sex for security as some young *pingueros* commented: 'I don't do it because I like it, I do it just for the money' (Hodge 2001: 22). In the Dominican Republic a sanky panky (a term playing on hanky panky) caters for both men and women, either straight or gay (Cabezas 2004: 5), but the term mainly refers to middle-aged, white, foreign women and young, fit, dreadlocked, black men (Herold et al. 2001; Sánchez Taylor 2001). See also Chapter 5.

5 FOREIGN AFFAIRS

Sex is an emotion in motion

Mae West

It has become a truism that we live in a world of intensified mobility, one in which we are frequently told that distances and boundaries rarely function as the barriers to the passage of people and goods that they once were. Migrants, tourists, economic entrepreneurs and others travel in increasing numbers to take advantage of whatever it is they believe they might find as they move from one economic, social and political space to another. Some of this travel leads to enduring ties with the places visited, and most of it entails crossing borders. Even for migrants, the passage to other places is rarely the one-way ticket that it used to be, and regular movement back and forth between old and new 'homes', as well as frequent virtual contact, characterize the lives of the transnational migrants now widely documented in the ethnographic literature. Some of the theories advanced to understand these global processes argue that as a result of all this movement and interconnectedness the world is becoming increasingly alike, while others disagree and suggest instead that the ideas, goods and practices that are spread through increased travel are always appropriated and moulded to the local cultural setting, thereby ensuring the continuation and even amplification of difference. And while some see the transnational flood of goods and people as indicative of the weakening of borders and even as a sign of the nation-state's demise, others argue that national boundaries have in fact been strengthened and intensified, selecting out with growing sophistication those who may pass from those for whom access is denied.

In this chapter we ask how and where sex and sexual intimacy feature in these processes, questions on which the literature has until recently been comparatively and surprisingly silent given the many studies published on the economic and political consequences of transnational movement and the 'softening' of borders. When the dynamics between sex and borders have been examined, the emphasis has usually been on the political, financial, legal and human consequences of transnational prostitution (see, for instance, Jeffrey 2002). Here, however, our focus is less on the global capitalist relations within which transnational forms of sex occur – on which there is a growing literature (e.g. Altman 2001) – or on the human rights dimensions of people trafficking and international sexual indenture, although these provide the broader frame within which we write and are themes to which we return later in the book. Rather, our concern in this chapter is with people's sexual subjectivities and with how and when their sexual relationships, experiences and understandings have been affected by transnational movement, and with the ways in which cross-border sex is represented. We explore what it means to cross borders and how border crossing can lead to radical transformations of sexual value and meaning for those engaged in intimate encounters. We look particularly at erotic desire in the context of migration – at its shifting shape and forms of accommodation and transformation – at the role of tourism in shaping the lives and practices of sex workers and their partners, and at other kinds of women and men who cross or live at borders in order to sell or buy or otherwise transact sex.

Throughout the chapter we also try to show how borders have very different implications for the rich and the poor, and so too for the kind of sex they can realize and imagine there. As Altman (2001) has argued, cultural studies of sex have too often ignored the political, economic and other material realities of its practice in favour of emphasizing the representational, the discursive and the textual. But at borders it is virtually impossible to ignore the inequalities of power that structure relationships there, in sex just as much as in other aspects of everyday life. Borders may be contact zones where people and cultures meet and mix in dramas of creativity and exchange. Yet for many, if not most, they are sites of control and domination, where movement and entry are (sometimes forcibly) regulated in patterns of exclusion and incorporation. Not everyone is similarly placed to realize the possibilities that borders offer or to travel to and across them, and the examples below show how inequalities of power shape the sex we find there. We begin by examining the border sex trade.

BORDERLESS BROTHELS

State borders are stereotypically known for offering a variety of commercial opportunities to the everyday entrepreneur in search of a bargain or an exotic product not readily available at home. Disparities in labour costs, tax regulations and customs duties are among the many factors that ensure that borders are often thriving centres of economic activity. Labour migrants, commuters, cross-border shoppers and smugglers all take advantage of and derive economic benefit, and in some cases their livelihood, from the economic differentials that borders often offer, where merely moving goods or people from one side to the other can be sufficient to turn a profit. So too different legal codes and variations in the vigour with which the law is enforced on each side of a border can clearly affect the kinds of activities that take place there or what can be bought, and some people cross in order to shop for what they cannot otherwise buy or to engage in behaviour outlawed at home. Throughout the 1960s residents in the Irish Republic, for example, where the government was strongly influenced by the Catholic Church, had to visit Northern Ireland to purchase condoms, while Prohibition in the USA from 1918 to 1933 meant that the only alternative to bootleg liquor was to purchase alcohol by crossing the border into Mexico. Border zones thus act as convenient locations in which to conduct business that can profit from the economic, legal and political disjunctures between adjacent jurisdictions.

In border markets sex is often just another product available for sale. The same forces that facilitate and shape the border trade in general also shape the forms of sex we find there, and, as we shall see below, these are also determined by a range of factors including supply and demand, periodic clamp downs and inequalities of wealth and power. Although various forms of 'adult entertainment' are frequently available, such as strip clubs and massage parlours, much of the sex trade at borders involves prostitution. Indeed, social scientists have long remarked on how prostitution thrives at borders, where it is evident in 'large doses', to use Oscar Martínez's (1988: 11) somewhat loaded phrase, and it appears to flourish at borders where a lower standard of living, poor wages and underemployment on one side are juxtaposed with a ready flow of comparatively prosperous potential clients on the other, as many examples testify (on Morocco and Spain see Driessen 1992: 182–8; on Mozambique and South Africa see Gordimer 1990: 73–4; on Mexico and the US see below). Sometimes the gap is between a comparatively stable economy and one characterized by collapse or transformation, as between former 'Western' and 'Eastern' Europe. At other times it may be between a developing economy and one recovering from war, as in the border markets ankle-deep in mud where Thai clients brave checkpoint signs that warn of AIDS to visit Cambodian prostitutes (French 1996). So although prostitution is obviously neither inevitable nor unique at borders, it is certainly well documented there, and many borders have long enjoyed notoriety for their sex and vice (on the economics of prostitution, see Chapter 4).

Popular cultural images of crossing borders are often tied up with a seductive image of sexual discovery; they symbolize the crossing of sexual boundaries and hold out the promise of real sexual emancipation and fulfilment. Structured by disparities of wealth and power, which they both reflect and help to reproduce, such images are sometimes explicit, as exemplified by a series of titillating tabloid-like textual and web-based representations of the US–Mexico border (recalling the graphic Tijuana cartoons of the 1930s and 1940s; see Adelman 1997). Widely represented in the US throughout the twentieth century as a source of sexual thrills, with its rows of sleazy bars, easy sex and debauched men, the border with Mexico has been sensationally described in Ovid Demaris's ironically titled *Poso del Mundo* ('The Sink of the World') as a 'sixteen-hundred-mile pleasure strip ... oriented to gringos with low libidinal thresholds' (Demaris 1970: 4). It has thus 'long been imagined as a border that separates a pure from an impure body, a virtuous body from a sinful one, a monogamous conjugal body regulated by the law of marriage from a criminal body given to fornication, adultery, prostitution, bestiality, and sodomy' (Gutiérrez 1996: 255–6). Despite a succession of 'clean-up campaigns' on both sides of the border, this image persists. Some contemporary websites capitalize on the border's reputation for vice and decadence by advertising pornographic videos purportedly featuring 'illegal Latinas' in a variety of sexual positions with men wearing the uniform of the US Immigration and Naturalization Service's Border Patrol.

Allegedly 'shot by our own film crew on location', one site markets videos of young women whom the site claims were intercepted trying to cross the border illegally and who were offered a choice between providing sexual favours and being deported. In an image that suggests a twice-over dominating exercise of power, a banner headline on the site and a photo gallery of mug shots, each stamped 'DEPORTED', gloats that many of the women were deported even after providing sex.[1] These images reveal the marketing potential and almost mythic status that border sex continues to enjoy among at least some sections of North American popular culture. The overriding tone of the website text, the photographs of uniformed men with naked women and even the sexual positions depicted merge in an imaginary that reflects and reworks in sexualized code the inequalities of the US–Mexican border itself. We shall return to this theme of 'policing bodies' later.

Whatever the popular view of border prostitution, the realities of sex along the Mexico–US border as documented in the social scientific literature sometimes evoke a no less striking set of images. Certainly the picture that these images portray is one that juxtaposes politico-economic power and wealth with poverty and unemployment, a picture that both reflects and underwrites the inequalities that are such a feature of life and social relations across this border generally. The Mexico–US border has been famously described as a border at which the 'Third World grates against the first and bleeds' (Anzaldúa 1987: 3). The economic consequences of this for the Mexican side, and the centrality of the sex trade to the economic viability of the region and the Mexican state, have been summarized elsewhere (see Donnan and Wilson 1999: 93–5). Drawing on this discussion here, we outline how the many disparities between Mexico and the US have helped to shape the settings, styles and structure of border sex and how this has altered in response to shifting relations between the two countries.

In the early days the sex trade along this border was moulded by American military might. During the American occupation of Chihuahua in 1916, General Pershing controversially introduced a system of regulated prostitution in an effort to control the spread of venereal disease amongst his troops. Pershing designated particular areas for prostitution at the edge of camp and instituted regular health checks for the Mexican prostitutes that he brought to live and work there. Not everyone approved, even among his troops, and those in the nearby military hospital complained of being covered in 'whoredust' when the wind was blowing in a certain direction, although this was nothing compared to the 'foul stench' that the border sex trade was later said by an Episcopalian pastor in California to cast across the border to the north (cited in Machado 1982: 350). Such censure reflected the growing moral reform then gripping the US, which with the introduction of Prohibition in 1918 led to most of the south-west's 'merchants of sin' relocating to Mexico (Martínez 1988: 114), where northern visitors could now 'break our laws [rather] than their own', as one Mexican sarcastically remarked (cited in Demaris 1970: 5).

American servicemen continued to stimulate the demand for the border sex trade, now mainly in Mexican hands, well into the 1940s and 1950s, with a new and ready market in the thousands of American servicemen from the massive military bases just to the north. Once again the economy was booming, with prostitutes among the highest paid women in border areas and sex work being used by some as a means of supplementing income from other more recent sources of employment in the mostly American-owned factories and assembly plants (*maquiladora*) located just across the border on the Mexican side (Fernández-Kelly 1983: 142–4). In the minds of many people, even these *maquiladora* were often closely associated with prostitution, both as sites where prostitutes worked and as places where prostitution was actually carried out, and they also had a reputation for more general promiscuity among the workforce. To enhance productivity, some *maquiladora* even integrated sexuality into the structure of production (Salzinger 2000). As one Mexican woman told Pablo Vila (2005: 123):

> The maquilas are just fucking prostitution [*pinche puteadero*], nothing but fucking corruption [*pinche corrupcion*]. I think that a fucking cabaret [*chingada cantina*] is cleaner than the maquilas.

Working for foreign employers is itself seen as a form of prostitution, which then becomes a sexualized discourse for talking about the inequalities and hierarchies of this kind of cross-border employment.

By the late 1950s prostitution was a major contributor to the border economy, with untold sums being pocketed as bribes by members of the police and municipal bureaucracy. Attempts to 'clean up' the area and eliminate corruption were persistently compromised by a dependency on the income from the very activities which the Mexican government has sought to eradicate since the early 1960s. State attempts to shut down the sex business were frequently short-lived; ridding border cities of prostitution was highly problematic 'because of the considerable financial returns that such activities provide both legally through taxes, official fees, and personal income as well as illicitly through various forms of corruption' (Arreola and Curtis 1993: 106).

What social scientific accounts reveal is a highly structured and profitable business, one in which to varying degrees the state itself and its agents have been implicated in a messy world of cross-border politics, sex and power. Two main kinds of prostitute are usually identified in the literature: the 'freelancers' or *clandestinas* who work solely for themselves and the *ficheras* who work for a particular bar and who are entitled to a percentage of the income from the drinks they encourage patrons to purchase. Bars which provide prostitution are themselves of a number of types and may be variously classified according to the arrangement which they have with the prostitutes who work for them (see Roebuck and McNamara 1973), as well as by their clientele and geographical location. Historically, the first *zonas de tolerancia*, as the neighbourhoods associated with prostitution are known, developed in or near the commerical centres of the border towns themselves, often in close proximity to, or on the margins of, the major traditional tourist trails, as with the Zona Norte in Tijuana. As efforts to attract a different kind of tourist were made, many of these *zonas* were allowed to decay or were removed altogether. In many cases the action simply shifted out of town, to areas difficult to reach and flanked by industrial estates, railways or low-income housing. These 'boys' towns' and 'bull pens' were purpose-built with a range of bars and other facilities within a walled enclosure, access to which was controlled by strict policing of a single entrance. Within the enclosure itself, prostitutes and establishments were hierarchically ranked, largely on the basis of cost and perceived desirability to potential clients, with the least attractive women consigned to the rear of the compound where business was transacted in tiny cabins or 'cribs' that opened directly on to the street. *Zonas* can be ethnically segregated, catering mainly either for a Mexican or an American clientele, or for black Americans or white Americans; they may also be segregated depending on whether it is heterosexual or homosexual sex that is on offer. Here border sex is clearly shaped by race, nationality and class, a structure manifest in concrete form in the layout of the *zonas* themselves, even those undergoing the modernization of Mexico's sex industry (see Kelly 2008).

According to Pablo Vila (2005), many of those on the Mexican side of the Mexico–US border have come to understand their own lives in terms of the widespread border sex trade, alongside which they must live irrespective of whether they are actually involved in it or not. As we shall see in the Turkish example below, this is also the case elsewhere; where commercial sex is part of border life, it is not unusual to find it incorporated into people's self image as one way in which they understand and define themselves. Thus in Mexico the border sex trade has become an integral element of border identity. Mexican borderlanders use it as a way of talking about themselves, about the distinctiveness of the region in which they live and about the differences they perceive between themselves and North Americans. They also see it as something which distinguishes them from their fellow Mexicans who live further south. In other words, border sex has become a boundary marker that simultaneously both reinforces the state lines that articulate a sense of national identity and nuances the ties of Mexican ethnic self-identification. Paradoxically, then, border sex would seem to help to draw the lines around a national identity (distinguishing Mexicans in relation to Americans), at the same time as it helps to differentiate within it (between border Mexicans and southern Mexicans).

A reputation for sex and vice thus gives to the Mexican border a kind of stigmatized distinctiveness, and it is for this that it has become so widely known. Some border towns and cities have particularly bad reputations; Ciudad Juárez and Tijuana have become bywords for prostitution and libertarian values and behaviour throughout the US, Mexico and beyond, generating a 'metaphorical overlay of feminization and abjection' (Castillo et al. 1999: 388). The result has been the emergence of a stigmatized 'border city identity' and a distinct regional discourse that generates a powerful sense of borderland belonging by emphasizing the kinds of commercialized sexual activities outlined above (Vila 2000: 25). Vila (2005: 112–13) refers to this as the 'city of vice' discourse, which he sees as composed of a constellation of key narrative themes and characters. Central among these is the figure of the *libertine Fronterizola*, a role that Vila suggests easily transmutes into the male or female prostitute. Other narrative themes similarly emphasize liberal or libertarian attitudes and morals, and he notes how the location of Juárez as a border town in the middle of the desert has helped to produce the *liberal Fronterizo/a* who displays a more tolerant and relaxed approach to sexual behaviour and who is the Mexican counterpart of a third character in the 'city of vice' discourse, the *liberal American*. Throughout the narratives that Vila collected in and about Juárez, where he did his fieldwork, these themes and figures appeared recurrently, sometimes together or overlapping and sometimes individually. Talk about the town was full of such images – of male and female prostitutes and of liberal and libertine borderlanders – even when the focus of the conversation was not explicitly about sexual matters. In other words, this regionally specific discourse with its roots in the border sex trade became a way of talking about all kinds of issues and relationships and not just the sex trade itself. Mexico becomes 'a concept, not a country, a way to understand morals and ethics, morals and ethics that allegedly were characteristics of a country named Mexico' (Vila 2000: 117). Border sex thereby supplies a repertoire of images, metaphors and characters that can be used to talk about what it means to be Mexican and the unequal relationship to the American 'other' to Mexico's north. In a world where everything may seem increasingly similar, even a stigmatized sexual distinctiveness can be a resource.

One consequence of inequality at borders is of course that it is often easier to cross from one side than it is from the other. Thus at the Mexico–US border Americans have generally found it easier to cross than Mexicans, reflecting the stark disjunctures that characterize the region. That 'gringos' could travel south for sex was tolerable, legally if not morally, and was even sometimes something to be facilitated and encouraged, but the possibilities of a sexual flow in the other direction were somewhat more tightly regulated, as we examine next.

ALIEN BODIES

Following the influential work of Mary Douglas (1966) and Judith Butler (1990), it is now a commonplace in anthropology to note the synecdochal relationship between the margins of the human body and the boundaries of the social. Butler's observations on the contamination and dangers of 'unregulated permeability' for social and bodily boundaries are often cited by those who note how border crossing is expressed in sexual metaphor and image (Borneman 1986). The perceived permeability of the Mexican border, for instance, is readily resignified in terms of the margins of men's and women's bodies in a popular discourse that emphasizes the boundary transgressions of prostitution and male homosexuality; like the border, such bodies are believed to be at risk of 'foreign pollution' because of their openness to the 'other' (see Vila 2005: 114–15, 132). Evident in such discussions is a dual process by which the sexual body is both subjected to and can stand as a metaphor for the wider political fields of nationalism, minority and majority politics, ethnic and other social and political movements, and international and inter-state relations.

Geopolitical borders are frequently conceived in this way as boundaries of the body politic, a protective skin that guards against disease, moral degeneration, sexual 'penetration' and genetic corrosion. 'Leaky' borders are thought likely to result in 'infection', a danger to the nation that must be averted through rigorous policing. 'Transitional beings', as we know from Victor Turner (1967: 97), 'are particularly polluting, since they are neither one thing nor another; or may be both; or neither here nor there'. Border guards thus become 'body' guards, who safeguard the body politic and scrutinize the bodies of all who pass for tell-tale signs of contamination.

Prevention of disease has long offered states a rationale for border controls and may provide a justification for quarantine, refusal of entry or repatriation, practices with the potential to become highly charged politically when they intensify conflicts over bordered terrain (see Porter 1997) or when they block the free passage of identifiable categories of entrant.[2] Many examples suggest that sexually transmitted diseases and HIV are 'nationalized' by being particularly blamed on foreigners: the Greek media blame Albanian migrants, while Albanian health officials attribute the proliferation of new viruses to movement in the opposite direction (Seremetakis 1996: 490); in Uganda it is Tanzanian soldiers, Kenyan long-distance lorry drivers and Western tourists and development workers who are said to have brought AIDS (Lyons 1996); while among Mexicans who migrate to California it is seen as an exclusively North American illness (Bronfman and Moreno 1996: 66). The processes at work here are unsurprising to anthropologists, who have long documented the element of danger associated with the stranger and that naturalizes their undesirability in justificatory mechanisms of exclusion and closure. 'Infected' travellers are likely to find themselves excluded, like the Haitian asylum seekers held by the US in an HIV detention camp in Guantanamo Bay in the early 1990s, or the young Romanian and Russian women whose entry to Northern Cyprus depends on a certificate of health clearance additional to that required by other visitors, a formal border entry requirement that simultaneously constitutes the sexualized category it sets out to regulate (Scott 1995: 391, 401). Alien bodies, it would seem, are likely to be pathologized as disseminators of disease, as the embodiment of the viruses they are said to carry, so that difference and undesirability are made integral to their very being. 'Otherness' is quite literally 'in their blood'.

Both the body and the body politic are thereby put at risk by borders that threaten to leak, in a leakage that is at once both physical and moral, and consisting of people and contaminating substance in the parallel flow of bodies and bodily fluids. Although the threat is often most visibly represented by the bodies of prostitutes charged with the spread of sexually transmitted diseases, all who cross may be considered potentially polluting. Many different borders are thus personified and gendered in this form and examples from Turkey–Syria (Stokes 1994), Turkey–Georgia (Hann and Bellér-Hann 1998) and Mexico–US (Gutiérrez 1996: 258) all testify to the perceived close association between borders, sexual infection and moral decline.

The US has a particularly well-documented history of vetting hopeful entrants for disease, and strict medical examination and quarantine regulations were enforced throughout the nineteenth and twentieth centuries to screen out those thought to be polluting. Such procedures also screened for migrant sexuality and sexual practice. Both men and women were scrutinized for evidence of 'immoral' behaviour and attitudes, and might be barred from entering the US not just because of what they had actually done but also because of who they *were* and what it was thought they *might* do. Such judgements were frequently made on the basis of gender, class and race in a manner that both reflected and helped to reproduce the very inequalities from which these criteria arose in the first place. In the nineteenth and twentieth centuries, the US immigration authorities increasingly codified and refined a range of procedures intended to exclude 'immoral' women from entering the country (Luibhéid 2002). Female migrants were classified as wife, prostitute and lesbian, with only the former likely to be granted entry. These categories were not self-evident or pre-existent, but were constructed through the practices of those who worked at migrant reception centres and who consequently helped to determine the sexual identities that they sought to regulate. According to Luibhéid, preconceptions and prejudices that associated certain kinds of sex with a particular class, race or ethnicity further influenced decisions to grant or deny entry. Thus working-class Chinese women were targeted by immigration officials who believed that such women were likely to be prostitutes, a suspicion generated by the convergence of their gendered, class and racial identities (Luibhéid 2002). Other 'peripheral sexualities' were also excluded on the grounds that they threatened the nation; 'the amoral and despotic pimp, the fecund woman whose reproduction was uncontrolled, the gold-digging hussy intent on snaring an American husband, and the foreigner who threatened miscegenation' were all thought to be too 'dangerous' to be granted entry (Luibhéid 2002: xiv–xv). Prostitutes and lesbians were considered especially dangerous to the nation's 'heterosexual imperative'; even after the ban on lesbians was lifted in 1990, lesbian immigrants still faced discriminatory practices, including the fact that, unlike heterosexuals, their intimate relationships with US citizens did not entitle them to legal residency (Luibhéid 2002: xix). Such women were denied entry on medical grounds, with lesbians barred as part of the 'intent to exclude all aliens who are sexual deviants' (Luibhéid 2002: 78).

In a crudely embryonic form of biometrics, immigration officials believed they could identify the sexuality of intending entrants from their bodies, which were closely inspected for sexual 'contamination'. While Luibhéid (2002: 84) suggests that the use of visual cues to monitor the border is still not well understood, particularly 'where immigrant women of color with diverse sexualities are involved', she is nevertheless able to show that dress, demeanour and the physical body itself offered themselves for judgement and were taken to reveal the secrets of erotic desire and practice. Immigration doctors were instructed to look for signs of syphilis, gonorrhoea and 'abnormal' sexual appetite, but they were also required to look for indications of pregnancy, which regardless of marital status could be grounds for exclusion since it was thought likely that pregnant women would become a drain on public welfare. The hair of the female migrant was a frequent focus of attention, with its relative lustrousness or lifelessness regarded by some immigration doctors as a useful diagnostic tool to determine pregnancy, while hair 'cut shorter than some women's' contributed to the deportation in 1960 of a Mexican woman since it made her look 'like a lesbian' (Luibhéid 2002: 9, 80, 81). Some bodily features were positively assessed, and a Chinese immigrant might overcome preconceptions associated with her gender, race and class by her modesty, youth and prettiness, or by the fact that her feet had been bound, something considered by immigration officials as reliable evidence that she was unlikely to be a prostitute (Luibhéid 2002: 49). Some female immigrants sought to conceal their sexuality, and others sought to pass as men. In one colourful case that caught the eye of sexologist Havelock Ellis, a female immigrant was found to be a woman only after her death, although her two wives continued to maintain that she had been a man. Apparently she had worn 'a very elaborately constructed artificial penis. In her will she made careful arrangements to prevent detection of sex after death, but these were frustrated as she died in a hospital' (Havelock Ellis, cited in Luibhéid 2002: 12). In yet other cases dress revealed rather than concealed, and prostitutes, for example, were regarded as readily identifiable by the style and colour of their clothing.

The meaning of the sexual body here takes on a particular inflection when read in a manner that is specific to the regulatory 'culture' of the border, where the sexual identities of those who wish to cross are confirmed and shaped in the dialectic between formal regimes of control and the quotidian practices of the officials who apply them. As Luibhéid (2002: 84) argues, such mechanisms of control are deeply embedded in 'histories of racism, sexism, imperialism, and exploitation', and this makes them particularly pervasive and resistant to change. Moreover, where entry can be denied on the basis of sexual practice or condition, how migrants experience their sexuality, and the bearing their sexuality has on their future, are directly susceptible to fluctuating interpretations and applications of this border policy.

Once migrants are granted entry, these gendered, class and racial hierarchies continue to provide the frame within which alien bodies are understood, as well as the context against which the migrants themselves experience the erotic. Yet amidst all the research on migrants, even that on gender (Luibhéid 2002: 138), there is surprisingly little on their sex lives that sees their sex lives as other than a threat. One study that seeks to move beyond images of migrants as sexual predators or prostitutes is Gloria González-López's (2005) account of sexual intimacy among Mexican migrants in Los Angeles, in which she explores the sexual narratives of a group of Mexican heterosexuals to show how what takes place in the 'privacy' of their bedrooms is shaped by the wider context of their new migratory circumstances. The focus on heterosexuals is significant, she suggests, as an example of 'studying up' in a field (the sociology of sex) that has focused largely on how other sexualities have been shaped within structures of power where heterosexuality is privileged, dominant and 'normative'. Moreover, it raises questions about how a dominant sexual identity as heterosexual intersects with marginalized social identities as migrants, Mexicans and monolinguals.

In contrast to acculturation and assimilationist models of migration which view it as a process of incorporation into the values and practices of the host society, González-López shows how the sex lives of Mexican migrants are no simple and direct response to their new environment. Instead, the transformations are 'complex, nonlinear, and diverse', responsive to new and sometimes perplexing political, economic and social forces within contexts of inequality based on gender, race and class (González-López 2005: 26). Because sexuality is perpetually in flux, in Mexico just as in the US, models of 'before' and 'after' simply cannot accommodate or explain post-migration sexual transformations. Instead, migrants rethink their sexuality in response to the shifting circumstances of daily life – as they enter full-time employment, find a better job and renegotiate their relationship with their partner – as one Mexican woman explained:

> I work and support myself so I don't have to have sex with my husband if I don't feel like it... In Mexico, I worked in a factory, but here I became an apartment manager. Before, he used to do whatever he wanted to. If he wanted to have sex, I had to go right there and do it, day or night. I had no choice. But now that's all over! That's history! (González-López 2005: 18)

Mexican women are more likely than men to report sexual gains as a result of their migration (González-López 2005: 218). Financial independence has given many migrant women a new sense of control and self-sufficiency in their relationships that has transformed their sex lives and shifted the power dynamic in erotic encounters. This might mean the confidence to engage in sexual practices they would not have considered or even known of before or to take the lead themselves in intimate affairs. But it has also meant a willingness and openness to talk about sex and to share their sexual experiences and concerns with other migrant women, whose sexual advice, support and information are mutually transformative of the participants' sex lives in a way that does not just automatically 'Americanize' them (González-López 2005: 27, 163ff.). Sometimes such sexual emancipation may cause friction between partners, particularly if a woman is thought to have become over-empowered, or it may result in 'a power revolt across generations and beyond borders' as daughters pressure their parents to be allowed to date boyfriends and enjoy novel forms of sexual opportunity (González-López 2005: 194; see also Vila 2005: 138–9).

While working outside the home may have enabled migrant women to reclaim sexual agency and autonomy, it has done so in a context where their sex lives are framed by threat and danger as well as pleasure. For some Mexican women the new-found sexual freedoms of migration to Los Angeles are accompanied by new-found sexual fears for themselves and their children about HIV, promiscuity and sexual violence which temper the sense of sexual emancipation. Other forces outside their control also constrain and shape migrants' sex lives, as one man explained:

> The woman gets off from work and the man gets off from work, they invested eight hours at their work places, and two hours of overtime, and after that ... do you think she is going to be willing to flirt with or to be teased by her husband? Or to wear intimate and beautiful underwear? Or to allow her man to be romantic with her... By 8 or 9 pm, they are fried. All they want to do is to lie down and go to sleep. (González-López 2005: 154)

Under the pressures of time and work in a busy society where the fast-paced demands of capitalism have invaded the bedroom and limited the opportunities for sex, the sex lives of some migrants have deteriorated (González-López 2005: 151–60, 173). For others, the change is particularly dramatic, and the pressure of an impoverished and structurally disadvantaged position in the Los Angeles economy forces less advantaged migrants into periodic sex work. Here the inequalities that shape migrant sex lives become especially acute as sexual identities intersect in destructive ways with identities of race and class. Many of the *jornaleros* (day labourers) who migrated to California to find work could not have imagined that they would become objects of desire for American consumers who would transform the labour relationship into a sexual transaction. As González-López (2005: 206–7) points out, while white, middle-class gay men may be disadvantaged relative to white, middle-class heterosexuals, when they hire poor Mexican men for work and sexual pleasure, they become 'the protagonists of a hegemonic masculinity because of their different class, ethnicity/race, citizenship, and language'. Sexual harassment and coercion are common experiences among poorer migrant men, whose image as dark, passionate and exotic makes them just as vulnerable to sexual exploitation as unemployed migrant Mexican women. At the same time, these men (like migrant lesbians) are subject to the heterosexual pressures of their fellow migrants, and thus become caught between 'the racism of the dominant society and the sexist expectations' of their own community (Espín 1997: 175, cited in Luibhéid 2002: 144).

Under circumstances characterized by great inequality, such as those at the Mexico–US border, migrant men and women thus 'face painful alternatives ... [and] ... play out their few choices via their sexualized bodies' (González-López 2005: 209). As we see next, these choices are frequently full of ambivalences and ambiguities as border crossers become entangled in the complex intersections of gender, sexuality, ethnicity and class in a *mestiza* world of multiple and shifting subjectivities (see Anzaldúa 1987).

AMBIVALENT LIAISONS

Girls have come from Russia
They are all over the coast
The river in our valley
Flows in excitement
Oh, Natasha...

The border at Sarp has been opened,
People came to sell their goods,
Those fed up with their wives
Now sleep with Natasha.
Oh, Natasha...

(from 'Natasha Disco' by Erkan Ocaklı,
cited in Bellér-Hann 1995: 231–2)

So far we have considered the economic and other inequalities that shape the sex lives of those who live at or seek to cross state borders, and we have noted at length the commodification of sex that so often seems to be a feature of relationships there. We have also noted how sex and its commercial transaction become ways of talking about the border and about those who live and work on either side, a discursive embellishment that reflects and renews the inequalities of international relations and becomes an idiom for imagining the nation. In this section we extend these themes to include examples of cross-border sex that are less obviously and more ambiguously commodified or not commodified at all, and where the ways in which sex has been shaped and altered by the fact of having crossed the border are rather more ambivalent. Seeing borderland sex solely in terms of prostitution and threat, as much of the popular press and even academic literature seem to do, greatly oversimplifies the forms that this sex can take and may not only fail to disentangle economy, commodity, romance and desire but also undermine the agency and subjectivity of those involved. We must be careful, therefore, not to overemphasize the 'exploitative power relations' in cross-cultural encounters, but to explore as well the potential empowerment of sexual involvement in border settings (Campbell 2007: 262, 264; Lindquist 2002: 137).

Lurid accounts of 'streets of shame', such as the E55 highway between Germany and the Czech Republic where sex is sold along the roadside, still have the power to generate moral panic across much of northern Europe and beyond. But the line between sex work and other forms of sexual involvement that may entail economic exchange is particularly blurred among female migrants such as those who crossed the borders between Eastern and Western Europe following the collapse of communism. In the early 1990s women from Eastern Europe began to cross the borders into the West in vast numbers, alongside suitcase traders and small-time smugglers, and like them became a feature of the new markets that sprang up everywhere selling goods and services that had been unobtainable before. Taking advantage of the relaxation of the border with Turkey, for example, women from the former Soviet socialist republic of Georgia were quick to 'cash in on opportunities to provide services' previously only available in Ankara (Hann and Bellér-Hann 1998: 250; Hann and Hann 1992), services for which they might initially demand as much as one million *lira* even if, in the end, they were prepared to settle for less. In these circumstances, sex clearly became a potentially very lucrative commodity. However, the position of these women and their sexual attachments are more complex and subtle than sometimes thought. Despite the tight jeans, distinctive hairstyles and seductive postures that make these women highly visible, and lead to their being locally categorized as immoral, their sexual engagements are rarely 'prostitution' or 'sex work' in any straightforward or clear-cut sense of these terms. Instead, their sexual liaisons with local Turkish men are complex intimacies that entail love, romance, sex, money, food, housing, marriage and much else besides. In this sense, 'sex work' is better seen as one strategy amongst others, rather than as denoting a category of person (cf. Keough 2004: 22).

It is important to remember that these women do not form a homogeneous group, but have their own internal hierarchies and differences that shape their opportunities and sexual capital (Bellér-Hann 1995: 222). Some are relatively well-educated and from urban backgrounds, yet their sexual transactions when they cross the border are, in some parts of Turkey at least, with rural Turkish men who have had little or no education. Their sexual involvements thus confound and invert the popular stereotype of white middle-class men seeking sex for cash from vulnerable, lower-class women and contrast sharply with the sex sought by the German businessmen who cruise the E55, and with the pay-for-play border sex trade we explored in the Mexico–US context. The ambiguous class identity of these foreign women when they cross the border thereby complicates the relationship between sexual power and inequality (cf. Constable 1997: 542). In her study of Trabzon on the Black Sea coast, Uygun (2004) comments on the anxieties and disjunctures that arise in such circumstances, arguing that the sexual liaisons between the Georgian 'Natashas', as they are locally called, and the local Turkish men must be seen within a broader context than a one-off trade of sex for cash. Rather, these women enter into a variety of relationships with Turkish men that include those of lover, wife and mistress as well as prostitute. All of these relationships at some level involve an exchange of sexual services for material benefits including money, but they also encompass accommodation and everyday subsistence and support. Some of the women Uygun met denied that they were engaged in 'sex work' at all, perhaps not surprisingly given local moral strictures, though they admitted that some of their close friends were so involved. Because of their physical appearance, many of the women were readily identified as 'Natashas' whom Turkish men stared at in the street, even though they said they tried hard not to draw attention to themselves by carefully avoiding settings in which cross-border sex workers were known to gather. Olga, for example, was a masseuse but was ambiguous about whether or not she was involved in 'sex work'. On arrival in Turkey she had conducted a series of affairs with married men, the most recent of whom was paying for her accommodation while she pursued her ambition of contracting a 'formality marriage' that would enable her to claim Turkish citizenship. Similarly, Tatayana was the mistress of an elderly married patron whose financial support was eventually replaced by that of her neighbour, with whom she subsequently began an affair, eventually marrying this man's son in order to obtain citizenship. Uygun argues that both of these women had to balance the contradictory and ambivalent demands faced by young single migrant women. Honourable but sexually available and desiring as well as desired, their relationships entailed complex combinations of service, respect and erotic longing in a livelihood that depended on the ability to provide sexual services to their patrons while distinguishing themselves from full-time sex workers (Uygun 2004: 36).

The political and moral narratives that have come to characterize the transnational flow of women into this part of borderland Turkey mirror the ambiguities of the ambivalent liaisons that are found there. In addition to the moral anxiety that so often accompanies the sexual penetration of borders, which is usually expressed in the imagery of sexual threat and moral decline that we noted above, another kind of narrative has accompanied the Natashas, one that sees them in a very positive and liberating light as sophisticated cosmopolitans who bring the promise of modernity to this long-neglected corner of Turkey. Uygun records some revealing remarks about these women by local Turkish men who have become involved in relationships with them. These describe how the women introduced the men to a range of novel experiences, such as romantic restaurant dining, seeing a woman comfortable with her own nakedness and oral sex. Men who described themselves as coming from a traditional rural background said that they had seized this opportunity 'to get "educated" in the art of desire and romance' and to learn 'how to use knife and fork, how to make love, how to shave and be clean-cut, how to dance' (Uygun 2004: 38). Although Uygun is sceptical about the modernizing potential of these developments, and particularly about their ability to effect long-term change to the existing conservative conceptions of gender, it is clear nevertheless that there is an ambivalence about the way in which the arrival of these women is discursively elaborated. Such ambivalences are found elsewhere too, and Julie Scott (1995: 400) reports from Northern Cyprus that migrant Russian and Romanian women are similarly characterized by a paradoxical mix of desirability and revulsion, being viewed as modern and attractive as well as deviant and dangerous. In Cyprus, however, these ambivalences are mirrored in emerging transformations in the sexuality of young Cypriot women themselves and so help to highlight the unresolved contradictions in women's contemporary status on the island. In both these examples, then, the sexualized discourse around those who cross borders is once again a way of commenting on and articulating community identity, as we have already seen in a number of the examples above (cf. Constable 1997; Demetriou 2006).

Notions of modernity are thereby effected and defined in the context of the new forms of sexual opportunity and adventure to which increasing transnational flows of people and ideas give rise. Transnational mobility has extended sexual possibilities and introduced new ways of being in the cosmopolitan environments it has generated, and although these themes may be played out in different ways in different places, the ethnographic record confirms that the varied and particularized local forms they take reflect the uneven access to political and economic resources of those involved. As Brennan (2004a, 2004b) shows in her account of sex tourism in the Dominican Republic, while border crossing may generate aspirations to sexual modernity, this is clearly not equally available to all.

Since the 1990s the town of Sosúa in which Brennan did her fieldwork has become a major destination for sex tourists, principally from Canada initially but subsequently also in large numbers from Germany as the town's reputation spread and the cost of transatlantic air travel declined. Although some foreign women enter into relationships with sanky pankies, Dominican men with whom sex is exchanged for gifts including money (see Chapter 4), most of the sex tourists are heterosexual men seeking sex with their romanticized and orientalized image of a dark and sensuous Venus, images propagated via the Internet on websites that have appropriated Sosúa as a sexual playground in what one site refers to as the '*Deutsches* Dominican Republic'.

The arrival of thousands of foreign tourists and the rapid expansion of a resident expatriate community of retirees, restaurateurs and hoteliers has accelerated Sosúa's transformation into a transnational space by adding to the mixed population of Dominicans, Haitians, German Jews (who had fled Nazi Germany in the 1930s) and other Europeans who already lived there. The town's progressive incorporation into global structures means it is impossible to consider the local sex workers' activities in isolation from the transnational networks in which they are now entangled. Sosúa has become a 'transnational sexual meeting ground', an increasingly complex contact zone and 'a kind of border town/transnational space' (Brennan 2004a: 15, 17) within which the local Dominican and Haitian women with whom the visiting German men become sexually involved are just as firmly located as are the German visitors, even though these women themselves might never move. Like the Germans who repeatedly return to the Caribbean, the women also have a stake in more than one place, and though only a small number of them might ever have the opportunity to visit or live in Germany, their daily lives entail maintaining regular contact with their German partners there – often simultaneously with more than one partner – via fax, telephone and money wire. They may be immobile but their lives, livelihoods and relationships nevertheless depend on the ability to span borders, and this in turn helps to shape the nature and durability of the sexual liaisons into which they enter.

Brennan encourages us to abandon any lingering preconceptions about sex work. While exploitation is certainly involved, Dominican sex workers are rarely simply power-less victims and, insofar as they can, they in their turn try to take advantage of foreign men who are prepared to pay for sex, exploiting them as dupes who might provide a passport out of poverty (see also Cabezas 2009). Operating mainly without pimps, the women control their own earnings and conditions of work and see their sex work as a strategy of 'advancement' and not just as one of survival. Involvement in sex work is seen as more than just a way to support one's family; it potentially provides a route out of Sosúa, and many young women dream of finding a European man who will support them financially, perhaps marry them and maybe even relocate them to Germany (just as male 'romance entrepreneurs' in Indonesia seek out foreign women as a 'ticket to a better life'; Dahles and Bras 1999). Their sexual careers and income from sex work thus often come in spurts, as they move in and out of relationships of greater or lesser durability and as their participation in sex work is correspondingly episodic, fragmentary and interrupted. To see them solely as sex workers would thus be greatly to simplify their sexual involvements, which for many entail a cyclical passage through a range of liaisons as sex worker, girlfriend, lover, mistress and wife; sometimes they look like sex worker and client and at other times like a 'couple' (Brennan 1999: 28). Similarly, to see them only as exploited and not also as exploiters would be to mask the ambivalence of their liaisons, which, as Brennan succinctly puts it, requires them to be 'at once independent and dependent, manipulating and exploited' (2004a: 25).

Twenty-two-year-old Elena, for example, entered sex work initially to support her daughter, two sisters and a friend. On meeting Jürgen, a German businessman in his mid-forties, she began a long-term relationship at first underpinned by transatlantic transfers of money but subsequently confirmed by marriage, with Jürgen returning to Sosúa to set up home with Elena, renting an upmarket apartment and furnishing it with the kinds of goods beyond the reach of most Dominicans. Sex work and the transnational relationship that it gave rise to had clearly transformed Elena's situation, enabling her to give up sex work and to realize every sex worker's fantasy of finding a supportive European partner. But it was not to last. Although expecting his baby, Elena began to see less and less of Jürgen, who without warning eventually packed up and returned to Germany. Elena's situation was quickly reversed and she had to sell up, take her daughter out of school and move back into her old neighbourhood. For Dominican sex workers like Elena, life is often boom or bust, reflecting the relative impermanence of both their 'successes' and their 'failures' (Brennan 2004a: 25). She had begun as a sex worker, become girlfriend and mistress and then wife, only to end up as marginal as ever, a cycle she repeated some years later when she married a second German man who within a year had also returned to Germany and stopped sending money.

The precariousness and ambivalences of such sexual careers are closely tied to their transnational basis and to the global inequalities that ensure unequal opportunities to travel, earn and exploit, with the nature of the sexual liaisons that ensue being a manifestation of these inequalities at the same time as they help to underwrite and recon-firm them. While Jürgen and the other German tourists are free to enter and leave the Dominican Republic with no more than a passport, the opportunities for overseas travel for Sosúan sex workers are wholly dependent on the fickleness and unpredictability of their transnational affairs. Although many of the German men who visit Sosúa are of relatively low social and economic status at home, their access to visas and their right to be mobile grant them a capital whose value is greatly enhanced as soon as they land in the Dominican Republic, where, as one website promises, there await '18-year-old girls for less than the price of a good steak'. In Sosúa their modest status at home is inverted and even the unattractive or 'otherwise undesirable' can find partners (just as in Cuba foreign tourists of doubtful attractiveness are privileged when seeking local men to have sex with; see Allen 2007: 196). It is this threat of exploitation that local actors in Sosúa (and in Cuba) strive to convert into an opportunity, exercising 'conscious choices' within the constraints of 'material realities and historical interpellations' based on global hierarchies of race and class (Allen 2007: 199).

Brennan argues that we can understand these processes through an adaptation of Appadurai's (1990) concept of the 'scape', and she conceptualizes Sosúa as a 'sexscape' with three key defining characteristics: the availability of commercial sex; international travel from the developed to the developing world to purchase sex; and the presence of historical and current inequality. In Sosúa, as we have seen, inequality follows from differences in race, class and nationality as well as gender, differences which Brennan (2004a: 16, 32) suggests become eroticized and commodified in order to fuel the racialized sexual imaginings of overseas visitors. Sosúa as sexscape is a world of unequal opportunities and asymmetries where the foreign 'buyer' is at an advantage over the local 'seller' not only in terms of determining 'price' but also in terms of realizing their desires. It is the foreign traveller rather than the local who extracts the greatest benefit, she argues, since 'race, class, gender, citizenship, and mobility create undeniable power differentials among the actors' (Brennan 2004a: 16, 32). Given such disparities, foreign affairs thus always 'fall short of mutual exploitation' (Brennan 2004b: 713).

But even here, in the midst of such undeniable differentials, there may be ambivalences and disjunctures of meaning. At the local level the negotiation and outcome of these global hierarchies are often subtle and complex and not always what we might expect. In the Dominican Republic, as we have seen, they draw young women from modest backgrounds into ambivalent and volatile transnational relationships characterized by a shifting mix of support and exploitation, desire and romance, with men whose relatively low status at home is elevated and even inverted by their access to international mobility. Yet despite continual disappointments with their German partners, Elena and other Dominican sex workers like her sustain their belief in an image of the idealized foreign partner whose drunkenness and infidelities they repeatedly excuse. Nor is the outcome of these transnational relationships unequivocal in every context, and those who enter such erotic encounters may adopt strategies that subvert their evidently unequal nature, struggling to wrest control of their meaning and symbolism at least.

A striking instance of symbolic subversion that illustrates an attempt to manage the meaning of an otherwise asymmetrical sexual act is provided by Bowman (1996) in his seminal account of a sexual encounter between a rich American woman and Salim, a Palestinian trader in the tourist markets of pre-*intifada* Jerusalem. Sex with foreign tourists, Bowman suggests, was one way in which disenfranchised Palestinian youth like Salim could demonstrate a power which objectively they did not possess in this Israeli-dominated and disputed border zone. Given the transience of their tourist customers and the general similarity of the goods they offered, business was unpredictable for these traders, who compensated for their uncertain fortunes by telling tales of their economic and sexual successes to amuse friends and fellow merchants in the bars and cafes of the quarter after hours, much as Greek men boast of sexually 'harpooning' (*kamaki*) foreign females (Scott 1995: 387). These tales were usually graphic accounts that celebrated how the traders were able to 'screw' the tourists in more ways than one, triumphing sexually as well as economically. Salim, for example, described how he had conned a wealthy American by selling her a Bedouin dress for $400, reducing it from its $450 price tag so that she believed she had got a bargain even though the dress was worth much less. According to Salim, the woman was rich, beautiful and married and although she declined his invitation to meet him that evening, she had clearly been captivated by his charm. Calling at her hotel anyway, he found her exquisitely dressed and anxiously awaiting his arrival. Salim told of how she could not resist his virile attractiveness and, leaving her husband asleep upstairs in their expensive hotel room, went with him to 'a dirty little room' where 'he fucked her till 5am'. In front of his fellow traders Salim made much of the woman's wealth and nationality, using his narrative to subvert the global hierarchies that otherwise denied him power. This is what seemed to be most important to him; the carnality of the encounter gave Salim no pleasure, his account striking in its failure to mention that he himself might have been sexually aroused. As for his partner, she

> was ecstatic about both the size of his 'Palestinian cock' and his technique, and was carried to heights of sexual fulfilment. He, on the other hand, was dropped into disgust and depression by the whole experience. Looking down on her, supposedly flushed by orgasm, he told her she was 'just a slut' and that he was sure 'she fucked with everyone in all the countries she'd been in'. She was, he said, deeply offended, but he claimed that saying this 'made him feel good afterwards'. (Bowman 1996: 93–4)

Salim told of how this was one woman he had certainly 'screwed', 'with the profit and the fuck thrown in'. But he went on to add that, once married to a fellow Palestinian, he would 'take out [his] cock and piss on all the foreign women' (Bowman 1996: 94), comments which suggest the significance of his penis as a tool of subaltern power rather than of reproduction, pleasure or bodily relief.

For Salim and his friends, it is the seduction and conquest of 'foreigners' which count and in their eyes trump a power that is based on wealth and national position. As Bowman (1989: 88) explains in an earlier account of Salim's adventures, the structurally 'fucked' become the 'fuckers' in a symbolic inversion whose sexual domination of foreigners restores the masculinity of those 'feminized' by their economic and political marginality. The American woman is simply incapable of protecting her economic and bodily integrity, despite her advantages and structurally more powerful position, which in his sexual bragging at least Salim manages to confront and reverse (Bowman 1996: 95). Oppression thus 'does not erase agency', as Cabezas (2009: 111, 137) puts it in another context, and foreign affairs enable some to renegotiate their class and racial status even within the disparities of late capitalism.

ASYMMETRICAL SEX

The cases of Salim and Elena are instructive in the present context for they not only offer us a view on how the hierarchies of race, class and nation are variously negotiated in transnational space by those whom these hierarchies most acutely disempower, but they also do so from differently gendered perspectives, with Salim and Elena responding as active agents to border asymmetries in distinctively sexualized ways. Such examples suggest that the mapping out and enactment of power in sexual liaisons that span borders cannot always be read off the asymmetries of power that underlie the borders themselves, at least not in any straightforward way. Socio-economic inequalities may be relativized or inverted, for foreign gay men and visiting heterosexual women alike (Parker 1999: 196–200). There is always the possibility of subversion and challenge and this must be recognized and understood if we are to acknowledge the agency of those involved. At the same time, of course, and as we have seen throughout this chapter, the partners to foreign affairs bring to their relationship often radically unequal access to resources, and it is the negotiation of these within the context of their erotic engagements that we have here considered as a feature of an emerging global sexscape. It is in this sense that the politico-economic asymmetries of borders offer a suggestive indication as to the kinds of sex that are likely to be found there. The potential empowerment or disempowerment of any sexual intimacy is here amplified by the inequalities of the border, where the sexual body becomes – in that well-worn but suggestive phrase – 'an especially dense transfer point for relations of power' (Foucault 1981: 103).

Borderland sex lives also play a major role in the narrative elaboration of the self and the nation, whereby these are imagined in contrast to the sexual representations of others beyond. In many cases national understandings about the reproduction of the nation are closely tied to ideas about the contaminating potential of sex across borders, whether this is in the form of disease or moral corruption. Such notions might be explored, for example, in relation to local beliefs about the family and the reproduction of the nation. In the United States, for instance, where in middle class eyes the family and the nation are underpinned by ideas about conjugal sex (see Schneider 1980), the 'whoredust' that still threatens to blow across the border remains something to be feared. Or they could be further explored in relation to notions of gender that conceive women's role as reproducers of the nation to be threatened by 'foreign' affairs and imported sexual 'perversities'. We take up some of these issues in Chapter 6, where we consider how negotiations over sexual inclusion and exclusion shape the ways in which the nation is imagined, enacted and transformed.

Borderlands clearly offer up new sexual possibilities, just as they have helped to generate novel cultural and economic opportunities. But some of the material presented in this chapter encourages us to be cautious about the impact of novel sexual opportunities created by border crossing and transnational flows. Borderlands may constitute liminal zones, 'experimental region[s] of culture' (Turner 1982: 28), where artists have access 'to many languages (discourses) from different communities' (McMaster 1995: 82). They may constitute festive arenas of play and cultural mixing, the crossing and coming together releasing creative (and libidinous) energies that some scholars have argued are inherently liberating. What we have suggested here, however, is that while new sexual and other cultural forms may come into being through the erotic journeys that transnational travellers undertake, the borderlands which they traverse remain zones of domination and control as well as of cultural play and experimentation. Foreign affairs may generate sexual possibility, but it is power that always seems to realize desire.

NOTES

1. In one well-known case that came to court in 1993, a Mexican migrant woman claimed that she was raped at the border when she refused an agent's offer of release 'in exchange for … giving him sex'. In contrast to the commentary on the website,

documented cases suggest that women are released rather than deported once they have had sex (Luibhéid 2002: 123, 129). The potential for sexual violation at border crossings is not new and aggressive sexual imagery was sometimes used as a threat on territorial boundary markers. For example, a twelfth-century sandstone pillar on an island near Bombay depicts a woman being sexually violated by a bull as a warning to border transgressors that their women will be dishonoured in this way (British Museum n.d.: 32). The relationship between women's bodies and the boundaries of the nation is well documented (see Chapter 6; for an overview see Mayer 2000: 1–22).

2. In the case of immigrant workers, public health is sometimes compromised to keep the flow of labour coming, suggesting that concerns for their health are less a philanthropic gesture than a medicalized rhetoric for controlling the workforce.

6 FORBIDDEN FRONTIERS

When we had made love I slowly recovered my wits... 'Don't you think we ought to find out more about each other? How we live, how we think, what we are? I know your geography pretty well now, all your hills and valleys. Hadn't we better study each other's sociology and anthropology?'

(English colonial officer to his Anglo-Indian lover;
John Masters 1956: 261, 264)

In the last chapter, we examined how transnational movement could radically alter the personal, cultural, economic and political meanings and value of sexual intimacy, as well as how it is culturally represented and understood. In this chapter we develop the focus on how perceived differences of race, ethnicity and nation can shape experiences of sexual intimacy, influencing reactions to it by encouraging the stimulation or the suppression of inter-ethnic erotic desire. We concentrate here on everyday relations at these racial, national and ethnic boundaries – at what is sometimes called the 'ethnic frontier' – in order to understand how sexual relationships are negotiated and regulated in a zone that is perhaps more often analyzed in terms of its political and economic significance in studies which marginalize sex as colourful or spicy anecdote. Accounts of the expansionist injustices and brutalities of the American 'Wild West', for example, occasionally allude to the capture and sexual incorporation of young, white female settlers by the Native Americans whose land was being appropriated, but they do little to probe the role of sexuality in this contact or to portray these women's voices (Courtwright 1996; Wickstrom 2005). Similarly, Linda Colley's (2003) historical overview of 'captivity narratives' in the seventeenth to mid-nineteenth century Mediterranean is generally brief and reserved in its treatment of inter-ethnic sexual involvements when compared to her elucidation of their political ramifications. In this work we are often left wondering how such liaisons were regarded, how they worked out and with what consequences for those involved and their offspring. What did it mean for people to push against a politico-moral code that discouraged sex with those of another race or nation? For the individuals engaged in these relationships, how did they and those around them feel about it and react? And what does this tell us about wider issues of social and cultural order and disorder? The growing body of studies on which we focus below strives to answer such questions by showing how sex is central to many other aspects of the mixing and non-mixing at the frontier, forming the basis of elaborate and shifting moralities that determine behavioural standards, everyday practice and representations of the Other. The chapter is therefore concerned with exploring the dialectic between personal intimacy and the global flows and interconnections that both featured in the colonial past and pervade the increasingly mobile present.

As we noted earlier, sexual representations of the ethnic and racial Other are a common feature of ethnic frontiers, which provide rich and fertile ground for the sexual fantasies that seem easily to take root in the gaps that national and ethnic differences open up. Edward Said (1978) has shown how images of the East as seductive and voluptuous systematically misrepresented it in ways that legitimated the West's understanding of itself as a civilizing, rationalizing and modernizing force, images that both reflected global inequalities of power and were constitutive of them. The product of the Orientalists' own ideological and cultural prejudices, such imagery became a means to subordinate and dominate as well as titillate. Although perhaps less visible now than they once were, similar images continue to inform popular culture. For example, one instalment of the French comic-book adventure series 'Insiders' features a naked female captive bound and immobilized at the mercy of a group of bearded Afghans with unsheathed phallic blades in hand (Garreta and Bartoll 2005). So too the sexual possibilities generated by the uncertainties and edginess of life along the frontier were used as an exotic backdrop to stoke the passions of young men in America between the 1950s and 1970s in the so-called 'sweat magazines' which graphically depicted full-bodied and barely clad young white women in the clutches of a succession of grossly stereotyped imagined ethnic Others. One can only speculate on the view of the world beyond America held by young men raised on titles like 'Sex and the Leopard God', 'Mufti Marshouk's Pleasure Dome of 29 Nudes', 'Blonde Captive in Tibet's Torture Temple', 'Love Queen of the Pygmies', 'The Sex-Crazed Kidnap Cult of the Tanganyika Lion Men' and 'The 1000 Sex Slaves of the Whip-Mad Sheik' (see Collins and Hagenauer 2008). Yet tantalizing and provocative as these storylines were clearly intended to be, it seems likely that they functioned more as cautionary tales about the perils of crossing ethnosexual lines than as a licence and invitation to those who might be tempted to transgress in this way.

Certainly, the personal risks and penalties implied or graphically depicted are grim, both in these men's magazines and in other works of popular culture. A well-worked theme of anglophone fiction on both sides of the Atlantic is sex with someone from 'the wrong side of town', a narrative device that is used to strike fear into middle-class hearts by drawing together characters from diverse backgrounds in explosive meetings that blow social worlds apart, revealing the power of unbridled sexual passion and the precariousness of the moral, cultural and political principles designed to contain it. Rules and regulations may proliferate, but sex seems always at risk of breaking out. In this chapter we explore the forbidden frontiers where ethnic and racial lines are crossed and the efforts made to redress or prevent this.[1] Many factors can complicate the management and negotiation of sexual intimacy at the ethnic frontier. Relations across ethnic and racial boundaries may be qualified by those of age and class as well as by the political-economic context in which they occur, and while we sometimes touch on these latter factors below, it is the former that are our principal focus here. We begin by looking at the regulation of and response to sexual intimacy in war and violent conflict, when, as we shall also see in many of the other examples that follow, ethnosexual intimacy may paradoxically reaffirm and strengthen the very barriers it might otherwise appear to transcend.

CONTROLLING PASSIONS

> Near to the metro stop … a crowd was following a woman who was entirely naked. Her head had been completely shaved, and on her breasts two swastikas tattooed in Indian ink. I trembled at the idea that this woman would no longer be able to undress herself in front of a man without showing the shame that was on her body. (Manouchian 1974: 73, cited by Virgili 2002: 137)

This brief account describes one incident during a procession through the streets of Paris following the liberation of France at the end of the Second World War, an incident that was repeated throughout the country between 1943 and 1946, when an estimated 20,000 women had their heads shaved for allegedly collaborating with the occupying German army (Virgili 2002). Such processions superficially exhibited some of the features of the carnivals mentioned in Chapter 3, including the joyous and riotous behaviour of over-indulgence and licensed self-gratification that was a 'letting go' after years of Nazi occupation and oppression. Like carnivals, they were also often ambiguous, ambivalent and liminal events, as might be expected at a time of passage from war to peace, and usually mingled celebration of freedom with a desire for revenge and reparation in a confusion of passions that was barely contained. Thus the witness of the event cited above goes on to describe how the crowd lost control, pushing and shoving the woman, shouting insults and throwing stones, in a frenzy of hate that ultimately ousted any pretence at the festive.

Many other accounts of French women's sexual humiliation for collaboration with the occupying Germans describe how they were beaten, abused or tarred and feathered as well as shaved before being paraded barefoot or naked through the streets (Virgili 2002: 157). While in France such punishments were inflicted for a variety of offences, including political and financial collaboration, the majority of such accusations (57 per cent) were made against those who had 'slept with Germans' and who had engaged in what became known as 'horizontal collaboration' (Virgili 2002: 15). Elsewhere they were meted out exclusively for sexual collaboration, as in Norway and Denmark (Warring 2006: 88–9).

These punishments for sexually transgressive behaviour that involved crossing ethnic lines were not confined to liberation France or to the Second World War, even if they were not practised elsewhere to the same extent. When widespread street violence erupted in Northern Ireland in the early 1970s, local women had to be careful to maintain their distance from the troops dispatched by the British government to contain it, particularly those who lived in Catholic and Republican neighbourhoods where violent resistance to Britain was greatest. A woman thought to be the girlfriend of a British soldier, or believed to have slept with one, risked having her head shaved, being tarred and feathered and sometimes also beaten 'for fraternizing with the enemy' by Irish Republican paramilitaries who saw these soldiers as an army of occupation (Taylor 1997: 108–9). As the following contemporary quotation makes clear, the sexual boundary between local women and the British army was rigorously policed and its transgression just as firmly punished in Northern Ireland as in liberation France:

> A bucket of tar, a cluster of feathers and a pair of scissors – the implements of IRA 'justice'. On the night of November 9/10, 1971, the mediaeval practice of tarring, feathering and hair-cutting was applied to 19-year-old Marta Doherty, a Roman Catholic from Londonderry's Bogside, who was then tied to a lamppost. Marta's 'crime' – she had fallen in love with a soldier. (Government of Northern Ireland 1972: 4; a full-page photograph accompanies the account)

While war might have exposed the sharp end of the penalties to be paid for transgressive sexual relations in Northern Ireland, the boundary between the British army and local women was not the only sexual frontier to be patrolled there. Intimate contact between the Catholics and Protestants who made up 40 and 60 per cent of the country's population respectively was similarly proscribed and was a boundary that had been effectively sustained by a social system that had kept the two apart since Northern Ireland's establishment through the partition of the island in the 1920s. While the literature on Northern Ireland's deeply divided society tends to emphasize the commercial and political issues surrounding the segregation of Catholic and Protestant, the institutions that underlie this separation can just as well be seen in sexual terms, as providing a way to regulate sexual affairs between the two sides. Residential, educational and occupational segregation may have been instrumental in ensuring the continued marginalization of a Catholic population that was thought to threaten Protestant political and economic privilege, but it also produced parallel political, cultural and social worlds in which the two stood back-to-back, a position that without substantial contortions was hardly conducive to sex.

Such contortions could occasionally be observed in everyday life among the few courageous, rash or blasé mixed-religion couples who, to brave the risks entailed by their affair, had to develop strategies for addressing the many obstacles in their path – exercising caution about their status in public, socializing only with trusted friends, avoiding each other's homes – strategies that offered rich material for works of fiction which depicted the difficulties of 'love across the barricades'. The strength of the antagonism towards these mixed relationships varied historically, and in response to the level of violence at any particular moment, as well as in relation to socio-economic class and the area of Northern Ireland in which one lived. But such variation was along a scale of intensity of hostility, and no one at any time or in any place actively sought out such relationships or was pleased when they occurred. Rather, with varying degrees of vigour, mixed relationships attracted the hostile attentions of family, friends and neighbours, all intent on discouraging them from continuing, sometimes by force if necessary (Donnan 1990). Thus the sexual attributes of the Other were a forbidden and dangerous fruit which if plucked risked retribution. As the statistics show, few of these relationships blossomed into marriage, confirming in practice the cultural preference among both Catholics and Protestants for endogamous unions within their social group.

Within this context, it is not surprising that subversive desire was more likely to flourish in thought than in deed, generating sexualized imaginings about the unknown and exotic sexual Other, much in the manner of well-known analyses of orientalist and colonial fantasy.[2] Although not much written about outside fiction in the Irish case, such a sexualizing of Catholic–Protestant relations can be found encoded in cultural artefact, popular saying and folk belief, as well as in more explicitly sexual and often vulgar statements (and graffiti) about the sexual proclivities of the other side. Among young Protestant men, for example, a popular and enduring belief extols the sexual willingness and virtuosity (if not virtue) of Catholic girls, particularly those who are convent-educated. Once again, contortions feature in the accounts. So too some key iconic moments of the past are remembered in sexualized form. In Protestant accounts of the siege of Derry (in 1689), much is made of the fact that the city walls were never breached by James II's besieging Catholic army. The Catholic Other was repelled and the virtue of the 'maiden' city, as it is now known, secured intact by the prompt action of the Protestants inside who closed the city gates. Transgressive fantasies and fears (of sexual violation) are inscribed in daily life in similar ways, and sometimes come together in descriptions of particular acts. Thus one subversive schoolboy limerick compares the battering of (cannon) balls against Derry's walls to a more intimate act of attempted penetration involving a mixed-religion heterosexual couple.

A vulgar vernacular for sexual body parts and sexual acts was also drawn upon in certain contexts to describe the ethnic violence that has for so long characterized relations between Catholic and Protestant, particularly during the final thirty years of the last century, when death and killing were talked about by paramilitaries in a language heavy with sexual associations. According to Allen Feldman (1991: 69), paramilitary assassins feminized the male objects of their violence by referring to them as 'cunts' – slang for the female genitals – where a 'cunt' was someone understood as 'a passive recipient prior [to] and during the application of violence to the body'. Such 'cunts' were 'given the message', a phrase that in peacetime Northern Ireland had depicted the male role in heterosexual intercourse, but which among paramilitaries during the conflict referred to murdering someone. By being 'given the message', cunts are consequently converted into 'stiffs' (i.e. corpses), the act of 'stiffing a cunt' itself indexing killing and marking a 'shift from the feminized and passive recipient of political codes to the phallic stiff, artifact of power and disseminator of political codes' (Feldman 1991: 70). The sexual allusions are very clear to those who know the argot – even allowing for critics of Feldman's over-interpretative style – and the underlying reference in such violent enactments between Catholic and Protestant, as Feldman notes, is to sexual dominance.

That the Irish war was just as much a sex war as one about religion, culture and politics is evident from what was (and is) one of Irish Protestants' most enduring concerns: the fear that they will be 'bred out' by a higher Catholic birth rate. Many Protestants are quick to allege that this has already happened in the Irish Republic, and that if Protestants in Northern Ireland are allowed to enter mixed-religion relationships and so reproduce for Catholicism, this will spell the end. It is consequently critical that inter-ethnic sexual relations continue to be rigorously policed, and this should not be a matter only for the formal structures, rules and institutions of Northern Irish life in which the sexual boundary between Catholic and Protestant has been long embedded. In a modification of the famous wartime maxim, some diehard Protestant evangelicals even go so far as to claim that in the sectarian battle for souls (and votes) 'careless sex costs lives'; by which, of course, they mean unprotected and thus reproductive sex with Catholics, the only sort possible in Protestant eyes given their perception of the conservative Catholic position on contraception. 'Safe sex' here takes on a whole new meaning. Vigilance is consequently crucial, and everyday social relations become a fragile and delicate process of distinguishing appropriate from inappropriate sexual partners in a situation where skin colour and other physical attributes offer few or no visible clues.

For most people in Northern Ireland, both Catholic and Protestant, choosing a sexual partner thus entails a complex process of sectarian sifting to navigate successfully those contexts where Protestant and Catholic might meet. Rosemary Harris (1972: 148), for example, has documented how everyone 'looks automatically for slight indications from another's name, physical appearance, expression and manner, style of dress and speech idiom to provide the clues that will enable the correct categorisation to be made'. First names, place of residence or the school in which one was educated all provide clues to religious identity in Northern Ireland's divided society. Thus someone called Séamus or Sinéad is more likely to be Catholic than Billy or Sammy, and one's postal address can be promptly located within Northern Ireland's segregated sectarian map. So too less overt clues identify the Other. Slight differences in pronunciation are a giveaway to the practised ear, which identifies how Catholics 'pronounce a as "ah" and h as "haitch", in contrast to Protestants, who say "ay" and "aitch"' (Buckley and Kenney 1995: 7). Many other commentators have also noted this ability to read the religion of the Other from a repertoire of signs, interpreting this process in the context of political conflict, where the ability to 'tell' someone's religion, and by extension their political and national belonging, is a crucial way of managing the possibility of violent antagonism and dispute in the flow of daily life. Less often mentioned, however, is that it is also a way of managing sexual relations, part of the habitus that ideologically divides up the world into political allies and opponents but also into preferred and proscribed sexual partners. So while this ability to tell religion may have been used to identify targets for sectarian attack, it has also been and still is used much more routinely as a means of directing sexual desire along the recommended ethnic routes.

This underlying and usually tacit sexualization of the boundary between Catholic and Protestant in Northern Ireland fits well Joane Nagel's (2003) model of the ethnosexual frontier. Nagel suggests that ethnicity and sexuality converge to form:

a barrier to hold some people in and keep others out, to define who is pure and who is impure, to shape our view of ourselves and others, to fashion feelings of sexual desire and notions of sexual desirability, to provide us with seemingly 'natural' sexual preferences for some partners and 'intuitive' aversions to others, to leave us with a taste for some ethnic sexual encounters and a distaste for others. (Nagel 2003: 1)

Nagel argues that although the relationship between sexuality and ethnicity is often hidden or unarticulated, ethnic boundaries are also sexual boundaries and the power of each is magnified by the co-presence of the Other. She begins with an example from her own adolescence, explaining that while her family's move to the white middle-class suburbs of Cleveland – like that of many similar families throughout American cities – was rationalized in terms of improving 'quality of life' and providing access to 'better schools', it also had the effect of removing her from the possibility of sexual contact with Afro-Americans just as she reached puberty. The decision to move thus had a sexual dimension that was 'part of the invisible foundation upon which ethnic boundaries rest' (Nagel 2003: 3).

Sexual relations across these ethnosexual divides can take many forms according to Nagel and may result in permanent relationships, in temporary, recreational sexual adventuring and experimentation, and in the violent sexual assaults on the ethnic Other that are sometimes characteristic of war. The intersection of sex and ethnicity can be a volatile mix and, as we have already seen in the examples cited above, ethnosexual encounters are often regarded as something to be rigorously policed. They can help to reinforce ethnic (and racial and national) boundaries, but they can also resist them, as subversive and transgressive acts that violate the ethnosexual order. Such violations can contain a range of powerful and contradictory messages about the representation and classification of the ethnic self and Other, about domination and control, and about the practical limits imposed on personal intimacies, not only in times of war or conflict as we examine next.

FATAL ATTRACTIONS

Among the most violent and shocking punishments for violating ethnosexual boundaries were the lynchings and castrations inflicted for transgressing the colour line in the American South. Although lynchings were carried out for a number of reasons, including allegations of murder, they were chiefly seen as a means of racial control in a context where white women were believed to be at threat from the powerful sexuality of African American men. There were often clear political and economic reasons for such attacks, and in the nineteenth century white anxiety about interracial sex can be shown to be closely linked to concerns about black men's growing independence during this period. Nevertheless, such attacks were generally justified in overtly sexual terms. In one such case in Georgia in 1870, the Ku Klux Klan arrived at the home of Henry Lowther, a prosperous, black shopkeeper with political ambitions. Despite being advised of a likely attack in a warning that suggested castration – Lowther had been asked by a white man if he was 'willing to give up [his] stones to save [his] life' – Lowther did not escape, and he later recalled how he was dragged off to a swamp in the middle of the night to be castrated (Hodes 1993: 64; Nagel 2003: 113), an act which the Ku Klux Klan repeatedly insisted was punishment for his illicit sexual relations with a white woman rather than for his political activism.

Such punishments for sexual transgression can seem symbolically overdetermined. As Wiegman (1993: 224) has argued:

> Not only does lynching enact a grotesquely symbolic – if not literal – sexual encounter between the white mob and its victim, but the increasing utilization of castration as a preferred form of mutilation for African American men demonstrates lynching's connection to the sociosymbolic realm of sexual difference. In the disciplinary fusion of castration with lynching, the mob severs the black male from the masculine, interrupting the privilege of the phallus, and thereby reclaiming, through the perversity of dismemberment, his (masculine) potentiality for citizenship.

There is certainly a lot going on here and although to some it may seem overfanciful, it can be hard to resist an analysis of lynching and castration that interprets the message these violent acts inscribe upon the body as an ethnosexualized political code, much as in Feldman's (1991) reading of sectarian violence in Northern Ireland. As Wiegman suggests, the victim is subject to a two-stage process of gendering, first as a *hypermasculinized* 'rapist' requiring punishment and subsequently as the demasculinized body that has been *feminized* through ritualized castration, acts which, as Wiegman (1993: 225) puts it, perform 'the border crossings of race, sex, and sexual difference'. It is an act which, in Wiegman's terms, realigns the newly enfranchised black man with those who still do not have the vote, rendering him both sexually and politically impotent and thereby restoring the ethnosexual frontier.

Such symbolic interpretations may be less fashionable than they once were, at least in certain forms of anthropology, where they are criticized for floating free of any documentable empirical reality anchored in the voices or acts of those most closely involved, but they remain seductive and suggestive and resonate with the kind of sexual and gendered inversions that many anthropologists have noted in the context of the transgressive carnivalesque (for a summary, see Gilmore 1988). Surely more than just flights of analytical fancy, they must be treated seriously, if only for generating debate about what these kinds of acts might have 'really' meant. Nevertheless, it can be difficult to ground them in anything other than the literature and novelistic accounts of the day.[3]

The consequences of crossing the colour line were rather different for white men engaged in sexual relations with black women, particularly before slavery was ended by the passage of the Thirteenth Amendment in 1865. Although interracial sex was outlawed in many US states by anti-miscegenation laws, the law was likely to overlook instances where white men were involved; their sexual entanglements with black women were much less likely to reach the courts than were those between black men and white women (as also under South Africa's Immorality Act of 1927; Bland 2005: 32). Legislative changes in the early nineteenth century which prohibited the importation but not the reproduction of slaves, and which classified the child of a black mother and white man as 'black', had the presumably unintended consequence of encouraging mixed-race unions, since the changes provided whites with economic incentives for such ethnosexual relationships. Thus Nagel (2003: 106–7) notes that slave owners not only introduced breeding programmes to organize and promote sexual contact between male and female slaves, but also were encouraged by the legislation to view their own sexual transgressions as a further means of increasing the size of their labour force, since any offspring from the union would be seen as 'black'. Such light-skinned slaves fetched a much higher price in the slave markets and were the favoured 'fancy girls' and mistresses of slave owners' lust. These liaisons between white men and black women were an 'open secret', subversive intimacies that were morally reprehensible and publicly denounced, and while everyone knew who had fathered the mixed-race children in any particular household, no one could acknowledge them for their own (Nagel 2003: 108). As we shall see below, mixed-race children raised similar issues in colonial south and southeast Asia and their re-classification as belonging to one 'race' or another is often used as an 'elementary strategy' in ethnic boundary making to escape the ambiguity of their stigmatized hybridity (Wimmer 2008: 1039).

While white men could therefore freely cross the colour line, black men were likely to be lynched, reflecting the clear structural and racial inequalities between them. However, race was not the only factor shaping responses to sexual transgression. The gender of the transgressor was also a major element: where white men might expect to avoid overt sanction, the same was not true for white women sexually involved with blacks. These women were generally scorned as lower-class degenerates and were seen by other whites as no better than prostitutes. Black women were equally antagonistic to white women having sexual relations with blacks, and they too saw them as moral degenerates guilty of initiating the sexual seduction of black men. Thus in 1827 one black woman, a free woman and not a slave, was imprisoned for 'assaulting a white woman who associated with black men' (Hodes 1997: 43, cited in Nagel 2003: 110). Clearly 'being assaulted' was nothing like the punishment meted out to black men, but it does suggest that there was an intolerance of sexual transgression on both sides of the colour line, one that was typified by a racialized and gendered inversion of blame in which white men blamed black men while black women blamed white women.

Denigrating the virtue of women who cross the colour line is a widely reported feature of the ethnosexual frontier, as Micaela di Leonardo's (1997) essay 'White Lies, Black Myths' so compellingly bears out. Years after she was raped by a black man, di Leonardo (1997: 55) married a black colleague and began to experience the world in 'both black and white'. When she and her husband applied for jobs at a southern university, it was di Leonardo who was 'the victim of the sly, sexually insinuating remarks made by male and female faculty' (1997: 55), an experience that recalls that of a mixed-race woman in

Britain who complained that everyone who knew her was 'horrified' that she had 'slept with a black man' (Olumide 2001: 107). But men could also be the butt of disparaging comments, as Nagel illustrates with reference to 1960s America, when black women saw black men's sexual affairs with white women as a betrayal, irrespective of whether these affairs were politically or erotically motivated. Even though black men themselves might feel that they were proving their manhood or making a political point by crossing the ethnosexual frontier, black women branded such men as inadequate and dismissed them with a colourful clarity: 'only the rejects crawl for white pussy' (Wallace 1990: 10, cited in Nagel 2003: 118). Intimacy across racial lines was thus as likely to strengthen as to transcend a dichotomized view of the world that saw it in terms of black and white, and even activities that repeatedly crossed social and geographical boundaries – like the 'slumming' parties of the white, middle-class sexual adventurers of early twentieth-century American nightlife who frequented mixed-race nightclubs – contributed to a binary notion of racial difference (Heap 2009).

Nagel includes national as well as racial boundaries within her concept of the ethno-sexual frontier and suggests that implicit within the notion of the nation are certain prescriptions and proscriptions about with whom it is acceptable and unacceptable to have sex. Disciplining those who threaten national boundaries by transgressing these forbidden sexual frontiers is a powerful means of reinforcing national solidarity and of defining the nation, since it clearly distinguishes members from non-members. This is, in part, why in violent conflicts such ethnosexual frontiers are sometimes deliberately transgressed by military rape, when women on the opposing side are systematically sexually assaulted in a strategic deployment of sex as a weapon of war that unsettles the national order of things.[4] During the war in former Yugoslavia, for example, women were represented as the borders of the nation – whose territories were 'feminine spaces ... open to invasion' – an eroticizing of nation that sought both to control and to valorize their sexuality (Mostov 2000: 91). Some less shocking sexual subversions are no less disruptive of national boundaries. The comfortable boundaries of colonial rule and the national orders which they endeavoured to separate were repeatedly endangered and ultimately transformed by the ambiguous status of anyone who straddled them, as Ann Stoler (1992) has shown for the offspring of mixed unions (*métissage*) in French Indochina at the end of the nineteenth century. Stoler's meticulous historical anthropology traces the consequences of the colonial fascination with the exotic and the implications of the colonizers' sexual transgressions with those they governed. As Stoler (1992) shows, anxieties at 'home' in France about what it meant to be French (provoked by the loss of Alsace-Lorraine, the Dreyfus affair and the ambivalent loyalties of the newly classified French citizens in Algeria) were exacerbated in the colonial setting, where the nation's 'interior frontier' was thought to be threatened by interracial unions that blurred the lines of national incorporation and exclusion. Not only might French officials involved in such relations 'go native', but the divided loyalties of their offspring could be politically dangerous to colonial stability and national belonging if the increasing numbers of mixed-race children (*métis*) were recognized as French. The challenge for colonial Indochina thus became how to accept some *métis* as French while rejecting others, a fascination with the hybridized, 'miscegenated product' of illicit, interracial sex that was endlessly rehearsed in nineteenth-century theories of race and enacted in practice (Young 1995: 181–2).[5]

Stoler describes the case of Lucien, the nineteen-year-old son of a French naval employee and his Vietnamese concubine, who was brought to court and sentenced to six months' imprisonment for assaulting a German naval mechanic. His father's plea for a pardon was rejected by the court and he was compelled to serve the full sentence. At issue, according to Stoler (1992: 523), was whether Lucien could really be 'considered culturally and politically French', something that the court seemed to go out of its way to challenge and ultimately deny by consistently referring to him by his Vietnamese name – Nguyen van Thinh – and questioning whether his father had been sufficiently involved in the young man's upbringing to instil a proper sense of *patrie*. There were vague allegations too of improper conduct between them, which, Stoler suggests, may have been a coded accusation of homosexuality or a reference to the possibility that his 'father' was fraudulently making a claim to this relationship only to accord French citizenship to his 'son'. Clearly 'perversion and immorality and patriotism and nationalist sentiments were ... mutually exclusive categories' within a moral order rooted in middle-class European sexual standards (Stoler 1992: 524).

Some of the details of Lucien/Nguyen van Thinh's case recall the physical and cultural distinctions routinely made when identifying the ethnic appropriateness of sexual partners in Northern Ireland, as discussed above, and highlight the moral perils of culturally improper sexual mixing. Lucien (and his father) were judged by how the son looked and acted. What the court appeared to condemn was the father's plea for a son who had been allowed to grow up as Indochinese and who lacked the external attributes of being French, such as skin colour, language and cultural fluency, and so presumably lacked the affective and internal attributes as well. Far from being swayed by the demonstration of a father's love and support for his son, the court denounced the former's behaviour as a neglectful and morally profligate enactment of paternal responsibility – if he was not going to raise Lucien as French, he would have been better to abandon him all together – and ultimately judged both father and son as 'guilty of transgressing the boundaries of race, culture, sex, and patrie' (Stoler 1992: 524).

Stoler argues that such cases were permeated with notions of national purity, contamination and corrosion and were central to defining and managing the boundary between colonizer and colonized at the height of the imperial project. *Métis* children represented the sexual excesses of European men and indexed the failure to adhere to European standards of sexuality and parenting, even as the different ways in which these children were regarded by colonial society reflected the varied sexual contracts between their parents (cohabitation, prostitution, legally recognized mixed marriages). Whatever form it took, *métissage* became 'heavily politicized' not just because it challenged the boundary between 'ruler and ruled', but also for threatening to 'destabilize national identity' and what it meant to be a European (Stoler 1991: 87; 1992: 550).

In her analysis of sex and race in colonial Java, Margaret Wiener (2007) similarly shows how attempts to draw clear distinctions between Europeans and those they sought to govern were repeatedly confronted by the 'messy hybridity of practice', resulting in a 'twilight zone' of muddied racial ambiguities between white and native. Europeans in Java had not always been condemnatory of sexual mixing. When the Dutch East India Company was established in Batavia in the seventeenth century, it mainly hired single men who, prohibited from bringing European women with them, were encouraged to set up house with Indonesian women, adopting many local Asian practices at home and whose children were considered by law to be Europeans as long as their fathers admitted paternity. By the nineteenth century, however, the situation was much less relaxed and the boundaries between European colonials and the mixed 'Indo-Europeans' descended from the sexual involvements of an earlier age began to harden (as in Indochina, where concubinage was similarly subject to a shifting morality; Stoler 1989). Improvements in transportation had brought many more Europeans to the Indies and changes in Dutch emigration policy meant that many of them were women. Colonial concern increasingly focused on strengthening the distinction between those considered culturally European and those merely classified as such by law and with whom sexual relationships were now thought inappropriate, immoral, corrosive of European prestige and a danger to the stability of the colonial order. The deployment of magic (*guna-guna*) to influence sexual encounters, and understandings about who was and who was not susceptible to magic, including Europeans, seemed further to undermine a distinction between rational European and superstitious native.

According to Wiener, *guna-guna* was most likely to be used in mixed relationships by Eurasian or Javanese women attempting to trap a European man into marriage or to punish him for leaving her; she records no cases of the opposite occurring where European women have relationships with Asian men. In one case taken from a 'quasi-ethnographic' novel, a young woman (Betsy) classified as 'European' but with Indonesian ancestors directs her attentions towards a colonial official who:

> is happily married to a (blonde, blue-eyed) [woman] he met on leave in the Netherlands. Repeated ingestion of *guna-guna* potions draws him increasingly under Betsy's spell; he not only loses interest in his family but in his greatest passion, his work as a notary. (Wiener 2007: 508)

Guna-guna thus targeted male colonizers and drained their will, desire magically ousting duty, and stories about the seductive power of magic potions were increasingly used to explain why mixed relationships persisted in a context now antagonistic to them. Colonial men and women saw *guna-guna* differently; where white men self-servingly regarded it as absolving them from blame, white women were more likely to empathize with the predicament of native women jilted by their European lovers, or to regard the fear of a lingering death brought about by magic as a brake on mixed relationships. Certainly, as the unacceptability of cohabitation increased, it was revenge and not seduction that these stories emphasized, and Wiener recounts an intriguing meeting on the steamship home between Muller, a colonial official, and Geoffrey Gorer (an anthropologist and popular author). Upon ending a long relationship with a Eurasian woman whom he had refused to marry on account of her 'colour' – and who was legally classed as 'native' since her father had not recognized her paternity – Muller had been 'bewitched' by her uncle. Everyone he saw now looked exactly like her or the uncle and was the same colour, making his life and work impossible. Rejecting advice to commission a counter-spell, all Muller could do was flee the country, returning to Europe to seek psychoanalytical help.

Muller's case and the other cases analyzed by Wiener suggest that Europeans were just as susceptible to *guna-guna* stories as the natives with whom they consorted. Intimacy was dangerous for colonials, who might risk catching a 'belief in magic' by contagion, like a 'sexually transmitted disease' (Wiener 2007: 514). But his case also suggests that self-exonerating colonial male readings of *guna-guna* stories could not be pushed too far, since any attribution of efficacy to love potions made of nail-clippings, spit and hair was likely to undermine the boundary between credulous native and rational white. After all, as Muller told Gorer, 'we're in the twentieth century'. While *guna-guna* operated as an instrument of power by bending others to one's desires, it was also about mixing and bringing together what otherwise should remain apart, working against 'purificatory technologies of race and rationality' by indicating that Europeans were just as susceptible as natives (Wiener 2007: 506).

Stoler and Wiener show that for colonial authorities throughout Asia the ethnic and racial frontier remained a dangerous twilight world where intimacy between white and native was a potentially fatal attraction that demanded continuous boundary work to remedy or constrain. Indeed, it posed a fatal attraction at many different levels. Not only could sexual mixing challenge the social order through loss of colonial prestige and children of mixed parentage, but a shared vulnerability to some of the responses it provoked, and an admission that 'natives might be able to affect [Europeans], would be to lose control of white reality', risking national degeneration and decay (Wiener 2007: 522). In diverse colonial contexts, different forms of sexual control mediated by gender and race thus came to define what it meant to be colonizer or colonized, a process that was just as likely to require demarcation of the 'interior frontier' by specifying internal moral conformity among Europeans themselves, as it was to necessitate maintenance of the external boundary between 'Europeans' and 'others' (Stoler 1989: 651).

'GETTING A BIT OF THE OTHER'[6]

More than a century later some of these anxieties about miscegenation, sexual mixing and hybridity seem to be repeated in the post-colonial desires of contemporary expatriates. This should not surprise us. As Robert Young (1995: 27) has argued, social theory's recent interest in hybridity as a strategy of political emancipation may not be as novel or as distant from nineteenth-century racial theories as we like to think; nor is it necessarily any less essentializing of cultural identity than were the racial categories of the past (cf. Ali 2003; Brah and Coombes 2000). Anne-Meike Fechter (2007) implies the presence of parallels between the sexual encounters of contemporary expatriates in Jakarta and those of European colonials in the nineteenth- and twentieth-century Dutch East Indies. Although her account differs in its gendered perspective (citing the views of European women as well as European men) and its temporal focus (twenty-first century versus nineteenth century), what is striking is the apparent longevity of many of the sexual beliefs and practices at this ethnic frontier.

Following Stoler, Fechter sees the body as critical for the reproduction of a European identity at the boundary with Indonesians as well as within the expatriate community itself. Once again we find that Europeans are anxious about being contaminated by contact with Indonesian bodies such as those of their domestic staff, whose handling of food and care of their children might 'give [something] to the family' (Fechter 2007: 94). At the same time, however, European women feel sexually threatened by the exotic and slim figures of these Asian women, who are seen as the contemporary predatory equivalent of the nineteenth-century concubine, and whose sexual advances they resist by jokingly enlisting the divine in what Fechter (2007: 95) calls the 'expat wife's prayer': 'Almighty Father, keep our husbands from looking at foreign women and comparing them to us.' In one case very reminiscent of some of those described by Stoler and Wiener, an expat man set up house with an Indonesian woman while his wife spent the summer in the United Kingdom, ending the affair just before his wife returned. Persistent phone calls from the Indonesian lover followed, describing in detail to the wife the illicit couple's activities in the conjugal bed. Although *guna-guna* is nowhere mentioned, the psychological impact on the man recalls that on Muller all those years before, and while the substantive content of the stories might now be different from that of their nineteenth-century counterparts, similar kinds of cautionary tale inhibit post-colonial desire. For example, one widely circulated story recorded by Fechter (2007: 158–9) tells of how the teenage sons of an expatriate family contracted HIV after sleeping with their Indonesian maid.

There is also some hint in Fechter that sexual prohibitions among expatriates in Jakarta continue to be racially asymmetric and gender specific, just as Stoler (1991: 85) described for the Dutch East Indies. Today, as in the nineteenth century, white men might sleep with Asian women, but white women may not sleep with Asian men. Even wearing local dress may result in a European woman being rebuked for having 'gone a bit too far' (Fechter 2007: 99). Among these expatriates, then, we find a lingering sense that while men might philander, their wives remain responsible for the domestic reproduction of cultural and moral standards, just like their colonial forebears, and even today's independent, unmarried, professional elite women must act as custodians of national purity and moral integrity by maintaining a 'respectable' distance from local cultural involvement and intimate contact with the Other (a view that persists in the Netherlands, where Dutch women who marry Indonesian men are stigmatized; Dragojlovic 2008: 339).

So far our discussion of the gendered and racial asymmetries of ethnosexual frontiers has focused on heterosexual sex. This very much reflects the emphasis in the literature. As we have seen, Stoler, Wiener and Fechter all focus on the representations and regulation of interracial heterosexual sex, and so too does the work on Northern Ireland and the post-Abolitionist American South that we discussed earlier. As we have also seen, such sex is often most problematic when it is reproductive, posing the most threat when it results in mixed-race offspring, who then stand as the living and legally problematic embodiment of a culturally improper and reprehensible act. In this sense, sex that does not produce children has an advantage in being 'silent and unmarked', which according to Young (1995: 25–6) means that discussions of hybridity and interracial sexual mixing always contain within them an 'implicit politics of heterosexuality', something that may have contributed to the smaller number of studies of same-sex sexual relations across the ethnic frontier. However, same-sex sexual encounters are no less complex in their articulation of ethnic self-definition and national belonging.

Sasho Lambevski's (1999) forthright discussion of sex between Macedonian and Albanian men graphically analyzes the gendered, class and ethnic differences that are played out in the different sexual positions adopted by same-sex couples in Skopje's busiest gay cruising area at the city's main bus terminus. Once again the kinds of physical and other cues that we saw were so much an implicit part of sexual negotiations in Northern Ireland provide in Skopje a code through which to select a same-sex sexual partner:

> a breathtakingly handsome man in his mid-twenties entered my field of vision ... I started trembling silently in anticipation of numerous possibilities of enjoyment... However, at the very moment my eyes met his, I turned my gaze, filled with guilt, sorrow, frustration, and incomprehensible anger, away from him. In a fleeting moment, I understood that *this* could not happen, 'must not happen', because the man was Albanian. Although I had never seen or talked to this man before, I knew immediately that he was Albanian.
>
> It took only a few seconds to read his haircut, his dress, his bodily gestures, and his walk as signs of his Albanicity ... something within my body ordering me to stick to my Macedonian gender/sexual/ethnic script... I denied myself the thought of satisfying my desire for this other ... [in a] process of self-policing of my desire, of sublimating my gay desire, of exchanging it for a wish to be a 'good Macedonian'. (Lambevski 1999: 398, emphasis in original)

Being a 'good Macedonian', according to Lambevski, entails conforming to a heterosexual, homophobic national norm that this man found impossible to transgress and to which he had to subordinate his (homo)sexual longing. Acting on his desire would have meant him taking on the passive role as 'bottom' and allowing himself to be penetrated by the Albanian man, a possibility that sexually he was prepared and able to contemplate for reasons outlined below but which a visceral, embodied sense of ethnic Macedonian-ness precluded him from realizing. In the conventions of sexual contact between Albanian and Macedonian men in Skopje, Albanian men are the penetrators, adopting the dominant position as 'tops', an arrangement with which they expect their Macedonian male partners to comply and which enables them to sustain their self-image as heterosexuals even when engaging in sex with other men. The negotiation of relative positions (as passive/active, penetrated/penetrator and bottoms/tops) in homosexual encounters in Skopje is thus largely predetermined by national identity, while the position one is prepared to assume, or forced violently to adopt (since sometimes Macedonian homosexual men are raped), constructs and confirms one's ethnic and national belonging.

However, this ethnosexual frontier is visibly complicated by class, and asymmetries in sexual position and the performance of particular sexual acts are closely tied to and even inverted by asymmetries of status and other forms of social and cultural capital. Most of the Albanian men who have sex with men are working class and are socially and economically marginalized compared to their Macedonian partners, an inequality for which their sexual dominance is a kind of compensation according to Lambevski; this is one of the few contexts where they are in control and which consequently they are reluctant to concede. This is fine as long as the Macedonian men who seek sex with men are willing to self-identify as homosexual (rather than heterosexual) and to accept the role of the partner who is penetrated in these ethnosexual acts. But these conventional asymmetries are becoming unsettled by middle-class Macedonian 'gays' who insist on constant reversal of sexual positions in anal intercourse, a desire that clearly subverts the position and interpretation of the Albanian men involved.

In Skopje, class and national identities are thus central to negotiating acts of 'gay' sex, and ethnicity is a key element in determining what Albanian and Macedonian men do with one another's bodies, as well as what they permit or forbid in relation to their own (Lambevski 1999: 409). In this sense, nation trumps desire. Yet at the same time Macedonian men who have sex with Albanian men risk 'ambiguating' their ethnicity by flouting national expectations that a 'good Macedonian' conforms to a heterosexual ethnic script.[7] By allowing desire to override nation in this way, they put their identity at risk and can confirm their belonging only by curtailing their passion. Ethnicity, nation, sex and desire consequently cross-cut in ways that must be carefully negotiated, and where the outcome may be to harden or emasculate their Macedonian-ness as sexually and culturally defined.

Ethnicity is also crucial to the negotiation of interracial anal intercourse in Hong Kong, where we can see how its impact on the nature of the sexual act is modified by shifts in wider fields of power. Under colonial rule the positions of homosexual lovers were relatively fixed, with Chinese partners generally on the 'bottom'. But with the transfer of sovereignty over Hong Kong from Britain to China, Chinese gay men began to shift their sexual practices and the claims to power that these could represent, aspiring now to reciprocity of sexual position and expressing a diminished desire for the former privileged Western sexual object. Petula Sik Ying Ho and Adolf Kat Tat Tsang (2000: 305) offer a political interpretation of what they refer to as 'colonial anality', in which 'acts of penetration and reception ... not only articulate sexual positions but also political positions' that in different periods in Hong Kong can be read as reflecting domination or resistance to it.

Among the most interesting aspects of their discussion, however, are their comments on the interplay of pleasure and power, desire and domination, at this ethnosexual frontier and they implicitly caution against being too reductive in our interpretation of these shifting forms of homosexual act and seeing them mainly or only in terms of power. What their data show is that even where ethnic inequalities seem directly reflected in sexual practice, we must listen to the voices and subjectivities of those involved. Although they might now adopt the role of penetrator rather than penetrated, Chinese men continue to understand and experience their sexual subjectivity in terms of ideologies of penetration and sacrifice which emphasize giving pleasure to their partners, as one Western man with a Chinese partner explained:

> I think two different hierarchies of needs collide when Chinese and westerners engage in casual sex. Westerners operate with a hierarchy of sexual gratification and the negotiation process is geared towards getting to the highest level of mutual gratification. Mutual masturbation is fairly low in my hierarchy of gratification, oral sex somewhere in the middle and anal intercourse (passive or active) at the top. For my Chinese partners, it is the moral framework, of love, obligation, etc. which predominates … they will do [anal intercourse] on request regardless of whether or not they actually enjoy it. (Ho and Tsang 2000: 316)

As these examples from Hong Kong and Macedonia show, in any sexual encounter the dominant and most powerful sexual position is rarely self-evident but is a negotiated performance that is the outcome of many different factors, among which the ethnicity of those involved may be only one.[8] Power does not lie in the form of sex itself but in the meanings given to it, and the person in the passive role in anal intercourse may be the powerful agent by being able to demand to be served in this way. What is at stake, then, is more than ethnic domination, and people's subjectivities muddy over-dichotomized analyses that see every sexual act in terms of powerful agents and powerless dupes. Even where ethnicity clearly shapes the form that sexual encounters take – reflecting, reproducing or resisting the boundaries in the ethnic frontier – erotic desire is also about the 'quest for pleasure, relationship and identity' (Ho and Tsang 2000: 317). Crossing forbidden frontiers, then, is never just about a challenge to the social order, even if this is the interpretation that many academic analyses have a tendency to promote.

TRANSGRESSING FRONTIERS AND TRANSFORMING THE SELF

Most of the examples and authors we have considered in this chapter have emphasized how sexual intimacy across ethnic and racial boundaries is a potentially socially disruptive and perilous act which can endanger the structure and stability of society, unsettling the relations of power and subverting established moral codes. Sex, ethnicity and race seem almost always and everywhere to be a combustible mix whose conjunction can articulate the limits of society at the same time as threaten to rip societies apart. Racially and ethnically mixed relationships raise wide-ranging structural and conceptual issues, threatening the social and political order, as we have seen, but also raising classificatory and legal problems about how the 'ambiguous' progeny of mixed unions should be categorized and grouped, as well as questions about precisely how social relations should be structured and regulated to prevent those who should not come together from doing so and for dealing with them when they do. Consequently, as we have illustrated above, passions are policed and punished in ways that try to bring transgressors into line, and although the punishments can vary in severity – from the public shaming that spells the end of one's career to the castrations and hangings of the American South – they draw attention to the boundaries and help to ensure they remain intact even as individuals cross them in one of the most intimate ways imaginable. As Nagel (2003: 27) repeatedly makes clear, breaking social and moral rules provides an opportunity to define and reinforce ethnic and racial boundaries, leading her to conclude that 'the walls that divide ethnic groups' are re-established rather than transformed by such acts.

The emphasis on structures and social order evident in the examples we have included here follows from a long history in the study of boundary crossing and transgression in the social sciences which explains how boundaries can be crossed without being transformed as a result. Nagel's conclusion recalls the arguments so long favoured by anthropologists when writing about sexual rule-breaking and which stress how inversions and role reversals permit a licensed or ritualized sexuality that confirms the existing social order by acting as a social safety valve which releases tensions and conflict. Max Gluckman (1970), for example, described how some sexually permissive behaviours that visibly appeared to cross boundaries and challenge the structures of power (whether of kinship, class or ethnicity) were closely regulated by the 'rituals' of which they formed a part and were generally permitted only when the social order they appeared to challenge was sufficiently secure to withstand them. So too the subaltern sexual play and disrespectful vulgarities of the carnivalesque were often interpreted as confirmations of the prevailing social hierarchy even when they seemed to subvert it, so that once the festivities had ended, it was very much business as usual for the existing social order, which might even be strengthened as a result (see Stallybrass and White 1986). Rules might be broken and sexual boundaries crossed, but by being contained within certain social frames such acts were only rarely transformative. At best, to paraphrase Kelsky (1996: 187), 'flirting with the foreign' merely creates old orders in a new guise. So too the 'sociology of deviance' that characterized the social study of sexual 'subcultures' in the 1970s and 1980s explained how social norms and values were reaffirmed even by apparently deviant sexualities such as swinging and sadomasochism (Bryant 1977; Douglas 1970). These subcultures might seem like a threat and even help to push the boundaries of what was acceptable – expanding people's horizons of what was sexually possible and 'normal' – but they seemed just as often to underline the sexual standards of the day.

With its emphasis on structures and social boundaries, the literature examined here thus fits well within a tradition that sees sexual transgression in the context of social order and which considers whether or to what extent permissive sexual acts (those that cross these structures and boundaries) are a force for change and transformation of society. It draws less directly, however, on the insights of another body of theorists whose work emphasizes the experiential dimension of sexual subjectivities engaged in transgressions which can effect a transformation or dissolution of the self. The passions, infatuations and obsessions of erotic desire that underlie transgressive sexual dynamics, while sometimes touched on in the work cited above, as we have seen, are more usually subordinated to an analysis of social stability than systematically explored. Social power is stressed over sexual passion, whose role in shaping sexual subjectivities and generating novel social identities is thereby underplayed. However, the dynamics of erotic subjectivity are central to the work of Georges Bataille (1986), who emphasizes the meanings and experience of transgressive sexual practices for the actors over the social, political and cultural conditions in which transgression occurs. In his analysis of transgression, Bataille stresses the fusion of sexual categories and interrogates the boundaries that separate them in a process that rarely returns society to the status quo. This approach to experiential sexuality is clearly distinct from the 'structural' notion elaborated above (Jervis 1999) and yet it is an inherent part of its dynamic.

While for many the boundaries of sex, ethnicity, race and nation are all about sexual control and the containment of transgression as instruments and metaphors of power, for others these frontiers are zones of emancipatory possibility that can reshape sexual subjectivity and the self. Yet only by understanding both and by focusing on the inter-sections of social structure, sexual agency and erotic intersubjectivity will we grasp how people negotiate, deploy, redefine and subvert the possibilities and ambiguities of transgressive sexual encounters along this forbidden frontier.

NOTES

1. Joane Nagel's (2003) monograph has a similar title to this chapter and we draw on her book here for inspiration. We use the notion of 'frontier' to suggest a space of cultural mix and match, where the relations between cultures and communities are contested and dynamic rather than predictable and fixed (see Donnan and Wilson 1999).
2. Even in fiction, remorseful shock is likely to follow the realization of transgressive fantasy about someone of the other religion, as Geoffrey Beattie (1999: 175–6), an academic psychologist who has conducted research in Northern Ireland, vividly describes in his novel about young men growing up in a loyalist working-class housing estate in Belfast:

> I felt myself going numb. It was slowly dawning on me what I had just done. There was a sickening feeling in the pit of my stomach... I'd just had sex with a Roman Catholic, a Taig, a Fenian, a daughter of Rome. The numbness was running down my legs like the juices down hers.

3. Thus the central character (Bigger Thomas) of one novel comments on the racist culture in which he lives: 'Every time I think about it I feel like somebody's poking a red-hot iron down my throat' (Wright 1966 [1940]: 23), an image which Wiegman (1993: 235) interprets as the 'symbolic phalluses of white masculine power burning in Bigger's throat'. For Bigger, the white world is 'hot and hard' against him, denying him freedom and power in a symbolic castration. However, it is a castration that is also 'an inverted sexual encounter between black men and white men', evidenced when Bigger is trapped by the 'monstrous phallic image' of whites wielding a fire hose that coils itself around him (Wiegman 1993: 236).

4. Some of the most shocking images of the twentieth century are those that depict sex in the strategic and militaristic service of the nation, such as the rape of German women by Soviet troops advancing on Berlin in 1945 or the Serbian rape camps in the break up of Yugoslavia. Borneman (1998: 275) suggests that these tactics should be understood in terms of how heterosexuality functions 'in tandem' with territorial sovereignty. See Littlewood 1997; Nagel 2003: 182–6; see also Chapter 7 for a discussion of rape.

5. Such views persisted well into the mid-twentieth century when many British anthropologists and biologists continued to argue that procreation with evolutionarily 'distant' races was morally and physically disastrous. For example, Reginald Ruggles Gates – whose own marriage to the family planning activist Marie Stopes was never consummated according to his wife – held that sex between Europeans and 'more backward peoples led to physical, mental and moral "disharmonies"' (Bland 2005: 48).

6. With thanks to bell hooks (1992: 23).

7. This 'ambiguation' of ethnicity differs from the 'ambiguous ethnicity' of mixed race children in that it stems from one's own sexual actions while the latter results from the sexual actions of one's parents (see Benson 1981: 134–44). Nor does nation everywhere trump desire and, in contrast to Macedonia, national identity is not everywhere seen in heterosexual terms. Immigrant Russian lesbians in Israel, for example, stress their sexual identity to escape the stigma of being Othered newcomers while immigrant gay men imagine their belonging to the Israeli nation through homosexual fantasies (Kuntsman 2003, 2008).

8. In her discussion of these examples, Nagel (2003: 165–6) stresses their ethnic dimension but neglects their class complexities and the tensions that arise between passion and power.

7 SEX CRIMES

To be gazed at is one danger; to be manhandled is another

(Simone de Beauvoir 1997: 403)

BEYOND SEXUAL TABOOS

The range of activities encompassed by sexual violence is highly varied and contested cross-culturally, raising questions about how sex is related to violence and how sexual experiences differ among and between men and women when violence is involved. This chapter interrogates how sex is related to aggression and how sexual abuses are constructed and experienced through the biological, cultural and political dimensions of the sexual body. We tease out how sexually violent acts are circumscribed by definitions of sex and violence cross-culturally to reveal how slippage occurs between discourses of licence or prohibition that surround physiological experiences of sex, emotional engagements with violence and politico-legal frameworks. As we shall see, legal discourses which tip the scales in favour of an objectifying male perspective hide the complexities of how violence is manifested and experienced by men and women in different cultural contexts on a day-to-day basis. At another level, how perpetrators and victims are dealt with by others has ramifications for national discourses of sexual blame and purity which feed into constructions of masculinity and femininity and shape national and political sexual imaginaries.

Sexual violence is most commonly invoked to refer to the abuse of women's mental, physical and emotional health by men through acts of aggression such as rape, domestic violence, incest and the institutionalized violence of honour killings and bride-burning. Stereotypes of the relationship between sex and violence as well as sexually violent acts have largely concretized notions of sexual objectification as products of male domination, often seen by feminists as the central process within the dynamic of gender inequality (Dworkin 1989: 203; MacKinnon 1982: 201). Indeed, in many cultures the social, religious and political dimensions of sexual violence position women as inimical to male control, with severe penalties for their sexual transgressions. The effects of economic oppression upon women that stem from 'rape, forced prostitution, polygamy, genital mutilation, and pornography' are particularly harsh (Hosken 1981: 4). However, those who are unable to escape violent relationships or who find themselves locked into social structures and institutions of sexual violation often find ways to resist and challenge the abuse. Either they do not acknowledge that sexual misconduct has occurred or they may seek to resituate their tormentor within discourses of self-empowerment.

Of course, not all acts of aggression are conducted by men against women. Women can also be aggressive perpetrators of sexual violence, just as men may vent sexual aggression against other males. Varieties of sexual violence conducted by men and women may include harming the self or others through practices such as gang rape, domestic violence, sadomasochism and hard-core pornographic activities. As perspectives on sexual desires vary cross-culturally, so too do the rules that mark the limits between sexual pleasure and violence. Stanley Brandes (1981) shows, for example, how Spanish women could be accused of killing their husbands from too much sexual intercourse through their rapacious appetites for sex. This comparative analysis of situated accounts of sexual aggression will throw light upon male and female perspectives of self and other, domination and resistance, and oppression and sexual freedom cross-culturally. The sexual transgressions analyzed here are honour crimes, child sex abuse, pornography, sadomasochism and rape, and we also look at the effects of state-imposed reproductive regimes.

'GIVING IT AWAY'

In the West, the analysis of sexual violence is often divided between biological and sociological explanations that hang on perceptions of maleness, masculinity and patriarchy. Male violence has sometimes been rendered in biological or psychological terms (following Ellis or Freud) as an extension of male sexual urges that need to be met and that render women's sexuality subservient to these needs in ways that can be dangerous and exploitative. Lori Heise (1997: 424) questions such biological deter-minism through examples of other cultures where rape and wife abuse do not exist and argues that "'male conditioning" not the "condition of being male'" is to blame. Culture creates *conditions* in which expectations that men have of other men, as well as of themselves, are addressed by strategies of control over women to prove their own sexuality. Nonetheless, this view can be taken to be a stereotyped extreme, as evidenced in rape cases in the United States in which some men believed that sexual conquest made them truly male, a view supported by fathers who defended their teenage boys accused of raping and molesting girls, some as young as ten. Sexual invitation through the ensnaring performance of saying 'no' (Kulick 2003b: 288) and the ambiguity of female sexuality are frequently 'blamed' and used as justifications for sexual violence; as one father of these boys said, the girls were 'giving it away' (Gross 1993). Heise (1997: 426) argues that in order to address male violence societies need to redefine what it means to be a man and that, instead of praising virtues of conquest, domination, violation and predation, men need to be taught that masculinity can be constructed in very different ways that denounce these so-called virtues. In other cultures, the idea of 'giving it away' is unthinkable; as we shall see, amongst the Gerai of Indonesia the question 'How can a penis be taken into a vagina if a woman doesn't want it?' (Helliwell 2000: 808) invokes a very different response from that provided by Western theories of normative male dominance over female passivity.

Studies that discuss young American women's first sexual experiences in which they did not actively seek sex but in the end 'gave in, gave up [or] they gave out' (Thompson 1990: 358) suggest that force and coercion are not part of female sexual discourse, but neither is consent; rather, they relegate the act to an inevitability that is in some ways beyond their control because of the pressure of expectation, which, for some, may be related to fear of reprisal following refusal. In some cases, collective cultural and family expectations create an additional layer of oppression against which young women are powerless to act. Mary Hegland (n.d., cited in Heise 1997: 415) describes how young Iranian women in the United States can be forced to have sex with their promised husbands by being held down by relatives. Following an arranged marriage, accusations of rape cannot be brought because sexual intercourse is culturally acceptable whether it is forced or not. Even though a discourse of rape does not exist, this does not alter the fact that sexual abuse may occur, and in some countries where sexual violence against women cannot be openly discussed a 'parallel public sphere' has emerged to enable a debate to take place (Dewey 2009).

MARITAL RAPE

Due to the rights afforded to men and women over each other's bodies in marriage, it is perhaps not surprising that the most prevalent form of violence around the world is wife abuse (Heise 1997: 414). Marital rape is particularly difficult to address, because, along the shifting line between coercion and consent, the tendency is for women in abusive relationships to give in to and feel responsible for their abuse. There are, however, different degrees of coercion that can constitute rape in marriage. These range from male sexual satisfaction gained in physically abusive relationships of sexual non-consent; to emotional, verbal and mental coercion of women to effect sexual compliance; to resigned acceptance of sexual intercourse in marriages that are not based on any kind of overt abuse. In relationships that have no deliberately oppressive elements, women may still feel degraded or humiliated through their sexual experiences. Sexual experience, then, is closely related to personal value and respect. Violations of female integrity were expressed in six reasons that Mexican women gave as to why they resented men's sexual treatment of them (Folch-Lyon et al. 1981). The women in the focus group cited 'physical abuse; male infidelity; men's authoritarian attitudes; threats of abandonment if failing to meet sexual demands or demands for children; and a sense of depersonalization; humiliation and physical dissatisfaction during sex' (Hine 1997: 419). They felt their personhood was no longer visible to their husbands as their bodies were regarded as dehumanized property. The view of women as merely vessels of reproduction over which men can assert their rights is further supported by studies on the frequency with which pregnant women are battered in violent relationships. In the USA, one in six women on low incomes in abusive relationships was likely to be assaulted during pregnancy (McFarlane et al. 1992). In another study, the attack on pregnant women's bodies was shown to be levelled at the stomach, with 20 per cent of women in a survey of 342 battered women in Mexico City reporting this kind of violence (Valdez Santiago and Shrader Cox 1992).

STATE VIOLENCE IN FAMILY PLANNING

Sexual violence is seldom simply the domain of perpetrator and victim. More often, it is part of national concern bound by specific moral and cultural legislation. Some nation-states have institutionalized a moral approach to punishing violations against women. For example, Taiwan has incorporated rape into a more general prohibition of 'obscene offense against the morality of the society' (Luo 2000: 583). Rape, marriage and chastity are intimately intertwined here, where a woman who has experienced 'acquaintance rape' will still be advised to marry her rapist to protect her moral image (Luo 2000: 583).

In some countries, women's sexual behaviour is treated as a necessary dimension of national health policies, rather than as an integral expression of social womanhood and a woman's right to her own sexuality and pleasure. In addressing rights to family planning and contraception, some countries have been concerned to reduce the potential for disease and teenage pregnancy with prescriptions around condom use. Thus, while modern birth control methods have emerged in many different guises, rather than being wholly liberating they have also harnessed women's bodies to the medicalization of the state and the legalization of reproductive capacities. These can be forms of vicarious sexual violence by the state, whose policies have emotional and physical repercussions.

China's one-child birth programme has subjected women to contraceptive control not as a choice but as an imperative. The birth control programme has implications for the survival of the family and the harm experienced by women (Greenhalgh 1994; Greenhalgh and Winckler 2005). The one-child policy began in 1979, following earlier attempts to reduce the reproductive demographics from six children to three in an effort to improve the economic and living standards of the nation. By the 1980s 'birth control was virtually synonymous with what the Chinese call "the four operations": IUD insertion, tubectomy, vasectomy and induced abortion' (Greenhalgh 1994: 8), and families were fined if they had more than one child. In 1983 the state mandated IUD insertion for all women with one child and sterilization of the male or female for couples with two or more children (Greenhalgh 1994: 8). 'Remedial measures' (i.e. abortion) were required for all unauthorized pregnancies (Greenhalgh 1994: 8). Reproductive choice was therefore taken out of the hands of the individual and relegated to state policy. Sexual politics was thus a politics of coercion rather than intention.

Susan Greenhalgh's research uncovered examples of overt challenges to state policy. Information from 150 families comprising a total of 1,011 women showed that women made strategic use of silence against parts of the policy they did not like (Greenhalgh 1994: 9). In 1982 the system of fines began to collapse and was defunct by 1987. At the same time, the funds available for birth control operations also declined, increasing health risks for women. Women found new ways to circumvent the birth control policy and methods, as couples whose first child was a girl would arrange for her adoption out of the family in hopes of being allowed to try again for a son. The emotional strain on families trying to meet the national expectation was immense; some desperate parents would allow a second or third baby daughter to die (Greenhalgh 1994: 15).

The unauthorized removal of IUDs was difficult to monitor, but women did have them removed when they wanted more children. By resisting the national policy, women could take control of their reproductive desires, but they put themselves at risk of becoming known as troublemakers and having to endure more insertions and extractions of the device as well as possible late-term abortions. Women were therefore simultaneously victims and agents of state reproduction: on the one hand, they made themselves vulnerable to punitive actions of the state by resisting birth control policies, while on the other hand they repositioned female reproductive power, maintaining subordination to men, as sons became their ultimate aim.

SILENCING VIOLATION

Unregulated sexual activity threatens not only the individuals involved but also the religious values of the society or state in which excess occurs. Child sexual abuse occurred on a wide scale in the Catholic Church and the fear of this being discovered or resulting in a loss of support led to consistent cover-ups; offending priests were sent to special retreat houses, detox centres for alcoholism or given early retirement. These actions point to an institutionalized violence based on 'secrecy, impunity and almost totalitarian authority of Bishops and Cardinals' (Scheper-Hughes and Devine 2003: 16). In other cultures, rather than simply being seen as offending against a moral code, the violation of sex regulations may be punishable by death where the entire social fabric is considered to have been contaminated. These sexual acts are sufficiently transgressive to warrant the 'crime of honour' – the death penalty – because national agendas and religious identities are intimately entwined with female sexuality. The purpose of killing as part of a code of honour is to manage the public face of family sexuality represented by female genitals, since acts of murder are more justifiable than acts of sexual immorality.

In his coverage of the literature on homicide and suicide, Gideon Kressel (1981: 152) argues that institutionalized homicide in Arab Muslim countries is a consequence of hierarchical power structures amongst patrilineal kin groups and is not 'altruistic', 'egoistic' or 'anomic'. Murder is a group act that results from prior planning rather than instantaneous rage or uncontrolled outbursts. In this sense, the crime of honour is not equivalent to the Western 'crime of passion', which is defined by an individual's temporary insanity prompted by intense jealousy or heartbreak rather than premeditation. Instead, close scrutiny of a daughter's honour extends to continuous supervision in which young girls always have a watchful eye upon them that keeps them behind closed doors and means they are given away in marriage as soon as possible. Marriage, however, does not absolve the girl of her responsibility for protecting the family name. The response to adultery by married women is extremely harsh, with stoning as punishment, while the single woman may be whipped 100 times publicly (Kressel 1981: 142). In the Qur'an, public lashings are advised for a male adulterer, along with the prescription that they should only marry an adulteress (Kressel 1981: 142).

British rule resulted in changes to killings in the honour code. In the past, in Israeli Arab villages, for example, the immoral woman would be killed publicly and the murderer could advance his honourable status by parading the blood-stained weapon through the streets and covering his clothes in his victim's blood (Kressel 1981: 143). However, these practices were driven underground once the law intervened and perpetrators were caught and tried for their acts. While women are seldom involved in the attack on the guilty woman, they may be accomplices in assisting the attacker, either by spreading rumours of the misconduct or by bringing their daughters to the scene of the crime.

In Arab society, men are not merely protecting their reputations, they are idolizing the female hymen as the cocoon and haven within which their own reproductive power, political status and generational self-worth rests. Virginity is not simply an attribute that they wish to possess for demonstrating their masculine prowess; rather, it creates a man and his offspring and ensures their lineage. Women are not just owned, they are consumed by their husbands and their bodies become part of their husband's body. Thus, men may kill women if 'they fail to bleed on their wedding night, or if they dishonour and shame the family, by, for example, conversing with a man, smoking, coming home late, or engaging in a romantic relationship' (al-Khayyat 1990, cited in Shalhoub-Kevorkian 2002: 580). It could be argued that, when viewed as an extension of the male body, a husband may feel polluted as a result of his wife's sexual demeanour and her body becomes an aspect of self-loathing towards himself.

In a number of cases, the need to kill has been excused by the courts but as these offences are considered to be private rather than public, they do not sit easily under legal jurisdiction. Exemption from punishment for 'crimes of honour' is part of the Jordanian Penal Code (Shalhoub-Kevorkian 2002: 580). However, the partial status of the law is evident in the fact that only male relatives, husbands and male blood relatives can be pardoned for their offences against the woman; should a wife find her husband to be unfaithful, she has no equivalent comeback. A clear disparity between men's and women's sexual freedoms persists, also evidenced in the fact that men may have almost unlimited potential to take mistresses, conquests that are seen to enhance sexual status and power. However, the Qur'an is viewed as having improved the lot of women by giving daughters half (as much as sons) in an inheritance, limiting the number of wives a man may take to four, and equating the law for the adulteress to that for her partner in crime (Kressel 1981: 143).

These examples show us that both nations and families may be equally complicit in the implementation of oppressive sanctions on female reproductive capacities, some with extreme consequences. Yet, even in those countries that seek to shape supposedly healthy attitudes to sex and reproduction, the term 'family planning' may conjure up notions of mutual consent, negotiation and long-term vision between parents, while masking the possibility of violence occurring within relationships where rights to planning are not held equally by both husband and wife. In these places, women's rights to reproductive health and their rights to protect themselves from AIDS are not necessarily recognized due to the social stigma attached to discussing condom use and the subjugated role of women in negotiating safe sex. Often women cannot mention condoms for fear of male violence and the stigma attached, which would imply infidelity on their part, or they (mis)understand 'safe sex' and the use of condoms as about preventing pregnancy rather than STDs (García 2009: 612).

In countries where reproduction is a sign of social status, women may feel pressurized into accepting male views about the use of condoms as a challenge to male rights to reproduction. A woman may either accept her partner's view or, in some cases, subvert his insecurity by using a contraceptive method invisible to him (Heise 1997: 420), but she does so at her peril, for if discovered she may be beaten. This violence potentially opens women to an increased risk of STDs 'either through non-consensual sex or by limiting her willingness and/or ability to enforce condom use' (Heise 1997: 420). Where silence is maintained around family-planning issues in order to uphold cultural norms, it may promote a distorted view of what husbands actually think; although these women fear male abuse, this may not be a reality. Indeed, some studies have shown that men in these countries are actually open to family-planning issues (Gallen et al. 1986). In these contested spaces of reproductive possibility, male authority and roles as husband, father and head of the family are (re-)created and challenged by social expectation.

INNOCENCE REVILED

Since acceptable reproductive patterns are circumscribed by deference to social norms, it follows that child sexual abuse is its negative image, i.e. the abandonment of responsible socially prescribed adult roles. Silence also circumscribes these acts and telling someone else becomes the problem along with the abuse. Jean La Fontaine (1990: 78) reports one woman's recollection that:

> The worst memory is when I told him I was going to tell Mum what he was doing and he said if I did he would kill her and chop her into little bits. As a child I believed he would do this and by not telling anyone I felt as if I was protecting her in some way.

The term child sexual abuse should not be thought of as being synonymous with incest, although there are many reported instances of the incestuous abuse of children. 'Incest refers to sexual relations between certain types of relatives rather than to sexual activities between adult and child' (La Fontaine 1990: 24). Whether the abuse is by relatives or strangers, the defilement of children is self-gratification without regard for the victim, for others within the child's circle of friends or relations, or for society. La Fontaine (1990: 188) outlines the Hobbesian view that children by nature are relatively uncontrolled, un-socialized and selfish and that they represent the antithesis of disciplined, socialized adult life. They are in need of control, teaching and parental guidance. It is this dependency of the irresponsible child, who is also imitative, trusting, lacking autonomy and generally innocent of the adults who take advantage of them, that makes child sexual abuse so shocking. In the West when adults violate children sexually, there are implications for the child's ability to develop sexual control themselves in later life (see La Fontaine 1990: 189, 191). However, this may not be universally true and ethnographic data from places where sexuality is differently perceived complicate popular assumptions about the relationship between negative sexual experiences in childhood and subsequent adult sexual dysfunction (Montgomery 2009b: 184).

When child sexual abuse is carried out by parents, both husband and wife may be involved. The father is implicated most often in sexual violation and the mother may also be involved by complicit denial that the assault has taken place or by rejecting a child's story of the abuse. She may be afraid of speaking out against her husband, fear losing her economic status and security or be jealous of her husband's emotional intimacy with a daughter (La Fontaine 1990: 192–4). In one case cited by La Fontaine, a wife rejected her daughter after sexual relations with her stepfather, telling her: 'You stole my man' (1990: 197). The motivation for the abuse may also be placed upon a wife who is accused of having pushed her husband to seek sexual satisfaction elsewhere if she has refused his sexual advances, especially if she is ill or pregnant (Finklehor 1984: 26).

We have asserted in this volume that the emotional dimensions of sexual experience are often absent from anthropological analyses, and the case of child sexual abuse illustrates that this may be partly because the catalysts for this behaviour have no simple emotional causes. Rather, emotional needs are multifarious and it is has been argued that they have not been able to explain the real issues that pertain to child sexual abuse, which include both sexual and non-sexual motivations (La Fontaine 1990: 198). Nevertheless, mixed emotions of shame and disgust are often public responses to finding out about the details of any child sex scandal which may have graphic and extreme acts. La Fontaine (1990: 200) argues that the Cleveland case[1] showed that buggery was common, but also that in other cases there may be oral sex, rape, group sex, sadism and pornographic photography. Juries may not want to have to sit through the full details of what has happened to an abused child because of emotional distress, and the media seldom make explicit the exact nature of the violations. The shame of the act may be taken on by the viewer, creating a sense of contamination, as if by knowing the full facts those who hear somehow become complicit by their inability to act and, thus, disempowered by the full revelation of what has happened. However, not all cultures consider children to be innocent victims of abuse, especially in contexts where financial remuneration is given for child sexual services. Instead, by default, they may place the burden of shame and immorality upon a child's actions.

INSIDE CHILD RAPE: A HANDS-OFF APPROACH

In some countries, the ambivalent status of those who are being abused can shape national discourses of purity and immorality as defined by those who are being violated. Heather Montgomery (2001) discusses how Baan Nua child prostitutes in Thailand give up their identities as children because they lose their innocence and hence cannot claim the status of child-likeness or of victimhood. A child who engages in sex at a young age is called *dek jai taek* – 'a child with a shattered or broken heart', implying that they are no longer whole and are broken inside, impure and unfixable. For young girl prostitutes this transformed state condemns the child to another realm in which the recognition of lost virginity makes her permanently promiscuous, even if sex has first occurred within a loving relationship. Although child prostitution is often mainly associated with girls, it is also high amongst boys in Baan Nua (Montgomery 2001: 76). For both boys and girls, the lack of sexual control is viewed as deviant and thus sexual abuse is far more than a physical act of under-age sex as their impoverished status means that they become invisible to the state, employed illegally and vulnerable to exploitation with no voice or representative to acknowledge their position. They therefore experience a denigration of personhood, economic future and national recognition. Children brought up in these extreme circumstances are to be pitied, because their fate is one that will rob them of adult sympathies and of human rights, rendering them dangerous, ambiguous and threatening to others (Montgomery 2001: 134). Cultural perceptions of their irreversible moral state mean that some parents may condemn their own children to prostitution in order to get rid of them, while girls themselves may choose prostitution to escape their families (Montgomery 2001: 138). Yet as Montgomery (2009b: 198–9) describes, many of the girls she studied first entered prostitution out of a sense of filial duty, merely as a means to an end, and did not see their sexuality or involvement in paid sex as central to their identity. Their experience and understanding of sex are best seen in terms of duty and obligation and are thus 'profoundly different' from what many Western observers believe to be the case. While some turn to prostitution, others seek work in factories or on farms and construction sites, but all of them 'need knowledge of their rights, appreciation of all their options and ways of protecting themselves' (Montgomery 2001: 135–6). The paradox of victimhood is that, on the one hand, discourses about Thai child sex abuse construe children as innocent, weak and dependent (even though such children cannot claim innocence), while their clients are deviant abusers, and yet, on the other hand, the way in which innocence is constructed in Thai cultural attitudes to children fuels deviant desires and perpetuates their subjugation. Thus, these children have become commodities of the state and their agency and willingness to engage in Thai prostitution threaten Western moralities about how children ought to be protected from knowledge of sexual coercion.

Why do Thai organizations not try to address this problem? As child prostitutes represent an invisible group on the margins of society, the expectation is either that they will not survive AIDS or that they are beyond help, given the abuses they have suffered. Montgomery points out that many do leave prostitution and require help afterwards. This process involves 'complex long term intervention which punishes neither child nor parent, which accepts the children's justifications of their lives as valid and which does not rely on limiting stereotypes of what a child prostitute should be' (Montgomery 2001: 146). It is not an easy or quick solution and is one that requires an honest and inwardly critical assessment of the system that, by its lack of action, tacitly endorses the abuse it so strongly disparages. However, the difficulty of self-examination of sexual attitudes by the nation is side-stepped by putting the blame on the child-sex tourists, the foreigners who have become the symbol of Thai sexual immorality and the defilement of the country, rather than addressing the exploitation of the children per se. Child exploitation is glossed over and the problem of victimization is displaced on to the outsider.[2] Yet, the problem of victimization does not lie with the outsider alone. Within Thai society, the loss of innocence takes away a child's rights to personal freedom, self-respect and social recognition, locating them beyond the status of victim and making them unable to avail of the definition of human rights. Rights, then, take on new meanings where children feel compelled to earn money through prostitution, because they have no options open to them other than sexual exploitation.

PORNOGRAPHY AND SADOMASOCHISM

While the majority of discourses around child sexual abuse would suggest that nations revile the very possibility of sexual abuse against children, the truth is that child pornography has a significant market that is beyond the regulators in a multi-billion dollar web industry, connecting paedophiles for the sexual trade and exchange of children, as well as enabling them to produce and distribute new child pornography. Thus, the idea that pornography is detached from the body to codify sexuality for abstracted individual pleasure is only partially true. At one level, there is a certain degree of ambivalence within pornography that promises sexual pleasure which is beyond reach and has the potential to frustrate as much as fulfil. Where frustration reaches its climax, it may manifest in fetishistic representation that refuels the desire for more pornography, the effects of which are seldom dealt with in anthropological analysis.

Individualism has become the marker of much pornographic as well as S/M activity, but this was not always the case. Until the late 1700s, sexual images were intimately entwined with speech and debate in social life. A focus on the erotic impact of these images did not gain momentum until the 1800s. Sex then took on a force of its own, separating arousal from social value in a way that generated new discourses of obscenity and which led to the term pornography being coined in the 1860s. Obscenity referred to the power of corruption and depravation and therefore included a wide range of materials judged under the Obscene Publications Act (1857). Some of these works were anthropological, such as Ellis and Symonds' (1897) *Sexual Inversion*. The erotic power of pornography was viewed as something that needed to be closeted away from the masses but which in turn positioned discourses of obscenity as central to the freedom of speech (see Sigel 2002).

Anthropology has been seen as complicit with pornography in other ways, with parallels drawn between power relations in ethnographic practices and pornography (Hansen et al. 1991); in the rise of a commercial licence for erotic works in art and literature and sexually explicit anthropological accounts (Schick 1999: 78); and in the comparison between classic ethnographic film and illicit heterosexual pornography (see Nichols 1995). In the nineteenth century, anthropologists, along with lawyers and writers, were among the avid devourers of domination and submission as well as erotic anthropology that were on offer in the Victorian Cannibal Club.[3] They viewed their activities as an elite educational private practice, savouring a taste for racial and sexual difference that brought together science, anthropology and pornography in the search for hard erotic data (see Sigel 2002). These libidinal expressions have taken on different historical guises within the anthropological profession. Don Kulick (2006: 934) has called for a serious critique of what he calls the 'libidinal structure' in order to understand how anthropologists have derived a masochistic pleasure out of analyzing the powerless.

The rise in media technologies and unlimited access to Internet porn means that now 'the sexual culture of pornography is a formula for sexual self-abuse' (Sanday 2007: 213). For example, one of Sanday's (2007: 214) informants, John, testified to his addiction on a 'Quitting Pornography' webpage:

> My addiction was growing so fast I could hardly keep up with it... It kept getting sicker all the time. I need more books, more degrading sex, more abusive sex. Pornography showed me new ways of abuse and self-abuse.

The implications of this testimony are that pornography is a destructive influence beyond an agent's control. Rather than pornography serving sexual pleasure, eroticism has its own sadistic agency that can debilitate and victimize the viewer by virtue of their inability to choose to do otherwise.

Despite John's realization of his entrapment, not all analysts agree that self-harm, whether through pornography or other kinds of bodily modification or mutilation, is degenerative. Armando Favazza (1987: xi–xix) has posited that certain kinds of self-mutilation in general and sexual mutilation in particular can be forms of healing for mentally ill patients, in the same way that ritual mutilation may serve as a therapeutic resource for groups such as those who practise subincision or for Fakirs who practise tattooing in order to transcend the pain they inflict upon themselves.

The relationship between sexual pleasure and pain is a subtle one, either inflicted sadistically upon another person or masochistically upon oneself. Havelock Ellis (1921) argued that the distinction between the two was blurred as they complemented one another, and that the intention of either form of sexual pain was not for abuse. By contrast, Krafft-Ebing (1965: 86) invented the term masochism, viewing it as 'a peculiar perversion of the psychical sexual life' in which a person is 'unconditionally subject to the will of a person of the opposite sex; of being treated by the person as by a master, humiliated and abused'. Freud (1938: 570) also suggested that masochism was an extension of sadism as the two forms appeared in the same person. The terms masochism and sadomasochism derive from the names of two writers in the seventeenth and eighteenth centuries: Count Donatien-Alphonese-François de Sade (1740–1814), whose books describe outrageous forms of mutilation which some analysts regard as improbable, and Count Leopold Ritter von Sacher-Masoch (1836–95), whose most famous work, *Venus in Furs* (1870), concerns 'a nobleman who enjoyed being ordered about and whipped by an icy woman in furs' (Kulick 2006: 935). In reality, he asked his wife to beat him with cat-o'-nine-tails studded with nails, as well as seeking out other women to dominate him (Weinberg 2009).

Sadomasochism has been analyzed in recent times by sociologists, social psychologists and others in terms of 'pornonormativity', i.e. sexual scripts derived from images and narratives of porn (Bell 2006; see also Langdridge 2006; Plummer 1995 on sexual scripts); the politics of sexual citizenship (Binnie 1994); psycho-medical constructions (Taylor and Ussher 2001); and sadomasochism as a 'valid sexual culture' (Wilkinson 2009: 192). Culturally produced meanings have expanded over psychoanalytic interpretations (see Weinberg 2005). As research into sadomasochism has grown, it has been found that men tend to engage in more hypermasculine behaviours while women take on positions of humiliation (Weinberg 2005: 22). Sample studies in America show that more educated and single women tend to be involved in S/M activities, a minority of whom have a preference for playing a dominant role (Levitt et al. 1994: 472), and that the varieties of sexual practices are not randomly chosen but constitute a 'script' of 'structured patterns' (Santtila et al. 2002) in which fantasy plays a significant part in the arousal expectations for those in dominant positions but not for those being dominated (Donnelly and Frazer 1998). It has been argued that 'kinky' practices should be viewed as extensions of vanilla (natural) sex in a pluralistic sexuality that adds pleasure, parody and play, whilst making power inequalities in marriage visible and challenging structures of intimacy (Langdridge and Butt 2004: 43).

LEARNING SEXUAL TORTURE

So far we have seen how social and political systems that control and define sexual violence have within them the potential to depersonalize their victims, keeping them bound to exploitation whether out of socio-economic desperation, seduction or addiction. Sexual violence is often learned as part and parcel of cultural conditioning, legitimized and rationalized within the prevailing social order. All forms of sexual abuse, it might be argued, stem from violence as a cultural problem in which its agents must demonize the other in order to justify their actions. These crimes are not necessarily committed by people who stand on the edges of society as psychopaths; rather, as Robert Edgerton (1978) has argued, 'deviance' is an everyday occurrence into which others are socialized. Thus, the torturer learns the particularities of the skills required for carrying out the task and he or she is socialized into the legitimacy of the act (Argueta 1983). However, Janis Jenkins posits that this instrumentality of deviancy does not fully explain how feeling and sentiment are expressed as power and interest:

> We cannot be satisfied with the unreflective knowledge that the perpetrators are the creators of violence and the victims respond to it, for a political ethos is brought about in the conflictual interaction of both parties, and responded to – if only by denial – by both parties. (Jenkins 1998: 123, 140)

In order to interrogate how a political ethos is brought about, we turn now to perhaps one of the most disturbing ways in which sexual power and state interests have been played out: military rape. Rather than representing a neglect of power in dealing with abuse at a national level, such as in Thai prostitution, or conforming to seduction through power, as in pornography or S/M domination, wartime rape is the deliberate defilement and depersonalization of human life through torture.

Rape in wartime is perhaps most commonly associated with the legitimization of male aggression occurring under circumstances of trauma and extreme violence in which survival is marked in part by the biological urge for sexual aggression (Gottschall 2004). In Roland Littlewood's (1997) account of wartime rape, he shows how it may be an instrument of torture as well as a way of managing boundaries of inclusion and exclusion, delineating allies and enemies. Surviving the conditions of war may be marked by taking captive prized possessions, one of which may be rape as sexual conquest, booty for having been denied sexual satisfaction and facing death. In ancient Rome, soldiers were rewarded in sex rather than money as a motivation to encourage them to fight (Barkan 2002). In many wars, male and female enemies were sexually defiled by leaving corpses naked, mutilated, castrated or raped, just as other trophies of war were displayed. For example, 'Raped and "wasted" Vietnamese girls were left with U.S. military insignia placed between their open legs' (Brownmiller 1975: 105, cited in Littlewood 1997: 10). Such violation is intended to incite anger, suggesting that sexual violence begets sexual violence through militarism or 'reciprocal violation' (Littlewood 1997: 11).

Wartime rape was a means of collectively abusing and symbolically dismembering communities, and it was the domain not only of male atrocities to women but also of women to men and men to men. According to the Zagreb Medical Centre for Human Rights, 4,000 Croatian male prisoners were sexually tortured in Serb detention camps '… of whom 11 per cent were castrated or partially castrated (sometimes by women) and 20 per cent were forced to fellate their fellow prisoners' (*Independent*, 1996, cited in Littlewood 1997: 9). In some contexts, women combatants were reported as 'cutting off the penis to be stuffed in the live or dead body's mouth (a pattern which has recurred in Bosnia and Rwanda where women have been combatants)' (Littlewood 1997: 10). It has been argued that women who direct sexual violence against men are inciting sexual retaliation against themselves and other non-combatant women. In these cases, reciprocal violation cannot be so readily attributed to the dehumanization of women as standing for national symbols of purity and procreation; rather, these acts constitute 'the transgressive argument: the unchaining of a generally disallowed biological imperative of absolute desire and destruction following an increase in individual power over others' (Littlewood 1997: 11). Rape can become standardized practice under these conditions with aims beyond the violence, to infuse the genes of the enemy with those of the victor.

The ritualistic aspects of mutilating women's sexual parts and foetuses in the Bosnian conflict have been viewed as a 'hatred of femininity' (Seifert 1996: 38). Olujic's (1998) analysis of Bosnian women who were raped by Serbian soldiers shows how men further imposed their violence through language about the crimes committed against women. Olujic (1998: 42) describes how a nineteen-year-old Muslim woman, Sanela, was raped by four Serbian soldiers who then shaved and plucked her pubic hair, cut her, subjected her to obscene poses and threatened to kill her. Rapists' narratives use 'shaving' as a metaphor of male sexual domination, as well as referring to the 'peeled' penises of Muslim men, suggesting their power over both Muslim men and women by belittling circumcision (Olujic 1998: 43). Croatian women were repeatedly raped until they were pregnant and told to 'make a Serb baby', and they were held captive until it was too late for an abortion (Laber 1993, cited in Littlewood 1997: 15). The contempt for Muslim sexuality was a denigration of ethnic worth (Jenkins 1998: 128). On the one hand, then, these rapes can be read as acts of defiance and defilement of ethnic and religious purity; on the other hand, they may be seen as a means of drawing greater diversity into one's own group for the purposes of renewal.

Snyder et al. (2006) explain how rape in war was originally viewed as an inevitable practice that would eventually die out and was therefore both normalized and ignored in terms of its ramifications (Hansen 2001; Thomas and Ralph 1993). The experiences of raped women are largely silent in the historical war record, a 'public secret' which depicts men's conquests and heroics but nothing of their sexual aggression (as in memories of the Bangladesh war, see Mookherjee 2006). The conditions of collective incitement to violence and socialization into processes of dehumanization as military torturers offer initiates an arena in which their extreme acts are justified.

CONVINCING THE COLLECTIVITY: GANG RAPE

Collective incitement as justification for sexual violence is not confined to war but spills over into emotionally charged arenas such as ritual gang rape, where group bonding is central to the affirmation of male sexual identity. Acceptance within the group involves desensitization to the means of brutalizing others through techniques orchestrated by initiated members of the group. In her study of gang rape in some US fraternities, Sanday (2007: 148) combines symbolic analysis with an understanding of dissociative, mind-altering methods and ritual process to show how one initiate, Sean, is divested of self-worth and identity through a fraternity initiation ritual, leaving him vulnerable and amenable to adopting a new 'all powerful, male-defined self' within the brotherhood. His status gives him licence to engage a phallocentric discourse that legitimizes victimization because of male bonding through what young men perceive to be women's subjection of themselves to the rules of the fraternity. Sanday (2007: 193) argues: 'Women who resign themselves to victimization can be compared to ... [the young men] ... whose victimization is the condition of entrance into the fraternal order.' However, these women do not receive the recognition that accompanies the male rite of passage.

These 'party girls' are variously denigrated and disparaged for their potentially ambiguous role in being able to interfere with the power of male bonding (Sanday 2007: 184). Some girls actively seek equality through sex and alcohol, defending themselves when attacked; others act as 'pimps' and suppliers of women for the gratification of 'brothers' and earn a certain degree of joking acceptance in doing so, whilst other women submit passively to the victimization of the brothers (Sanday 2007: 192–3). Where gang rape is about the acquisition of power for the individual in the eyes of others, it can only make sense for the individual within the context of the fraternity which endorses it. However, just because one group of men adopts a position of collective domination to which others subscribe for the purposes of enhancing masculinity or controlling anxieties about sexual abilities and maternal separation does not mean that these logics apply in all cases of gang rape.

In reviewing the literature on ritual gang rape among the Xinguano in lowland South America, Celia McCallum (1994: 90–2) notes that there is a problem with ascribing an overarching theory of male domination to these practices, because Xinguano insist upon everyday attitudes of respect, emotional support and a lack of hostility. Furthermore, they express distress at the thought of sexual violence, especially if it occurs with any sense of approval. Scholars have looked to myth instead as a means of explaining rape and justifying a male model of domination, in some cases adopting neo-Freudian explanations of male fear of menstruation as a catalyst for aggressive behaviour towards women. Such analysis is evoked in the symbolic bullroarers and phallic flutes of one Xinguano community – the Mehinaku –instruments which women must not view upon pain of gang rape and death. However, the interpretation of these symbolic values varies depending upon the Xinguano community involved, as Ellen Basso (1985) shows for the Kalapalo, another Xinguano community whose rituals include sexual antagonisms and occasional violence as illustrated in the two major Kauka and Yamurikuma rituals:

> neither male sexuality nor female sexuality alone is inherently violent or merely aggressive, but in conjunction they become seriously threatening. As the myths propose and the Kalapalo enact during their musical rituals, this combination is socially lethal, and it can be extremely dangerous – even fatal to a member of the opposite sex. (Basso 1985: 261, 307)

In this context, it is the combination of male and female sexuality that creates a threatening environment in which gang rape may be meted out. However, both male and female performers have ambiguously dangerous capacities, embodied in the insatiable vaginal mouth and menstrual blood juxtaposed with male semen and the voracious penis (McCallum 1994: 98). For Kalapalo the mouths of the flutes are vaginas and the flutes themselves female sexual organs (Basso 1985: 304), which can be violated by the presence of men who stray too near the women during the Yamurikuma ritual. The flutes are said to menstruate when placed in the sponsor's house and, during Yamurikuma, women would attack a man who entered into the ritual plaza where the flutes are stored. They would beat him up, pull his hair and smear him with red body paint, which some informants say is symbolic of menstrual blood (McCallum 1994: 99). Similarly, McCallum notes that Thomas Gregor (1985) had been told by the Mehinaku that women could gang rape male intruders.

Although women control men's entry into their ritual space, men too control the degree of engagement that women have with the flutes. While men may watch women singing, women may be gang raped by men if women see them playing the flutes. This affirmation of collective male bonding against female sexual intrusion is done out of fear of harm for the group, who believe that the men will die if retribution is not taken. The complexity of the rituals and their multiple nuances around sexual prohibition and aggression are evidence that gang rapes in these contexts are not about universal desires to humiliate women (McCallum 1994: 110); they are responses to an intricate system of fertility, reproduction, illness, social engagement and ongoing ritual relations within and between Alto Xinguanos. Myth and ritual have often been analyzed as symbolic processes that order principles of masculinity and femininity, encapsulating the attributes of defiance and dependency upon which the continuity of social order rests.

In each of the examples discussed so far, we see that ambivalences surrounding sexual behaviours are typified by varying degrees of anxiety, some of which are represented by symbolic associations with bodily fluids from the genitals, which in turn shape boundary discourses of social life. On the one hand, a danger exists in viewing sexual violence as a symbolic category that is somehow separate from the erotics and subjectivity of sexual practices in everyday life. On the other hand, for some analysts, the potential for Western discourses to distinguish heterosexual practices from homosexual ones on the basis of eroticism is also problematic. As Deborah Elliston (1995: 850) has argued, the term 'semen practices' could be used to refer to either heterosexual or homosexual practices, thereby avoiding unreliable erotic distinctions.[4]

REPOSITIONING THE RAPIST: SUBVERSIVE SEX AND RACIAL DISSEMBLANCE

In Gilbert Herdt's (1982: 50) multivocal symbolic account of the Sambia of Papua New Guinea, masculinity and femininity are simultaneously examined through the flutes, not as a tool for gang rape but rather as a kind of pornographic icon that creates 'erotic arousal' through 'a fantasy system concerning the flutes and their sound'. Instead of being symbolic vaginal orifices as in the Kalapalo system, amongst the Sambia flutes come to stand for both the penis and the mouth by which young boys learn to fellate older bachelors. Herdt has been criticized for conflating semen practices and pleasure when he says they 'always entail erotic arousal at least for the inserter' (Herdt 1984: 7), because the majority of the boys that he interviewed were repulsed by and afraid of engaging in the practices and only succumbed after 'threats and seductive pleading' of elder men (Herdt 1982: 76; see also Elliston 1995: 854). Anger, however, is characteristic of the violence that has been meted out to these boys:

> The bachelors get soundly thrashed and nose-bled and they otherwise suffer much. This is how it should be, the elders assert, for the youths must become 'strong' and 'angry' because of what has been done to them. But they can 'pay back' that anger by doing to younger initiates what was done to them: beating and otherwise traumatizing them. In addition, they can do something equally laden with power; they are urged to channel that anger and relax their tight penises, by serving as dominant fellateds. (Herdt 1981: 56)

Coercion, fear and abuse seem to characterize this practice and thus it is not surprising that it entails the potential for payback when boys are old enough.

While many studies have analyzed strategies for managing the aftermath of sexual abuse, few critically compare and contrast how these strategies differ emotionally and practically and thus whether rape means the same thing for everyone either within or between cultures (however, see Elliston 1995). One study which demonstrates that different notions of rape exist for women within the same culture and that they reconstruct abuse in their own terms is Day's (1994: 172) account of London prostitutes, who hold a particular definition of rape at work as distinct from rape outside work – one which is broader than the majority public view. By divesting themselves of the inner vulnerability of intimacy and intimate contact, prostitutes ensure that the term 'sex' applies only to personal relationships outside work (Day 1994: 175). More often than not, studies tend to focus on the physical dimensions of rape and the psychological harm associated with it, and whether consent was involved. For prostitutes, consent is not the defining feature of rape.

Rape outside work is considered to be a greater personal assault than it is within the working environment, and any rape that involves physical attack is also viewed as extreme. As we saw in Chapter 4, the domain of work is identified by material boundaries, including using different rooms and beds, covering beds with towels which are washed separately, and ensuring sexual barriers are maintained by the use of condoms (Day 1994: 174). The working body, too, is divided into private and public parts, where the mouth and anus are out of bounds, as is emotional intimacy (Day 1994: 174–5). The maintenance of sexual boundaries is paramount to the notion of sex work and when these boundaries are violated by condoms breaking, coming off or being taken off, or when a client's cheque bounces, prostitutes consider that they have been 'raped at a distance' (Day 1994: 180). Thus, rather than rape pertaining to a notion of non-consent, there is 'a form of violence in which an agreement is apparently negotiated and accepted, only to be broken' (Day 1994: 179). Physical assault outside work, by contrast, is seen as a personal violation of the moral and emotional self. For prostitutes, then, the problem is often that the notion of consent underpins the characteristics of their job and so rape is a contradiction, and yet it is clear from prostitutes' perspectives that rape exists in a variety of forms. In Salvador, Kulick (1996: 5–6) shows how *travestis* are the perpetrators of violence against their clients during sex as much as they are victims of it, by pickpocketing, assaulting or threatening them with knives, razors, scissors or syringes filled with tomato juice which clients are led to believe is HIV-infected blood.

Rape, domestic violence and economic oppression have often been catalysts for protests against impoverished economic and social conditions and the discourses that surround them. Some discourses have been cast in racial terms by othering Black female bodies (Gilman 1985) and these have erroneously stereotyped Black societies as characteristic of rape, representations that Black women have employed in their own strategies of subversion. In the 1930s, Black women in the American South constituted 80 per cent of the workforce of personal servants and domestics (Hine 1997: 435) and were not equal in wages or status to their White female counterparts. The large-scale migrations that took place between 1915 and 1945 to the Midwest, with the formation of numerous Black women's clubs, suggest that a new culture of protest was being generated. Darlene Clark Hine (1997: 435) argues that Black female migration is a means of asserting personal autonomy over sexual abuse by both White and Black men and is a mode of self-protection and distancing from their violent pasts. Far from being passive subjects of patriarchy, these new migrants struggled for freedom over their own reproductive rights and capacities within adverse situations. Hine (1997: 436) argues that women developed 'a cult of secrecy, a cult of dissemblance, to protect the sanctity of inner aspects of their lives'. So while appearing outwardly engaging and easy to relate to, Black women veiled their innermost antagonisms to sexual oppression. Their inner selves were closed to those looking on and they erected a shield against the negative stereotypes held by society at large of Black women and their sexual history.

These women were not merely reactive participants in the construction of Black sexuality set against an antagonistic, dominant White culture; they were deliberately formulating their own expressions of resistance against it, but ones which did not prevent them from being able to move and work within White culture to their own benefit. This alternative history of the migration of Black women is starkly juxtaposed with the representation of victimization suffered by Black men who were compelled to leave the South because of lynchings in the late nineteenth and early twentieth centuries (see Chapter 6). The strength of opposition to racial and sexual abuse and stereotyping of Black women gained collective force in the founding of the National Association of Coloured Women's Clubs (NACW) in 1896, which had a following of fifty thousand members by 1914 (Hine 1997: 437). But this sexual counterbalance was not simply aimed at putting Black women on an equal footing with White women; it also served to construct Black women as morally superior because of their abuse.

One dissemblance strategy the NACW used to counteract negative stereotypes was that of sexual disassociation. By denying female sexuality, eroticism and femininity, the NACW fought back against a male chauvinism that impugned Black women's virtue. Aiming instead for the political recognition which would make the rape of Black women as unacceptable as that of White women, the NACW sought to take Black women out of the contexts in which their sexuality was being degraded. With increasing education, economic possibilities and involvement in women's movements, Black women took on the attitudes and values of the White middle class, including options for birth control and options not to have children. By separating their reproductive capacities from their Black status and achieving educational and professional qualifications, they were able to achieve recognition and support from the community. Financial security gave Black women sexual autonomy and the right to choose what to do with their bodies. However, choice is not always clear-cut where sex is concerned, and, in the almost exclusively private context of rape, the boundaries between consent and coercion can sometimes be finely drawn or blur into each other.

As rape is culturally determined in a multitude of ways, some of which we have explored in the form of extreme military mutilation, the erasure of female identity in campus fraternities, the care taken by prostitutes over their clients' misdemeanours and sexual disassociation by Black women, it is clear that rape is neither biologically determined nor culturally ubiquitous. Indeed, Sanday (1981) has shown that cultures exist which are void of rape.[5] Christine Helliwell (2000) illustrates how amongst the Gerai of Indonesian Borneo rape is unthinkable – it does not have a term or sanction in Gerai law equivalent to its Western counterpart. Their particular cultural perception of the genitals is in part the reason why men's and women's responses to the notion of sexual assault ranged from 'puzzlement to outright incredulity to horror' (Helliwell 2000: 798). Male and female genitalia are essentially the same and are distinguished primarily by location, albeit variously on the outside and inside of the body, rather than by function or the potency of the penis as an agent of dominating sexuality (Helliwell 2000: 803). Gerai, therefore, combine an equal understanding of male and female sexual capacities with reproductive labour. They say: 'We all must nurture because we all need' (Helliwell 2000: 800). In order to promote social harmony, uncontrolled aggression is devalued and punished when it takes the form of slapping, beating and knifing or murder, although men are expected to have the skill and courage to fight in appropriate circumstances. Both men and women are considered able to menstruate and engage in pregnancy and childbirth, because they share the same genital fluids required to create a baby, although reproduction is viewed as women's work related to the processes of rice selection and storage. It is the fact that women know how to hold rice seeds in their baskets that they are able to hold rice seeds in their wombs (Helliwell 2000: 807). Male domination, aggression and oppression are not part of the Gerai world-view, because the sustainability of rice production managed by women and the development of the rice field managed by men would not be possible if women refused to cultivate the seeds after field preparation. The ethos of Gerai sexuality is premised on the basis of gendered labour relations whereby need is reciprocal; therefore, sexual coercion is unthinkable because it would destroy the spiritual balance of the rice group and invite disaster upon everyone (Helliwell 2000: 808). Consequently, women do not fear rape because they do not view their genitals as vulnerable or capable of being despoiled by men, since in one sense there is no sexual division between men and women but rather a division on the basis of rice selection and storage and the clearing of trees to make a rice field, whereby mutual engagement is life enhancing for the group (Helliwell 2000: 807). What a woman fears is her rice seed being bewitched by an enemy who attacks the core of her being, which can result in the seed failing to sprout, causing personal illness as well as child deformity and death (Helliwell 2000: 811).

CONCLUSION

The multiplicity of catalysts for violent responses to sex, as well as the absence of sexual violence and lack of fear of abuse in some cultures, show that any tendency to reduce such violence to natural or unnatural, psychotic or deviant, phallocentric or patriarchal discourses is bound to fail because sex is rooted in the particular conditions of cultural beliefs from which it arises. Moreover, the roles that pleasure, fantasy and desire play in the creation of social regulation and restriction do not necessarily entail sexual violence per se, although, when taken to excess, they may lead to expressions of violence. Pleasure, fantasy and desire do, however, create discourses of power that shape how people are viewed in terms of their political, moral or economic engagements with sex and entail the Other because of their outwardly directed ends. As Kulick (2006: 941) shows, 'desire' has a voiced and unvoiced dimension that exists only in relation to the Other. The same may be said for other sexual emotions, as well as for the terms used to define different kinds of sexual engagement.

Terms for sexual violence like 'rape' and 'pornography' cannot be understood simply by their content in any one context or else they become tautologous. They should be viewed as systems of representation that define heterogeneous sexual engagements that are differentially subject to legal, political and religious ramifications cross-culturally. They also contain within their parameters historically discursive shifts of meaning regarding the place of sexuality in society and ways of regulating it. Sexual discourses have powerful effects, as sociological studies have shown in cultures, for example, that value male dominance, hierarchy and prowess and which correlate with high rates of violence.

Within the anthropological endeavour, there is often an uneasy tension around analyzing sexual violence that oscillates between what Littlewood (1997: 13) calls 'a wish to condemn and a wish to comprehend', and that is underpinned by a professional ethical agenda to identify with the disenfranchised and to avoid the perversion of justifying injustice. Some theorists argue that discourses of sexual freedom have swung too far beyond social and moral responsibility and that a new sexual revolution is needed to counteract growing sexual violence.

We have attempted to offer a balance of discourses and perspectives on the reality of violations experienced by men and women cross-culturally in order to highlight the complexities of sexual abuse. We have shown how sexual violence is delimited as much by cultural, moral and political perceptions of sexual (in)decency, the changing boundaries between pleasure and pain and national agendas of reproductive, erotic and militaristic control, as it is by gendered forms of aggression, transgressive behaviours and the consequences of sexual risk-taking. The comparative critique of national, religious and political concerns invites ongoing anthropological reflection about how to deal with sexual violence in discourse and practice when it embodies an uneasy or unhealthy rivalry between the ravages of power and desire. As we shall argue in the final chapter, this nexus of passion and dominance is further complicated by its circulation in global arenas bringing sexual ethics and sexual rights of cross-cultural intimacies to the fore.

NOTES

1. Between February and July 1987, 125 children from 57 families were taken into care as a result of having been diagnosed by two doctors in Middlesbrough General Hospital as having been sexually abused (La Fontaine 1990: 3).
2. The exception to addressing sex victims is where foreign paedophiles are concerned, but the emphasis on this category ignores any reference to the majority of Thai and Asian clients (Montgomery 2001: 153).
3. The Cannibal Club was a London diners' club founded in 1863 in response to the intellectual interest arising out of the newly formed Anthropological Society; members included the Africanist Richard Burton as well as the writers Swinburne and Milne (see Kennedy 2005: 168).
4. Elliston (1995: 848) strongly criticizes the idea that homoeroticism is a cross-cultural category, because the term disguises distinctions between Western and indigenous practices that it ought to problematize. Instead of adopting the notion of homo-sexuality, Elliston argues for 'semen practices' to be analyzed in relation to indigenous meanings around such practices.
5. Sanday (1986) argues that any idea of rape among the Minangkabau is unthinkable and would cause serious consequences for the community.

8 INTIMATE CULTURES

Intimacy builds worlds; it creates spaces and usurps places meant for other kinds of relation

(Lauren Berlant 1998a: 282)

Globalization, perhaps more than any other influence, has been responsible for creating dramatic paradigm shifts in cultural categories of sex and the experiences that they entail. Transformations in intimacy have occurred as cultures touch and brush against one another, travelling further than ever before. Boundaries of intimate behaviours, sexual values and concepts of acceptance, consent and access are being reshaped as they move across and between countries in physical and virtual ways. By widening access to sexual diversity, global audiences are being exposed to what some people may consider greater perversity, in turn influencing how normalizing processes are reconfigured. Indeed, what was once thought to be sexual perversion is often celebrated as essential to the diversification of selfhood in the global sex market. Yet, the desire for freedom and liberty within individual sexual rights brings with it other outcomes for participants who may be subject to partiality, exploitation and misrepresentation, thereby placing the issue of human rights at the centre of contemporary debates about sex and sexuality.

Throughout this volume we have focused on many varieties of sexual experiences within comparative social, economic, political and religious domains in an effort to demonstrate how parameters of intimacy are negotiated, contested and reformulated cross-culturally. We have taken the nature of subjectivity to be foundational to the analysis of sex and among other things have asked how we can understand sex; how sex has changed; and what is new about sex today. Some scholars have offered a definitive answer to these questions, suggesting that sex is different now primarily because of its role in the global economy. Others have emphasized the historical perspective, arguing that particular meanings of sex have characterized specific phases of history and even become iconic of them. While some of this work draws on the comparative ethnographic record, much of it does not and might thus be criticized for presenting arguments that depend principally on studies of sex in the West. Nevertheless, these perspectives are broadly sensitive to the dangers of reasoning about sexual subjectivities from mainly Western data and are generally careful not to universalize their arguments. They therefore offer useful frameworks in which to locate our discussion of sexual rights later in the chapter. We highlight four key perspectives through the lens of sexual subjectivity:

1. a periodization in which Steven Seidman and others (e.g. Zeldin 1995: 121–6) compare the historical shifts in meaning that have occurred around hetero- and homosexual sex and its relationship to love, desire and eroticism;
2. the deterritorialization of 'sexscapes' in which new possibilities arise for sexual flows, experiences and feelings in a mobile and technologically sophisticated world, a perspective espoused by scholars such as Zygmunt Bauman and Arjun Appadurai;
3. the denaturalization of 'sexscapes' through Anthony Giddens' notion of 'plastic sexuality', which allows sexual pleasure to be divorced from the sexual fabric of reproduction; and
4. the changing political economy of sex, as discussed in the work of Dennis Altman and those who have analyzed the shift towards the rise of global sex industries.

These approaches cannot be separated entirely from one another and their inter-connecting strands raise theoretical issues about the transformation of intimacies and the rights they entail. We begin this final chapter with a brief overview of these interlocking perspectives on sex, which, as we shall see later, are threaded through human rights debates internationally. This conclusion is a call to colleagues to consider how the political economy of sex is not merely about fulfilling sexual choice, desire and satisfaction but is also essentially a matter of sexual rights in a global world.

SEX THROUGH TIME

Changes in how people feel about sex and how it is understood can be mapped on to particular historical periods. Seidman (1991) identifies three distinct periods that typify (mainly middle-class) American attitudes to love and sex over the last couple of hundred years, arguing that these three phases have successively emphasized the reproductive role of sex, its place in symbolizing and strengthening romantic relationships, and its pursuit as a form of pleasure and recreation. The Victorians regarded sex as an essential but threatening component of love and marriage, relationships which stressed spiritual affinity and companionship but which could be disrupted if sex was not properly controlled. Sex was thus 'desensualized', with its erotic elements downplayed and its physical manifestations such as seed and semen seen as something to be carefully 'invested' rather than 'spent', pecuniary associations that resonate today in terms such as sperm 'banks'. By the turn of the twentieth century, however, 'modern' Americans had begun to feel and think differently about love, which over the next sixty years became progressively 'sexualized', with mutual sexual satisfaction and attraction now seen as a way of sustaining love in relationships of personal, social and sexual compatibility and companionship. Whereas in the past external pressures had sustained marriage, mutual love and sexual gratification now played this role, and people were as likely to value sex as a pleasurable activity within a sexualized, companionate, relational context than as a purely reproductive act. As the twentieth century progressed, the significance of the 'procreative rationale' for sex diminished and sex became increasingly uncoupled from its procreative goal (Seidman 1991: 82). By the 1960s and 1970s middle-class Americans understood their bodies to be sites of sexual pleasure and desire, so that even though 'sex continued to be valued in a context of romantic love' – which remained the dominant norm – it was now legitimated 'for its pleasurable, expressive and communicative qualities' quite independent of any romantic setting (Seidman 1991: 121). Sex and love were thereby unhooked, emerging as autonomous domains of pleasure and romance in a momentous historic transformation that Seidman refers to as 'eros unbound'. Sex became acceptable between consenting adults in virtually any setting, with or without romantic attachment, and took its place as an instrument of everyday human sociability that functioned as a form of play, pleasure and communication.

Other scholars have developed and refined Seidman's periodization of sex and love, by situating the increasing commodification of sex within the broader post-industrial changes in society and sexuality more generally. Bernstein (2007a), for example, contextualizes her concept of 'bounded authenticity' (see Chapter 4) within a three-phase model that emphasizes the nature of sexual ethics under early modern capitalism, modern industrial capitalism and late capitalism. These three phases are characterized, respectively, by sex that is procreative, companionate/promiscuous, and typified by bounded authenticity, and they map neatly onto Seidman's periodization of sex as successively reproductive, relational and recreational. Bernstein (2007a: 168–75) is careful to stress that each phase in her model does not supplant the preceding ones but exists simultaneously alongside the others, within society in general as well as within particular individuals. All three types of sexual engagement thus co-exist, both now and in the past, and, according to Bernstein, it is possible to discern forms of recreational sex even in those historical periods when reproductive sex predominated, just as today – in an age of sexual consumerism – reproductive sex continues to be the value and model accepted by many. What is new, however, is that sexual subjectivities detached from procreative and relational commitments – 'eroticism cut free from its reproductive and amorous constraints' (Bauman 1999: 27) – better match the need for autonomous and mobile individuals that contemporary economic life increasingly demands (Bernstein 2007a: 175).

DETERRITORIALIZING SEXSCAPES

Our analysis in this book has been largely informed by trying to tease out flows of sexual intimacy and eroticism within the political economy, a perspective that has received relatively little attention in scholarship until recently. Much is written, for example, on trafficking and prostitution through political and economic frameworks, but much less attention has been given to sexual affect and experience in a global context. Thus, we have sought to draw out people's experiential understandings of sex and sexual subjectivities, though we need to be mindful that sexual subjectivities are not ends in themselves and neither is the interconnected global sex arena a free licence to 'do your own thing'. As sex travels, so too do questions about how the aesthetics of intimacy may change and how inequalities may be created through movement. In comparing and contrasting sex cross-culturally, we have shown that, in spite of the global illusion of universal idioms of sex, sexual ideals, practices and beliefs are contested categories specific to the socio-political conditions in which they occur. In analyzing 'ideologies of intimacy' in a marital context, Hirsch and Wardlow (2006: 2, 9), for example, suggest that companionate marriage is a plural category, and their contributors elaborate a plethora of culturally specific ideals and expressions of courtship, fidelity and intimacy that are circumscribed by strategies of choice, demography and labour. Cultural conditioning shapes human responses to intimacy, which are further contoured by differential access to a range of sexual products, technologies, medical practices, values and educational programmes.

The flow of feelings conducted in virtual space and the explosion of arenas in which to try out sexual intimacies have meant that global 'sexscapes' are now domains of heightened intensity, risk and potential. 'Sexscapes' have become an almost essential global process shaping national agendas, state boundaries, regulatory transgressions and personal engagements. But what are the conditions for sexual change in these virtual arenas? Bauman (1991) has posited that mobility, renewal and speed of travel are the characteristics of transience in which non-permanence is desired and permanence is viewed as limiting. Where the interlocking strands of capitalism, military might and industrialization once combined to give a sense of stasis, movement not only destabilizes perceptions of permanence but also brings with it a fluid sense of social engagement which he terms 'liquid modernity'. As liquefaction spreads throughout modernity, it creates a more fluid and disordered structure that defies return to the conditions from which it was born (Bauman 1991: 230). Intimacy is inevitably caught up in this flux of social seepage and becomes part of the transience of sex and sexuality.

The implications for global sex are evident in that there are no absolutes in satisfaction, desire or commitment, merely the possibility of alternatives. Sexual freedom is an outcome of liquid choices which, like the consumers themselves, have been fuelled by transience and mobility. The effect of liquid modernity is its capacity to reconfigure stability by offering alternative sexual promise at the same time as it destabilizes social and sexual bonds by disrupting the modes of engagement that shaped them.

Arjun Appadurai (1990) also seeks to explain the deterritorialization of the global cultural economy. His theory is important in understanding changes in intimacy and sexual subjectivities. Deterritorialization is characterized by its complex, overlapping and yet disjunctive order comprising five dimensions: (a) ethnoscapes; (b) mediascapes; (c) technoscapes; (d) financscapes; and (e) ideoscapes (Appadurai 1996: 33–6). This approach is deliberately perspectival and seeks to recognize a multiplicity of irregular and potentially subversive 'imagined worlds' (Appadurai 1996: 3). The scapes refer to mobile landscapes of people and traffic; flows of technology, the dissemination of communication and investment; and the diasporic journey of ideologies and rhetorics. Within this intensely complex environment, sex travels in the flux of displaced movements and disjunctures between different kinds of cognitive, experiential and material landscapes. As we have argued (see chapters 5 and 6), global 'sexscapes' can create inequalities as well as opportunities across the fractured borders and boundaries based upon race, class, gender and nationality, and their politico-economic structures shape the manifestation of sexual intimacies within and between cultures. Questions of love in globalizing processes of sex trafficking are also highlighted in Padilla et al.'s (2007) edited volume *Love and Globalization*, whose authors consider the circulation of emotion in the global marketplace; the merger or recombination of cultural intimacies afforded by the Internet; and the impact of the media in influencing expressions of sexual intimacy.

DENATURALIZING SEXSCAPES

One of the concomitant effects of deterritorializing sex is that sex has also become denaturalized and this has had ramifications for legislation, cultural denotation, academic discourse and activist engagement. While sexual engagements have always been circumscribed by cultural expectation, obligation and legal ramifications, the idea that global sex can open up the way for the expression of a modern individual self somehow unencumbered by cultural constraint begs a reanalysis of Giddens' notions of the 'pure relationship' and 'plastic sexuality'. His notion of the 'pure relationship' is one where the erotic is central to social relations, not in a sordid or sexually perverse manner but rather in the 'generic quality of sexuality in social relations formed through mutuality rather than through unequal power' (Giddens 1993: 202). The individual self makes choices about how feeling, intimacy, seduction and response are invoked, manifested and reciprocated. The kind of agency involved in this choice is not restricted by regulation or sexual preference; rather, it is negotiated in the consensual moment with those involved. This idiom of sexual relationship contributes to the efflorescence of what Giddens calls 'plastic sexuality', which is bound up with the autonomous control of the individual self who is free to choose his or her sexuality aided by contraceptive options and freed from the structures that otherwise might have constrained reproduction in the 'pure relationship'. Psychological, physiological and emotional autonomy are at the heart of plastic sexuality and denote a rupture from the ideologies, values and structures that shape reproduction. Such autonomy invariably results in the formation of new kinds of loving and sexual relationships, which we consider below in relation to Internet cybersex. Giddens (1993: 63) suggests that one consequence of this autonomy is 'confluent love', evident in societies that do not condemn sexual inclusivity or plurality and allow for unorthodox behaviours as they give credence to the ability to negotiate relationships in multiple ways. The characteristics of 'confluent love' could be summed up as being predisposed towards tolerance, integration and the acceptance of difference as well as the foundational principles of negotiation, equality and autonomy found in the pure relationship.

For Giddens, however, 'confluent love' is far removed from the forever-and-always forms of romantic love upon which the imagination of sexual encounter in film and media is often based. Romantic love answers a need within both individuals to be completed by the other and thus to fulfil their sense of self-identity (Giddens 1993: 45). The romantic model once circumscribed by the cocoon of social expectation has become increasingly unsettled in a 'global ecumene' of incompatible ideologies and behaviours (Hannerz 1996). Giddens' view of sexuality is not universal, just as national sexual identities are not homogeneous, consistent or stable. Plastic sexuality and confluent love do not operate in those countries that have adopted state-driven systems of domination, such as India and Indonesia where various modes of coercion operate over women's reproductive rights. As material cultures, global commodities and technological capacities impact upon traditional lifestyles, so aesthetic choices around sexual display, eroticism, body adornment, sexual engagement and attraction are all girded about by a responsive reflexivity to global forms rather than mounting a retreat from them (see also Giddens 1991: 178).

A POLITICAL ECONOMY OF SEX

As intimacy and sexual subjectivity have become embroiled in a global marketplace, increasing attention has been given to a political economy of sex. Various scholars have shown that technology has transformed sex products and the desires associated with them. Cheaper and easier access has facilitated the potential for sexual business as well as the rise in sexual crime on an international scale. Altman (2001: 120) reports how an Internet group provided sexual images of children to people in over 40 countries which could only be accessed by a code allegedly originating from the former Soviet KGB. It might then be asked: to what extent do global sexual idioms offer alternative strategies for a new world sexual order? Or do they merely enslave and entrap individuals within a schema that is non-transparent, promising reified illusions of sexual liberation? It is ironic that the West embodies the ambiguity of promulgating moral codes that condemn particular practices whilst providing capital through processes of commodification that support them (see Altman 2001: 121). The tension between moral stricture and economic potential often leads to heated sexual politics and sexual panics around the political economy of sex. The effects of this tension create divisions between those who argue for the right to choose sexual pleasure and those who see such freedom as irresponsible. As agents of globalization, nation-states control the means to naturalize sexual perversions and to reconfigure sex meanings and norms through regulation. We might ask then whether states may be in danger of marginalizing and subverting the potential to disturb and unsettle the boundaries of transgression. Those who have examined a global 'queer' perspective have considered whether shifting discourses on to a global stage might create a tendency to essentialize and universalize human experience in ways that impose fixed Western understandings of sexual identity and, in doing so, 'marginalize, exclude and abject' other aspects of gender categories (Borneman 1996: 227).

Careful to avoid a reifying global discourse in their study of same-sex subjectivities in Asia, Blackwood et al. (2007: 7) argue that there is no evidence of an overarching and undifferentiated gay and lesbian global culture, and others point out that there is no 'universally legible grammar' to interpret lesbian and gay communities around the world (Wieringa 2005: 4; see also Jolly and Manderson 1997; Plummer 1992). Nevertheless, they note that there has been a misplaced emphasis upon examining 'queer' culture from above, and they highlight the fluidity between cultural placedness and global interconnectivity to show how 'queer' discourses and transgendered subjectivities are produced by asymmetries, tensions and struggles in this 'homoscape' (Parker 1999: 218–21). The growing support around sexual rights has also meant that the tensions and cultural differences between and across same-sex networks have become more visible, enabling individuals to engage more vocally with gay/lesbian rights global discourses and access these for culturally specific ends.

The kiss of one culture by another creates awareness of often quite distinct historical intimacies, trajectories and opportunities in which sexual practices have evolved. Changing sexual practices are not simply consequences of globalization, as they have always come about when external forces create conditions that shake the internal belief system or when indigenous groups question their practices in light of what are perceived as better alternatives. Although the notion of the activist is a product of contemporary sexual discourses, persecution and suffering have invited protest throughout history. For example, in China unsuccessful attempts were made by Manchu conquerors to ban the torturous practice of footbinding in 1665 and again in 1847, until pressure by the indigenous Anti-Footbinding Society along with the Western National Natural Foot Society generated a new view of modern life, health and beauty, resulting in its decline (Mackie 1996: 1001). In comparison with the time needed to effect cross-cultural engagement and sexual change in the past, the speed and plurality of virtual encounters today offer unlimited potential for sexual experimentation and a resulting diversification of beliefs. The values people hold about intimacy, sex, emotion and reproduction inevitably shape how global resources are used, and the rise of sexual diversity has led to an increasing emphasis upon sexual satisfaction and the burgeoning of sexual identities around the world. However, as sex and its effects travel, the challenge to existing sexual boundaries worldwide inevitably impacts upon all who are seduced in ways that highlight human rights debates.

GLOBAL 'SEX WARS'

The global discourses relating to sexual rights have taken different forms, historically gaining momentum in the sphere of pornography in the mid-1980s from feminists decrying its decensorship and promotion of violence. The anti-pornography campaigns of this period pre-empted a schism that was to form the basis of the 'sex wars' amongst feminists and activists who were embroiled in either support of women's agency, choice and sexual freedom or anti-violence campaigns that sought to expose and transform the underlying processes and structures of female subordination. Radical feminists rejected the inevitability of women's involvement in the sex industry, seeing it as supporting patriarchal relations. For example, Jeffreys (2009: 95) documents how women in San Diego strip clubs are lured by the myth of $2,000 per night, only to end up making closer to $45 as club owners rip off the profits. The purchase of sex is viewed as a violation of women's rights brought about by structural inequalities in the system (see Chapter 4). Fundamental to this perspective is the idea that the denigration of women's experiences is intrinsic to patriarchal ideologies; they become invisible or silenced in the reconstructed fantasies of male power. Female subjectivities and rights are thus invariably suppressed within the commercial transactions that enable sex flows to occur.

Liberal feminists, however, would argue that sex work is a matter of personal freedom and choice and a legitimate industry; they support the decriminalization of the sex industry to make prostitution a dignified profession. For example, where sex workers were once a product of Western sexual attitudes, the 'migrant sex worker' is viewed by liberal feminists as a global phenomenon operating in part through a utopian ideal of escape from abject poverty by engaging in the informal global sex economy. But radical feminists posit that there is a danger of normalizing harm, validating sexual exploitation and subverting the recognition of the oppression of women. Jeffreys (2009: 19) comments:

> It is more useful to see prostitution as the outsourcing of women's subordination, rather than the outsourcing of an ordinary form of servicing work which just happens to be performed by women.

Activist discourses have gained greater momentum on the international stage as the global sex industry has expanded commercial interests in non-Western countries with undeniably damaging effects, such as the website of a sadomasochistic Cambodian 'Rape Camp' for Vietnamese women that is designed to torture and humiliate (Hughes 2000). Where women were once forced into restricted and secreted brothels and subjected to military rape and prostitution, these activities are now perpetrated in full global view.

TRAFFICKING GETS THE RED LIGHT

When human rights are discussed with regard to global trafficking, sex laws are often the first to be considered rather than the emotional effects upon women and men involved in these situations. Scholars often highlight distinctions between what is considered legal and illegal and how customary or state laws may be at variance with international law. Yet, it is the processes of demand and supply, exploitation and coercion, profit and consent that mediate emotional engagements through global interconnectivity. The term human trafficking, for example, entails the concept of abuse around deceit, coercion, exploitation and travel within and across borders for adults and children. Many academics, along with activists, are vocal about the injustices meted out by participation in these contexts (see O'Connell Davidson 1998). Jeffreys (2009: 7) has argued that:

> the vagina becomes the centre of a business organized on an industrial scale though the vagina itself is still subject to the problems inevitably associated with the use of the interior of a woman's body.

The business-oriented vagina is seen as bringing harm to women for men's sexual pleasure. Discourses that highlight female subjugation and sexual harm often delineate measures for redress, such as those elaborated in a recent study conducted between 2007 and 2008 on sex trafficking in Ireland. The authors note that 'there is a need for society to move from patriarchal structures of dominance to social structures where gender equality and relational contexts of interaction are central' (Kelleher et al. 2009: 53), through 'cultural relational feminism' as outlined by authors such as Sanday (2002) and Chodorow (1978).

The Irish study worked with ten services involved in the sex industry, which identified 102 women and girls including many migrants.[1] (Of these, 11 per cent were children.) Their figures represent only a proportion of the total number of women involved (Kelleher et al. 2009: 31). Each day around 1,000 women are engaged in 'indoor prostitution', with the proportion of migrant women being between 87 and 97 per cent (Kelleher et al. 2009). The research examined the relationship between 'indoor prostitution' and 'victims of trafficking', a distinction that is brought into question because of the difficulty of establishing consent given the illicit nature of sex trafficking. The evidence given in the report demonstrates that a very high percentage experience physical violence, being held captive, threats to injure family or friends and being left in debt to the traffickers. Over 50 per cent of women were raped whilst being trafficked and almost 30 per cent were gang raped.

The authors of the report urge the authorities to recognize the harm caused to women by trafficking and to offer them compensation for their suffering. They have also called on the Irish government to criminalize the sale of sex in Ireland and to examine the legal and human rights implications in relation to the experiences of prostitution. They recommend the criminalization of buying sex and the decriminalization of selling sex by placing the moral responsibility upon men for seeking paid sex, the pursuit of which should be seen as a cultural taboo. They call for human rights education on prostitution and trafficking to be part of the school curriculum; greater communication around the role of sex shops; lap dancing clubs and the sex industry to be the subject of informed public debate (Kelleher et al. 2009: 38). These kinds of studies illustrate how the analysis of emotional harm is increasingly becoming the medium through which social change is examined.

CHILD SEX TRAFFICKING

As borders open up around the world, sex tourism and sex trafficking have flourished in a multi-million-dollar industry that invites exploiters to move freely from one country to another. Globalization has highlighted the tensions and debates around human rights perhaps nowhere more heatedly than in discussions of sex tourism, child sex trafficking, child prostitution and paedophilia. As we have seen, countries such as the Philippines may be guilty of vicarious exploitation as their economic basis depends upon the business generated from sex tourism, and they are complicit in allowing the exploitation of children who migrate to tourist areas to attract sex offenders. The sex industry invites transgression and facilitates the removal of restrictions as it opens up the possibilities of communication and sexual encounter as a global trade. International organizations such as ECPAT (whose acronym stands for 'End Child Prostitution, Child Pornography and Trafficking of Children for Sexual Purposes') are working to combat the potential for child abuse by increasing prevention strategies through offering educational materials on flights to sex tourist destinations, advertising against child sex and seeking to put regulations in place with tour operators.

In this volume we have shown that the issues surrounding the entry of children into prostitution and the reasons for sex trafficking vary enormously from one place to another; this is often recognized by campaigners but these cultural distinctions do not necessarily gain recognition and integration within legal arenas. The universal view that trafficking endangers child innocence, morality and personhood, whilst threatening a child physically, mentally and emotionally, is embodied in international law (see especially Article 34 of the United Nations Convention on the Rights of the Child). However, the view that laws can change behaviours ignores grass-roots issues of the complex cross-cultural dynamics of emotion in child prostitution or child sex trafficking. Furthermore, it stereotypes individuals within these domains dichotomously as agents or victims, perpetrators or abused, rather than attempting to understand the diversity of experiences and reasons for engagement, and how a continuum of abuses is perceived by children. And it also often does not fully grasp the importance of seeing the sexual exploitation of children within the context of the differential power associated with age, gender and ethnicity (e.g. Ennew 1986).

For example, in Chapter 7 we discussed how Montgomery's work on Baan Nua Thai children shows their independence in evaluating their status, morality and the effects of their actions upon social outcomes. She analyzed how child prostitutes differentiate amongst themselves for social advantage and distinguish between 'those who have no power to refuse or negotiate and those who do' (Montgomery 2001: 91). Socially, Baan Nua children become outcasts to their families but remain agents in their situation. However, not all child prostitutes make such distinctions. In Colombia, impurity for girls and women also stigmatizes them and confines them to prostitution. O'Connell Davidson (2005: 51) tells how a Colombian girl had become involved in prostitution at the age of ten and had asked her mother if she could come home, but her mother rejected her because she had 'already been damaged'.

GLOBALIZATION, NEW REPRODUCTIVE TECHNOLOGIES AND MEDICAL RIGHTS

Many human rights debates and laws centre around the disjuncture between etic and emic value judgements of sexual propriety evident in the tension between collective cultural rights and cultural expectations of the individual – often over female purity – and broader international human rights policies. This tension has fuelled competing global sex discourses in relation to sexual violence and intimacy focused around different ideological poles: by emphasizing universalizing biological tendencies, on the one hand, and sex as a product of particular social regimes with socio-economic and culturally specific effects, on the other.

Just as women's bodies have become profitable in their sale and exchange, so they have also become the skin upon which discourses and practices around reproductive rights, duty and honour are written. The effects of family-planning policies in different countries and issues over reproductive health, sterilization and birth control, as well as enhanced medical technologies, have impacted men and women around the world in different ways (see Chapter 7). Assisted conception, for example, enabled lesbians and gay men to realize their rights to be parents, often by entering into alliances and partnerships with one another, thereby referencing yet disrupting 'the unity of gendered opposites' that is the symbolic heart of heterosexual reproductive intercourse (Weston 1991: 180). These technological changes have also altered perceptions about the relationship between male and female essences in natural and assisted procreation. Martin (1997: 91) explains how the potential to view the microscopic journey of the sperm to the egg has offered scientists different ways of interpreting procreative agency. She asserts that, in spite of new discoveries such as a molecule *on the egg coat* that is key to fertilization, scientific discourses ascribe aggressive and passive roles to both sperm and egg that invoke plays of dominance and victimization between male and female substances. For example, the notion of the femme fatale still persists, where the egg swallows the unsuspecting sperm, rather than seeing them both 'as mutually active partners' (see Martin 1997: 90). Elsewhere, the sperm is seen as divine and thus it is ascribed a role that renders medical intervention outside of marriage as adulterous. In Sunni Islam, donated sperm stigmatizes a child as illegitimate, as does any form of procreation involving a third person, such as surrogacy (Fortier 2007: 29), or any form of adoptive kinship which would deny biological connection with the father. Divorce or the death of either partner also breaks the marital connection and although in-vitro fertilization is allowed between married couples, it is not permitted under these altered circumstances (see Fortier 2007: 31). In the West, the mixing of particular kinds of reproductive substances between different kin determines the extent to which such mergers should be condoned. Edwards (2004: 771) argues that in the UK the potential for incest restricts certain types of new reproductive technology procedures, as men, for example, do not donate sperm to sisters, and nor do sisters give ova to brothers. In the Middle East, IVF technologies also interrupt the conditions of marital sex and require sexual performance on demand in places that are not conducive to erotic desire, constituting an 'agonising ritual' that is often deeply embarrassing and psychologically scarring (Inhorn 2007: 46). Although new reproductive technologies offer possibilities for marital happiness, their procedures have not been given the same kind of consideration. As one Shia Muslim engineer told Inhorn (2007: 47):

> The first time I go to do it [masturbate for semen collection], I find one chaise longue chair. How will I do it? At least in the other center [in Tunisia], they give one room for me and my wife… We'd even pay extra for this. Give me one room, and we'll pay! … We pay for many things in IVF [at $2,000 per cycle], so why not this? Here [in the semen collection room], it's like a prison cell.

Inhorn (2007: 50) notes that although 150 ethnographies and edited anthologies have been published on experiences of reproduction, these are mostly written by women and seldom consider the sexual experiences and subjectivities of men's sexuality.

Sexual subjectivities inevitability speak to the issue of sexual rights, which is a large field and one to which anthropologists have contributed significantly in various ways, such as understanding the social impacts of HIV (see Brummelhuis and Herdt 1995; Parker 2001). The issue of sexual rights raises questions about how long one can be reproductively active and about the role of medical technologies in this process, with advances being offered by performance-enhancing drugs such as Viagra as well as HRTs (hormone replacement therapies). Issues of cross-cultural inequality have persisted, since Viagra is not available around the globe, but instead of pursuing questions of how sexual performance is experienced, anthropologists have focused upon sexual illness and the medicalization of sexually transmitted diseases such as HIV over enabling medical practices (see, for example, Aggleton 1996; Parker et al. 1991; Parker et al. 1995).

Most recently, the British popular press brought to public attention the case of seventy-two-year-old Jenny Brown, who over a period of twenty years spent 30,000 pounds sterling in America and Italy trying to conceive a child. This case raises ethical questions not just about her age, the fact that she is old enough to be the child's great-grandmother and could leave it orphaned, but also about the role of the industry in exploiting or supporting older parents. She justified her decision to pursue becoming the world's oldest mum by pointing to the increase in life expectancy and as a parallel right with men's ability to father children for a very long time.[2] These rationalizations raise questions about sexual rights for individuals and bring into focus other categories of people who straddle moral, ethical and biological boundaries and who have not received anthropological attention. For example, people with mental or physical incapacities form one group about whom anthropologists have remained relatively silent but which could bear further ethnographic research. Analyzing the specifics of potentially paradoxical cases can inform public policy and contribute to a deeper understanding of other people's lives, but the question arises as to what constitutes medical rights and in whose terms.

Some writers believe that the medicalization of the West has obscured other cultural visions, because arguments surrounding invasive procedures such as female genital surgeries hang on concepts of medical rights. As with those who condemn sex trafficking and prostitution on the basis of its exploitative and abusive dimensions, some feminists argue that women should not have to be subjected to medical treatments they do not need and which do not improve their health but could in fact damage it. These operations are viewed as 'unnecessary', just as Western cosmetic surgery procedures such as breast implants, nose jobs, tummy tucks, liposuction and other beautifying treatments are. The 'otherness' of female genital circumcision is often put down to a lack of choice on the part of the women undergoing the surgery, since it is the parents or grandparents who choose to alter the woman's body rather than the woman herself. The spotlight has usually been cast upon cases that have resulted in extreme health problems and death.

FEMALE CIRCUMCISION: HUMAN RIGHTS IN CROSS-CULTURAL PERSPECTIVE

In many cultures that practise female genital alteration, it has been argued that the latter has nothing to do with medical health but rather with beauty, desirability, fertility, reproductive capacity, gender equilibrium and traditional stability (see Boddy 1982; Gruenbaum 1996; Hayes 1975). Female purity does not just extend to the control of chastity but also to aesthetic judgements about what is suitably feminine in the construction of a woman's body, especially one being prepared for marriage. 'Tradition' has often been used to justify the perpetuation of female genital surgeries in order to ensure that women will be able to continue their heritage, experience female solidarity and remain as part of the group. Although culture is cited as the internal rationale for supporting female genital circumcision, critics argue that tradition has changed and that modernism presents its own challenges for indigenous societies. In some cases, this may mean that traditions become more concretized as they seek validity and perpetuity in the face of uncertainty, but they may do so even when original practices have died out. As Dorkenoo and Elworthy (1992: 11) note:

> Today in many of these societies the ceremonial has fallen away; both excision and infibulation are performed at a much younger age that cannot be construed as having anything to do with entry into adulthood or marriage, and the child's role in society does not change at all after the mutilation.

Feminist organizations have long argued that tradition is a cover-up for the subjugation of the female body. As the internal cultural consequences of defying normative expectations of female genital operations are ostracism, shame and prostitution, women are effectively coerced into sustaining the system that the practice of female genital mutilation creates. Feminist positions have, however, been accused of being essentialist and imperialist because they do not always consider the importance of culture in the experiences of women (Savell 1996: 795) and may be seen to speak for them by reconstructing their experiences in Western terms. Many women anthropologists thus argue that this is one area in which Sudanese and Egyptian women should now be left to debate the issue themselves (e.g. Scheper-Hughes 1991: 26).

Strong support has been shown for the practices in Kenya and Sudan, with 79 per cent of rural men and women in a 1989–90 demographic and health survey (n/a 1995: 6–7) declaring themselves in favour, although women with secondary education and those living in towns expressed much greater opposition. Critics argue that the support generated for these practices comes partly from community pressure where such practices are mandatory and if there was freedom of choice, the practices would not necessarily continue. Yet, the consequences of female genital circumcision are embedded within a whole array of socio-economic effects that impact upon women, including restricted travel, restricted access to land ownership, possible domestic violence and child marriage, since in many communities women's access to land and economic resources is through the male members of the family and husbands rather than direct inheritance (Savell 1996: 796). The symbolic power of participation may also be a factor that compels women to undergo the procedure, as it binds women together and gives them collective power, recognition and value within the male view.

Equally perplexing for some critics is the question as to why in places such as Senegal, where female genital circumcision was not traditionally practised after 1993, it has now become the norm to the extent that young girls willingly offer themselves for circumcision without parental pressure. It is clear that there are ambiguities around the experiences of female genital circumcision that allow women to feel accepted, morally upright, sexually empowered and carry sexual and economic capital, whilst at the same time recognizing considerable physiological and emotional costs that may also be oppressive.

Those looking on from outside have tended to focus on the oppressive aspects of the procedure and its social and medical effects and have appealed to international human rights standards to evaluate the treatment of women in female genital operations. Savell (1996: 805) notes that Burkina Faso, Egypt, Ethiopia, Gambia, Guinea, Senegal, Nigeria, Mali and Kenya, but not Somalia, have all adopted the United Nations Convention on the Rights of the Child.

Dorkenoo and Elworthy's (1992: 15) report, based on findings from forty-three Sudanese gynaecologists, shows unanimous agreement that the practice is harmful and should cease. Committees have been set up throughout Africa to eradicate female genital circumcision, but in order for them to be successful they need to develop terms of critique and debate that comment upon internal values. This is a difficult task, since the terms of the debate both internally and cross-culturally may change and organizations need to take account of the flux of the debate. Yet, in arguing that cross-cultural dialogue should articulate with external criticism, there is an attempt to reach more nuanced understandings of the debates from within in order to be critically supportive in ways that are culturally appropriate.

Obermeyer (1999: 80, 90) argues that epidemiological, demographic and anthropological insights need to be combined in order to tackle the problem effectively and asserts that if female genital surgeries are to be understood, they have to be considered in relation to the general conditions of life for men and women in the societies where they are found. Shweder (1996: 1) asks those outside the practice 'to imagine how it might be possible for a moral and rational person ... to rationally link ritual initiation and the marking and alteration of the genitals to virtues such as civility, loyalty, respect, purity and self control' and argues that we need to see inside the cultures that condone them. Savell (1996: 3–4) argues for greater cross-cultural dialogue in determining human rights issues around female genital operations. This should be a dynamic arena that does not see traditional cultural practices supplanted by moral judgements made externally to cultural norms, but rather one in which debates about and evaluations of different types of cultural constructs are positioned in relation to each other. She says that, rather than outlawing practices from ethnocentric moral and legal perspectives, there should be sensitivity to internal debates whilst at the same time provoking participants to think critically and in enlightened ways about their cultural practices.

GLOBAL SEX: DEALING WITH ABUSE IN INTERNATIONAL LAW

In the face of the global transposition of sexual forms, a renewal of tradition has accompanied global standardization, challenging the idea that universal human rights exist as desirable or possible, exposing the fissure between what is sexually acceptable in private and in public and how it is dealt with by law. Sexual abuses such as marital battering, marital rape, dowry violence, wife burning and genital surgeries (cited in the 1993 Vienna conference Declaration against All Forms of Violence against Women) are considered private acts. They are not legislated against in international law because of their private status and also because women themselves are the primary agents in some of these practices (Nagengast 1997: 353). In response, international human rights organizations have criticized governments for allowing such abuses, considering them to be an infringement of human rights; they are met with counterclaims that imposing cultural imperialist ideals upon religious traditions would taint and destroy cultural integrity and honour and lead to immoral sexual freedom. Against the background of this impasse, Nagengast (1997: 352) argues that the anthropological notion of cultural relativity that was intended to instil respect for cultural difference has since been taken up as a weapon against universalizing rights in order to justify cultural behaviours that others would deem to be human rights abuses. Therefore, one of the problems with applying the Universal Declaration of Human Rights (1948) is that it dissolves the boundaries of states and nations because it is predicated upon transcendent moral orders.

It also relies upon the assertion of cultural rules and customs to define transcendent orders, and thus the international human rights debate is paradoxically bound up within its own cultural relativism.

It is not easy to reach the middle ground and while the global opportunities afforded by human rights conferences such as the 1995 Beijing Conference have contributed to women becoming better educated about the kinds of choices they can make to prevent abuses to them, this does not mean they will be able to effect them. As Gruenbaum (1996) points out, it would be impossible for a woman who defied the norms of genital circumcision to obtain a husband, leaving her destitute and a social outcast. While human rights may have caught up with cultural constraints, changes needed within cultural expectations and traditions have not always been sufficient to accommodate them.

HARDCORE SOFTWARE

Discourses of human rights' violations are further complicated by the global traffic of ideas and practices, which has become increasingly difficult to police and regulate across the airwaves. Just as distinctions have been made between indoor prostitution and sex trafficking, so the sexual windows onto the Internet invite different forms of global engagement, many of which are beyond the regulators in the 'shadow zone of globalisation' (Pentinnen 2006). The sensorial effects of sex on the move are all-pervasive through the Internet, film and media, with implications for the legislation of sexual rights as well as the expression of new kinds of intimacy.

In countries like Ireland where advertising prostitution is illegal, the Internet offers an alternative source of world networking, allowing 800 women to advertise on the Internet in any one day (Kelleher et al. 2009). The possibilities of Internet interaction have altered sexual habits in both scale and kind. With the availability of pay-to-view websites, anonymous purchasing of X-rated videos, live sex shows and computer pornography, children have become a key target of the pornography industry, satisfying illegal lust and, in some instances, marking new characteristics of desire. For example, in Japan high demand exists for viewing schoolgirls in uniform on the web, while a Tokyo club provides the opportunity to molest young girls in a mock subway setting. These activities simulate reality, as evidenced in the finding of a survey in 2000 'that 72 per cent of teenage girls had been groped on their way to school' (Wood 2001: 23, cited in O'Connell Davidson 2005: 102).

The emotional effects of the Internet create a paradox between actual and online intimacy in which technological distance affords emotional proximity to the other and, in so doing, ruptures the patterns of emotional attachment within a committed relationship. Anonymity, self-disclosure and disappearance from the online forum all offer an appearance of relative safety, but they may also be beset by the conditions and feelings of deception, secrecy and potential discovery. As the Internet affords certain kinds of protection, it allows for greater degrees of intimacy and sincerity, on the one hand, but may also be beset by the same kinds of fears and emotional uncertainties as offline sex, on the other. It is difficult to generalize about these experiences because netsex activities are not all of the same kind, and nor are desires and experiences received in similar ways. One interactive sex site, CU-SeeMe, involves live streaming of men and women to each other involved in sex acts in public or private rooms online that have more in common with 'peep shows, strip shows and erotic postcards' than with virtual sex in chat rooms or other arenas where the participants are not physically present (Kibby and Costello 2001: 356). These sites allow women to perform erotically and sensuously with their whole bodies, while men, lacking a history of erotically seductive posturing, typically display their genitals in a close-up 'crotch cam' pose (Kibby and Costello 2001: 360–1). This is fantasy in reality at the same time as the participants are seeking intimacy with one another in a mistaken belief that exposure on the outside creates closeness inside. The delusion is afforded by the cyborg experience of the sexual extension of the body through the computer as a vehicle for intimacy, erasing the time and space between those involved:

> The participants' touch on the keyboard, mouse and body animates the image of their body and the bodies of others, and the tactility of the experience reduces the distance between the object and subject of the erotic event. (Kibby and Costello 2001: 366)

The rules of engagement are that each person must be able to see the other's erotic body parts, not their elbows or some part of their room. The perceived intimacies of the CU-SeeMe site are therefore distinct from other cybernet chat rooms that allow more impersonal encounters without direct video contact. This massaging of relationships in the mind operates through the absence of visual and physical intimacy with another person. The consequences of netsex are complex and paradoxical, bringing both benefits and potential stresses and emotional traumas. In a discussion of the effects of engaging with the netsex site Cybermind, Marshall (2003: 238) explains that the experience can be seen:

> as intense and as lacking, as disembodied and confirmed by the body, as authentic and as fake, as safe or as bringing new dangers, as oscillating between the 'truths' of the online and 'truths' of the offline.

Netsex thus unsettles the conventions of intimacy in offline relationships, as users look to sex online to experience new kinds of intimate bonding. This has led cybertheorist Ben-Ze'ev (2004: 46) to argue that online relations are characterized by dreams rather than deception. Virtual and real sexspaces coalesce in cyberspace, in chat rooms and phone sex in which the imaginary environment is acted out. This is a fictional arena in which one feeds into the imagination of the other but it is experienced as intensely as if it were reality. As one man told Ben-Ze'ev (2004: 4): 'Cybersex is closer to having a hooker than plain pornography because there is a real and active person on the other end. People are touching each other's minds in a mutual and cooperative way that silent fantasy does not permit.' As Ben-Ze'ev shows, cybersex is not necessarily a safe way to have sex in terms of emotional stability, because cyberadultery can threaten the mental resources reserved for offline relations. The effects of these global meeting places are both moral and emotional and are growing exponentially in the chaotic restlessness of the cyber dynamic. As people direct their attention towards the keyboard, so they open themselves to a vast array of sexual possibilities, which in turn could have the effect of altering concepts of infidelity and adultery; but these constitute only one end of a spectrum that includes a range of transgressive possibilities culminating in cybersex crimes, whose punishment is not always equivalent to that for the same crimes committed offline. For example, prostitution in the Philippines is a crime but prostitution in cyberspace does not fit the Revised Penal Code's requirement of paid corporeal sex experience. Many of the emerging Internet websites with illegal material are also beyond the control of cyberpolice, whilst the threshold for what constitutes obscenity varies from one country to another, making policing particularly problematic.

CONCLUSION

It is clear from the diversity of examples discussed here and throughout the book that the terms of sexual experience and emotion around the globe cannot be reduced to one set of arguments; nor are the emotional conditions of sexual variation easily comparable across different cultural contexts. Desires are now global commodities and political orientations that have become increasingly experimental. In some countries, new narratives of sexual needs, passions and longings underpin state economic policies in order to gain freedom from the political constraints of the past and mobilize possibilities for social action (see Rofel 2007; Yanagisako 2002). It has also been argued that in newly eroticized China the globalization of sexuality invites comparison between Western capitalism and traditional values and does not depoliticize everyday life. Instead, the generation of private desires is creating '"liberal" political values' that now overshadow Maoist politics (Farquhar 2002: 247). Any reorientation of desire is a difficult undertaking. Povinelli (2006) reflects upon how intimate love is continually shaped by moving discourses of individual choice and agency ('autology') as well as social constraint ('genealogy') within post-colonial liberal governance in Aboriginal Australia and America. She argues that 'intimate events' might appear to be delimited and normalized but they operate on a shifting perspective between 'the micro-practices of love' and 'macro-practices of state governance ... capital production, circulation and consumption' (Povinelli 2006: 191), and within this flexible dynamic they expose the operations of power that define difference. There are, therefore, no stable or easily bounded terms that can finally describe the sexual matrix of intimate socialities, and individuals may express different identities throughout their lives (cf. Lancaster and di Leonardo 1997: 67; see also Butler 1991: 14). In recognizing the dilemma of the uncertainty of the sexual encounter and the problematic relationship between feeling and identity in the London lesbian and gay community, one woman commented: 'you know, we are still supposed to be feminists as well – we are still sup-posed to have some recognition of the social construction of sexuality... But I don't know quite where to draw the line any more' (cited in Green 1997: 194).

We have tried to show that what anthropologists bring to the bed is a richness and depth of ethnographic material about the contexts in which sexual practices take place, contrasting accounts of individual experiences, a sensitivity to the social relations in which sex is embedded and a diversity of understandings in terms of how these are located in and transcend disparate cultural arenas (cf. Godelier 2003: 180–1). At the same time, this emphasis upon sexual plurality, divergence and difference has meant that the mundane aspects of heteronormativity have been viewed as relatively homogeneous and are often downplayed in analysis. Although a fascination with desires and intimacies has largely replaced a concern with incest, we should not overlook how sexual pleasures are 'embedded in mundane "reproduction"' or assume that 'the mundane is somehow less interesting or instructive' (Rival et al. 1999: 297, 316; see also Rival 2008). As Stevi Jackson (2008: 35) argues, 'whatever the lure of the novel and unconventional, the study of sexuality in the future should give higher priority to what goes on within less glamorous, more routine and normative sexual lives', since these can also illuminate multiplicities of sexual experience and desire. Yet, 'ordinary sex' has been less well studied around the globe than transgressive sexuality and has too often been assumed to mirror Western sex lives. While it is not possible to pin down sex to any one thing, this book has revealed that sex can be many things to many people, including but not limited to a blend of personalities, social rules, desire, intimacy and performance, moral order and national image that speak to processes of sexual embodiment, varieties of sexual practice and the dynamics of culture. Therefore, it is not enough simply to change Western discourses around sex, desire and eroticism in order to address this complexity; rather, it is necessary to attend to the multiple ways in which various cultural concepts of sex are produced and reproduced through the political economies, structures and experiences of sex at individual, local and global levels. Scholars who adopt the language of either universalism or cultural relativism, without considering how the social, economic and political frameworks of sexual violence, for example, are reproduced by them, are in danger of imposing and naturalizing particular kinds of sexual difference and oppression through the very discourses that are intended to liberate them.

A division has emerged in this overview of global sex rights between activists who feel their first priority is to speak out against bodily harm, abuse and exploitation and other academics who try to balance concern for human rights with a sensitivity to cultural distinction and practice. As the anthropological literature throws up conundrums around how other cultural idioms might best be interpreted cross-culturally, it has in the past largely reserved judgement and acted more cautiously with respect to acts and practices that may be deemed to have elements of abuse. However, it is clear that this situation is changing, and it is our contention that this is one of the effects of global sex. As sex practices have gained currency from the West within the rest of the world, so have perceptions about what kinds of values, desires and experiences need to be addressed, bringing into view questions about how to create appropriate methods to assess the nature of sexual value in both a cross-cultural and a global perspective. This is no easy matter and clearly the universal/cultural relativist arguments have only part of the answer. This book has attempted to show the complexity of the positions that anthropologists and others have taken in their approach to analyzing sex around the world and reflects the tension evident in many authors' writings as they negotiate the fine line between respect for cultural autonomy, individual agency and the advocacy of sexual rights.

NOTES

1. The Irish sex industry rakes in 180 million euros a year.
2. Miss Brown believed the child would look more like her if she carried it in her womb even though it would have been conceived by donated egg and sperm. This presumed connection between biological structure and associational affinity was not based on biological fact but upon emotional presumption.

REFERENCES

Abu-Lughod, L. (1988). *Veiled Sentiments: Honour and Poetry in a Bedouin Society*. Berkeley: University of California Press.

Adair, C. (1992). *Women and Dance: Sylphs and Sirens*. London: Macmillan.

Adelman, B. (1997). *Tijuana Bibles: Art and Wit in America's Forbidden Funnies, 1930s–1950s*. New York: Simon and Schuster.

African Population Newsletter (1995). Female Genital Mutilation in Kenya and Sudan, *African Population Newsletter* 67: 6–7.

Aggleton, P. (ed.) (1996). *Bisexualities and AIDS: International Perspectives*. London: Taylor and Francis.

Ali, S. (2003). *Mixed-Race, Post-Race: Gender, New Ethnicities and Cultural Practices*. Oxford: Berg.

Al-Khayyat, S. (1990). *Honour and Shame: Women in Modern Iraq*. London: Saqi Books.

Allen, J.S. (2007). Means of Desire's Production: Male Sex Labor in Cuba, *Identities: Global Studies in Culture and Power* 14(1/2): 183–202.

Allende, I. (1999). *Aphrodite: A Memoir of the Senses*. London: Flamingo.

Allison, A. (1994). *Nightwork: Sexuality, Pleasure, and Corporate Masculinity in a Tokyo Hostess Club*. Chicago, IL: University of Chicago Press.

Altman, D. (1996). Rupture or Community? The Internationalization of Gay Identities, *Social Text* 48: 77–94.

Altman, D. (2001). *Global Sex*. Chicago, IL: University of Chicago Press.

Anzaldúa, G. (1987). *Borderlands/La Frontera: The New Mestiza*. San Francisco, CA: Aunt Lute Books.

Anzieu, D. (1989). *The Skin Ego*. New Haven, CT: Yale University Press.

Appadurai, A. (1990). Disjuncture and Difference in the Global Cultural Economy, *Public Culture* 2(2): 1–24.

Appadurai, A. (1996). *Modernity at Large: Cultural Dimensions of Globalisation*. Minneapolis: University of Minnesota Press.

Archetti, E.P. (1999). *Masculinities: Football, Polo and Tango in Argentina*. Oxford: Berg.

Ardener, S. (1987). A Note on Gender Iconography: The Vagina. In P. Caplan (ed.), *The Cultural Construction of Sexuality*. London: Tavistock Publications.

Aretxaga, B. (1995). Dirty Protest: Symbolic Overdetermination and Gender in Northern Ireland Ethnic Violence, *Ethos* 23(2): 123–48.

Aretxaga, B. (1997). *Shattering Silence: Women, Nationalism, and Political Subjectivity in Northern Ireland*. Princeton, NJ: Princeton University Press.

Argueta, M. (1983). *One Day of Life*. New York: Vintage Books.

Ariëns, I. and R. Strijp (eds) (1989). Anthropological Couples. Special issue of *Focaal: Tijdschrift Voor Antropologie* 10.

Arnfred, S. (2007). Sex, Food and Female Power: Discussion of Data Material from Northern Mozambique, *Sexualities* 10(2): 141–58.

Arreola, D.D. and J.R. Curtis (1993). *The Mexican Border Cities: Landscape Anatomy and Place Personality*. Tucson: University of Arizona Press.

Ashkenazi, M. and F. Markowitz (1999). Introduction: Sexuality and Prevarication in the Praxis of Anthropology. In F. Markowitz and M. Ashkenazi (eds), *Sex, Sexuality, and the Anthropologist*. Urbana, IL: University of Illinois Press.

Babiracki, C. (2004). The Illusion of India's Public Dancers. In J.A. Bernstein (ed.), *Women's Voices across Musical Worlds*. Boston, MA: Northeastern University Press.

Baker, S. (2001). 'Rock on Baby!': Pre-teen Girls and Popular Music, *Continuum* 15(3): 359–71.

Baker, S. (2002). Bardot, Britney, Bodies and Breasts: Pre-teen girls' Negotiations of the Corporeal in Their Relation to Pop Stars and Their Music, *Perfect Beat* 6(1): 18–32.

Barcan, R. (2004). *Nudity: A Cultural Anatomy*. Oxford: Berg.

Barkan, J. (2002). Winter as Old as War Itself: Rape in Foča, *Dissent* 49(1): 60–6.

Barker, P. (1992 [1991]). *Regeneration*. Harmondsworth: Penguin Books.

Barthes, R. (1973). *Mythologies*, trans. Annette Lavers. London: Paladin.

Barton, B. (2007). Managing the Toll of Stripping: Boundary Setting among Exotic Dancers, *Journal of Contemporary Ethnography* 36(5): 571–96.

Basso, E. (1985). *A Musical View of the Universe: Kalapalo Myth and Ritual Performances*. Philadelphia: University of Pennsylvania Press.

Bataille, G. (1986). *Eroticism: Death and Sensuality*, trans. Mary Dalwood. San Francisco: City Lights.

Bauer, T. and B. McKercher (eds) (2003a). Preface. In T. Bauer and B. McKercher (eds), *Sex and Tourism: Journeys of Romance, Love and Lust*. Oxford and New York: Haworth Hospitality Press.

Bauer, T. and B. McKercher (2003b). Conceptual Framework of the Nexus between Tourism, Romance, and Sex. In T. Bauer and B. McKercher (eds), *Sex and Tourism: Journeys of Romance, Love and Lust*. Oxford and New York: Haworth Hospitality Press.

Bauman, Z. (1991). *Modernity and Ambivalence*. Cambridge: Polity.

Bauman, Z. (1999). On Postmodern Uses of Sex. In M. Featherstone (ed.), *Love and Eroticism*. London: Sage Publications.

Beach, F. (ed.) (1965). *Sex and Behaviour*. New York: Wiley.

Beattie, G. (1999). *The Corner Boys*. London: Indigo.

Bech, H. (1999). Citysex: Representing Lust in Public. In M. Featherstone (ed.), *Love and Eroticism*. London: Sage Publications.

Beetz, A.M. and A.L. Podberscek (eds) (2005). *Bestiality and Zoophilia: Sexual Relations with Animals*. West Lafayette, IN: Purdue University Press.

Bell, D. (2006). Bodies, Technologies, Spaces: On 'Dogging', *Sexualities* 9(4): 387–407.

Bell, D. and R. Holliday (2000). Naked as Nature Intended. *Body and Society* 6(3–4): 127–40.

Bell, D. and G. Valentine (eds) (1995). *Mapping Desire: Geographies of Sexualities*. London: Routledge.

Bellér-Hann, I. (1995). Prostitution and Its Effects in Northeast Turkey, *European Journal of Women's Studies* 2: 219–35.

Bennett, W. and J. Gurin (1982). *The Dieter's Dilemma: Eating Less and Weighing More*. New York: Basic Books.

Benson, S. (1981). *Ambiguous Ethnicity: Interracial Families in London*. Cambridge: Cambridge University Press.

Ben-Ze'ev, A. (2004). *Love Online: Emotions on the Internet*. Cambridge: Cambridge University Press.

Berlant, L. (1998a). Intimacy: A Special Issue. In L. Berlant (ed.), 'Intimacy'. Special Issue of *Critical Inquiry* 24(2): 281–8.

Berlant, L. (ed.) (1998b). 'Intimacy'. Special Issue of *Critical Inquiry* 24(2).

Berndt, R.M. (1976). *Love Songs of Arnhem Land*. Melbourne: Nelson.

Bernstein, E. (2001). The Meaning of the Purchase: Desire, Demand and the Commerce of Sex. *Ethnography* 2(3): 389–420.

Bernstein, E. (2007a). *Temporarily Yours: Intimacy, Authenticity, and the Commerce of Sex*. Chicago, IL: University of Chicago Press.

Bernstein, E. (2007b). Buying and Selling the 'Girlfriend Experience': The Social and Subjective Contours of Market Intimacy. In M.B. Padilla, J.S. Hirsch, M. Muñoz-Laboy, R.E. Sember and R.G. Parker (eds), *Love and Globalization: Transformations of Intimacy in the Contemporary World*. Nashville, TN: Vanderbilt Press.

Besnier, N. (1994). Polynesian Gender Liminality through Time and Space. In G. Herdt (ed.), *Third Sex, Third Gender: Beyond Sexual Dimorphism in Culture and History*. New York: Zone Books.

Besnier, N. (1997). Sluts and Superwomen: The Politics of Gender Liminality in Urban Tonga, *Ethnos* 62(1–2): 1–5.

Besnier, N. (2002). Transgenderism, Locality and the Miss Galaxy Beauty Pageant in Tonga, *American Ethnologist* 29(3): 534–66.

Besnier, N. (2004). The Social Production of Abjection: Desire and Silencing among Transgender Tongans, *Social Anthropology* 12(3): 1–23.

Binnie, J. (1994). The Twilight World of the Sadomasochist. In S. Whittle (ed.), *The Margins of the City: Gay Men's Urban Lives*. Aldershot: Ashgate.

Birdwhistell, R.L. (1970). *Kinesics and Context*. Philadelphia: University of Pennsylvania Press.

Blacking, J.R. (1977). Towards an Anthropology of the Body. In J.R. Blacking (ed.), *The Anthropology of the Body*. London: Academic Press.

Blacking, J.R. (1985). Movement, Dance, Music and the Venda Girls' Initiation Cycle. In P. Spencer (ed.), *Society and the Dance*. Cambridge: Cambridge University Press.

Blackwood, E. (1998). *Tombois* in West Sumatra: Constructing Masculinity and Erotic Desire, *Cultural Anthropology* 13(4): 491–521.

Blackwood, E., S. Wieringa and A. Bhaiya (eds) (2007). *Women's Sexuality and Masculinities in a Globalizing Asia*. London: Palgrave Macmillan.

Bland, L. (2005). White Women and Men of Colour: Miscegenation Fears in Britain after the Great War, *Gender and History* 17(1): 29–61.

Bloch, M. and J. P. Parry (eds) (1982). *Death and the Regeneration of Life*. Cambridge: Cambridge University Press.

Boddy, J. (1982). Womb as Oasis: The Symbolic Context of Pharaonic Circumcision in Rural Northern Sudan, *American Ethnologist* 9: 682–98.

Boddy, J. (1988). Spirits and Selves in Northern Sudan: The Cultural Therapeutics of Possession and Trance, *American Ethnologist* 15(1): 4–27.

Boellstorff, T. (2005). *The Gay Archipelago: Sexuality and Nation in Indonesia*. Princeton, NJ: Princeton University Press.

Boellstorff, T. (2007a). *A Coincidence of Desires: Anthropology, Queer Studies, Indonesia*. Durham, NC: Duke University Press.

Boellstorff, T. (2007b). Queer Studies in the House of Anthropology. *Annual Review of Anthropology* 36: 17–35.

Bolin, A. (1996). Transcending and Transgendering: Male-to-Female Transsexuals, Dichotomy and Diversity. In G. Herdt (ed.), *Third Sex, Third Gender: Beyond Sexual Dimorphism in Culture and History*. New York: Zone Books.

Bolwell, J. and K. Kaa (1998). Dance. In A. Kaeppler and J.W. Love (eds), *The Garland Encyclopaedia of World Music*, Vol. 9. New York and London: Garland Publishing Inc.

Bordo, S. (1993). *Unbearable Weight: Feminism, Western Culture, and the Body*. Berkeley, CA: University of California Press.

Borneman, J. (1986). Emigrés as Bullets/Immigration as Penetration: Perceptions of the Marielitos, *Journal of Popular Culture* 20(3): 73–92.

Borneman, J. (1996). Until Death Do Us Part: Marriage/Death in Anthropological Discourse, *American Ethnologist* 23(2): 215–38.

Borneman, J. (1998). *Subversions of International Order: Studies in the Political Anthropology of Culture*. New York: SUNY Press.

Borneman, J. (2007). *Syrian Episodes: Sons, Fathers, and an Anthropologist in Aleppo*. Princeton, NJ: Princeton University Press.

Boulware-Miller, K. (1985). Female Circumcision: Challenges to the Practice as a Human Rights Violation, *Harvard Women's Law Journal* 8: 155–77.

Bowman, G. (1989). Fucking Tourists: Sexual Relations and Tourism in Jerusalem's Old City, *Critique of Anthropology* 9(2): 77–93.

Bowman, G. (1996). Passion, Power and Politics in a Palestinian Tourist Market. In T. Selwyn (ed.), *The Tourist Image: Myths and Myth Making in Tourism*. Chichester: Wiley.

Brah, A. and A.E. Coombes (eds) (2000). *Hybridity and Its Discontents: Politics, Science, Culture*. London: Routledge.

Brandes, S. (1981). Like Wounded Stags: Male Sexual Ideology in an Andalusian Town. In S.B. Ortner and H. Whitehead (eds), *Sexual Meanings*. Cambridge: Cambridge University Press.

Brennan, D. (1999). Women at Work: Sex Tourism in Sosúa, the Dominican Republic, *Critical Matrix* 11(2): 17–41.

Brennan, D. (2004a). *What's Love Got To Do With It? Transnational Desires and Sex Tourism in the Dominican Republic*. Durham, NC: Duke University Press.

Brennan, D. (2004b). Women Work, Men Sponge, and Everyone Gossips: Macho Men and Stigmatized/ing Women in a Sex Tourist Town, *Anthropological Quarterly* 77(4): 705–33.

Brennan, H. (1999). *The Story of Irish Dance*. Dingle: Mount Eagle Publications Ltd.

British Museum (n.d.). *Little Book of Erotica*. London: The British Museum Press.

Broinowksi, A. (1992). *The Yellow Lady: Australian Impressions of Asia*. Melbourne: Oxford University Press.

Bronfman, M. and S.L. Moreno (1996). Perspectives on HIV/AIDS Prevention among Immigrants on the US–Mexico Border. In S.I. Mishra, R.F. Conner and J.R. Mangaña (eds), *AIDS Crossing Borders: The Spread of HIV among Migrant Latinos*. Boulder, CO: Westview Press.

Brown, L. (2007). Performance, Status and Hybridity in a Pakistani Red-Light District: The Cultural Production of the Courtesan, *Sexualities* 10(4): 409–23.

Brownmiller, S. (1975). *Against Our Will: Men, Women and Rape*. New York: Simon and Schuster.

Brummelhuis, H.T. and G. Herdt (eds) (1995). *Culture and Sexual Risk: Anthropological Perspectives on AIDS*. Amsterdam: Gordon and Breach.

Bruner, E. (1993). Introduction: The Ethnographic Self and the Personal Self. In Paul Benson (ed.), *Anthropology and Literature*. Urbana: University of Illinois Press.

Bryant, C.D. (ed.) (1977). *Sexual Deviancy in Social Context*. New York: New Viewpoints.

Buckley, A.D. and M.C. Kenney (1995). *Negotiating Identity: Rhetoric, Metaphor, and Social Drama in Northern Ireland*. Washington, DC, and London: Smithsonian Institution Press.

Bullough, V.L. (1994). *Science in the Bedroom: A History of Sex Research*. New York: Basic Books.

Butler, J. (1990). *Gender Trouble*. London: Routledge.

Butler, J. (1991). Imitation and Gender Insubordination. In D. Fuss (ed.), *Inside/Out*. London: Routledge.

Butler, J. (1993). *Bodies That Matter: On the Discursive Limits of 'Sex'*. London: Routledge.

Cabezas, A.L. (2004). Between Love and Money: Sex, Tourism and Citizenship in Cuba and the Dominican Republic, *Signs: Journal of Women in Culture and Society* 29(4): 987–1015.

Cabezas, A.L. (2009). *Economies of Desire: Sex and Tourism in Cuba and the Dominican Republic*. Philadelphia, PA: Temple University Press.

Campbell, H. (2007). Cultural Seduction: American Men, Mexican Women, Cross-Border Attraction, *Critique of Anthropology* 27(3): 261–83.

Caplan, P. (1987). Introduction. In P. Caplan (ed.), *The Cultural Construction of Sexuality*. London: Tavistock Publications.

Caraveli, A. (1982). The Song beyond the Song: Aesthetics and Social Interaction in Greek Folksong, *Journal of American Folklore* 95(376): 129–58.

Carsten, J. (2004). *After Kinship*. Cambridge: Cambridge University Press

Cassidy, R. (2009). Zoosex and Other Relationships with Animals. In H. Donnan and F. Magowan (eds), *Transgressive Sex: Subversion and Control in Erotic Encounters*. Oxford: Berghahn Books.

Castillo, D.A., M.G.R. Gómez and B. Delgado (1999). Border Lives: Prostitute Women in Tijuana, *Signs: Journal of Women in Culture and Society* 24(2): 387–422.

Chancer, L. (1998). *Reconcilable Differences: Confronting Beauty, Pornography and the Future of Feminism*. Berkeley: University of California Press.

Chapkis, W. (1997). *Live Sex Acts: Women Performing Erotic Labor*. New York: Routledge.

Chaplin, S. (2007). *Japanese Love Hotels: A Cultural History*. London: Routledge.

Chernin, K. (1981). *The Obsession: Reflections on the Tyranny of Slenderness*. New York: Harper and Row.

Chodorow, N. (1978). *The Reproduction of Mothering: Psychoanalysis and the Sociology of Gender*. Berkeley, CA: University of California Press.

Clarke, M. (1982). *Nudism in Australia: A First Study*. Deakin, Victoria: Deakin University Press.

Classen, C. (2005). The Witch's Senses: Sensory Ideologies and Transgressive Feminities from the Renaissanace to Modernity. In D. Howes (ed.), *The Empire of the Senses*. Oxford: Berg.

Cohen, E. (1979). Rethinking the Sociology of Tourism, *Annals of Tourism Research* 6(1): 18–35.

Cohen, E. (1982). Thai Girls and Farang Men: The Edge of Ambiguity, *Annals of Tourism Research* 9: 403–28.

Colley, L. (2003). *Captives: Britain, Empire and the World 1600–1850*. London: Pimlico.

Collins, M.A. and G. Hagenauer (2008). *Men's Adventure Magazines in Postwar America: The Rich Oberg Collection*. Cologne: Taschen.

Constable, N. (1997). Sexuality and Discipline among Filipina Domestic Workers in Hong Kong, *American Ethnologist* 24(3): 539–58.

Cook, S. (1998). Passionless Dancing and Passionate Reform: Respectability, Modernism and the Social Dancing of Irene and Vernon Castle. In W. Washabaugh (ed.), *The Passion of Music and Dance: Body, Gender and Sexuality*. Oxford: Berg.

Cooper, C. (1993). *Noises in the Blood: Orality, Gender and the 'Vulgar' Body of Jamaican Popular Culture*. London: Macmillan.

Cooper, W. (1971). *Hair: Sex, Society, Symbolism*. New York: Stein and Day.

Corbin, A. (2006). The New Calculus of Olfactory Pleasure. In J. Drobnick (ed.), *The Smell Culture Reader*. Oxford: Berg.

Courtwright, D.T. (1996). *Violent Land: Single Men and Social Disorder from the Frontier to the Inner City*. Cambridge, MA: Harvard University Press.

Cowan, J. (1990). *Dance and the Body Politic in Northern Greece*. Princeton, NJ: Princeton University Press.

Crowe, P. (1998). Vanuatu – Northern and Central Areas. In A. Kaeppler and J.W. Love (eds), *The Garland Encyclopaedia of World Music*, Vol. 9. New York and London: Garland Publishing Inc.

Dahles, H. and K. Bras (1999). Entrepreneurs in Romance: Tourism in Indonesia, *Annals of Tourism Research* 26(2): 267–93.

Daniel, E.V. (1987). *Fluid Signs: Being a Person the Tamil Way*. Berkeley: University of California Press.

Davis, D.L. and G. Whitten (1987). The Cross-Cultural Study of Human Sexuality, *Annual Review of Anthropology* 16: 69–98.

Davis, K. (1937). The Sociology of Prostitution, *American Sociological Review* 2(5): 744–55.

Day, S. (1994). What Counts as Rape? In P. Harvey and P. Gow (eds), *Sex and Violence: Issues in Representation and Experience*. London: Routledge.

Day, S. (1996). The Law and the Market: Rhetorics of Exclusion and Inclusion among London Prostitutes. In O. Harris (ed.), *Inside and Outside the Law: Anthropological Studies of Authority and Ambiguity*. London: Routledge.

Day, S. (2000). The Politics of Risk among London Prostitutes. In P. Caplan (ed.), *Risk Revisited*. London: Pluto Press.

Day, S. (2007). *On the Game: Women and Sex Work*. London: Pluto Press.

Day, S. (2009). Renewing the War on Prostitution: The Spectres of 'Trafficking' and 'Slavery', *Anthropology Today* 25(3): 1–3.

Day, S. and H. Ward (eds) (2004). *Sex Work, Mobility and Health in Europe*. London: Kegan Paul.

Dean, T. (2009). *Unlimited Intimacy: Reflections on the Subculture of Barebacking*. Chicago, IL: University of Chicago Press.

Deaver, S. (1978). Concealment and Display: The Modern Saudi Woman, *Dance Research Journal* 10(2): 14–18.

De Beauvoir, S. (1997 [1949]). *The Second Sex*. London: Vintage.

Demaris, O. (1970). *Poso del Mundo: Inside the Mexican American Border from Tijuana to Matamoros*. Boston: Little, Brown.

Demetriou, O. (2006). Owing the Seed: The Discursive Economy of Sex Migration among Turkish-Speaking Minority Urbanites in the Postsocialist Balkan Periphery, *Identities: Global Studies in Culture and Power* 13(2): 261–82.

Devereux, G. (1937). Institutionalised Homosexuality of the Mohave Indians, *Human Biology* 9(4): 498–527.

Dewey, S. (2009). 'Dear Dr Kothari...': Sexuality, Violence against Women, and the Parallel Public Sphere in India, *American Ethnologist* 36(1): 124–39.

Di Leonardo, M. (1997). White Lies, Black Myths: Rape, Race, and the Black 'Underclass'. In R.N. Lancaster and M. di Leonardo (eds), *The Gender/Sexuality Reader: Culture, History, Political Economy*. London: Routledge.

Donnan, H. (1990). Mixed Marriage in Comparative Perspective: Gender and Power in Northern Ireland and Pakistan, *Journal of Comparative Family Studies* XXI(2): 207–25.

Donnan, H. and F. Magowan (eds) (2009). *Transgressive Sex: Subversion and Control in Erotic Encounters*. Oxford: Berghahn Books.

Donnan, H. and T.M. Wilson (1999). *Borders: Frontiers of Identity, Nation and State*. Oxford: Berg.

Donnelly, D. and J. Fraser (1998). Gender Differences in Sado-masochistic Arousal among College Students, *Sex Roles* 39: 391–407.

Dorkenoo, E. and S. Elworthy (1992). *Female Genital Mutilation: Proposals for Change*. London: Manchester Free Press.

Doubleday, V. (2008). Sounds of Power: An Overview of Musical Instruments and Gender, *Ethnomusicology Forum* 17(1): 3–39.

Douglas, J.D. (ed.) (1970). *Observations of Deviance*. New York: Random House.

Douglas, M. (1966). *Purity and Danger: An Analysis of Concepts of Pollution and Taboo*. Harmondsworth: Penguin.

Douglas, M. (1973). *Natural Symbols*. New York: Vintage.

Dragojlovic, A. (2008). Dutch Women and Balinese Men: Intimacies, Popular Discourses and Citizenship Rights, *Asia Pacific Journal of Anthropology* 9(4): 332–45.

Driessen, H. (1992). *On the Spanish-Moroccan Frontier: A Study in Ritual, Power and Ethnicity*. Oxford: Berg.

Drobnick, J. (2005). Olfactory Dimensions of Art and Architecture. In D. Howes (ed.), *The Empire of the Senses*. Oxford: Berg.

Du, S. (2008). With One Word and One Strength: Intimacy among the Lahu of Southwest China. In W. Jankowiak (ed.), *Intimacies: Love and Sex across Cultures*. New York: Columbia University Press.

Dworkin, A. (1981). *Pornography: Men Possessing Women*. London: The Women's Press.

Dworkin, A. (1989). *Letters from a War Zone: Writings, 1976–1989*. New York: Dutton.

Edgerton, R.B. (1978). The Study of Deviance: Marginal Man or Everyman? In G.D. Spindler (ed.), *The Making of Psychological Anthropology*. Berkeley: University of California Press.

Edmonds, A. (2007). The Poor Have the Right to Be Beautiful: Cosmetic Surgery in Neoliberal Brazil, *Journal of the Royal Anthropological Institute* 13(2): 363–82.

Edwards, J. (2004). Incorporating Incest: Gamete, Body and Relation in Assisted Conception, *Journal of the Royal Anthropological Institute*, 10: 755–74.

Edwards, T. (1993). *Erotic Politics: Gay Male Sexuality, Masculinity and Feminism*. New York: Routledge.

Egan, D. (2006). The Phenomenology of Lap Dancing. In D.R. Egan, K. Frank and M.L. Johnson (eds), *Flesh for Fantasy: Producing and Consuming Exotic Dance*. New York: Thunder's Mouth.

Ellis, C. (1998). Central Australia. In A. Kaeppler and J.W. Love (eds), *The Garland Encyclopaedia of World Music*, Vol. 9. New York and London: Garland Publishing Inc.

Ellis, H.H. (1900). *The Evolution of Modesty, The Phenomena of Sexual Periodicity, Auto-Eroticism, Studies in the Psychology of Sex, Volume 2* (Watford); renumbered and subsequently known as vol. 1 of *Studies in the Psychology of Sex*. Philadelphia, 1901.

Ellis, H.H. (1921). *Studies in the Psychology of Sex*. Philadelphia, PA: F.A. Davis Co.

Ellis, H.H. (1923). *The Dance of Life*. Boston: Houghton Mifflin.

Ellis, H.H. and J.A. Symonds (1897). *The Psychology of Sex: Sexual Inversion, Volume 1*. London: London University Press; renumbered and subsequently known as vol. 2 of *Studies in the Psychology of Sex*. Philadelphia, 1901.

Elliston, D. (1995). Erotic Anthropology: 'Ritualized Homosexuality' in Melanesia and Beyond, *American Ethnologist* 22(4): 848–67.

Enck, Graves E. and James D. Preston (1988). Counterfeit Intimacy: A Dramaturgical Analysis of an Erotic Performance, *Deviant Behavior* 9: 369–81.

English, R. (1980). Alas, Alak the Representation of the Ballerina, *New Dance* 15: 18.

Ennew, J. (1986). *The Sexual Exploitation of Children*. Cambridge: Polity Press.

Espín, O. (1997). *Latina Realities: Essays on Healing, Migration, and Sexuality*. Boulder, CO: Westview Press.

Evans-Pritchard, E.E. (1970). Sexual Inversion among the Azande, *American Anthropologist* 72(6): 1428–34.

Farquhar, J. (2002). *Appetites: Food and Sex in Post-socialist China*. Durham, NC: Duke University Press.

Favazza, A.R. (1987). *Bodies under Siege: Self-Mutilation and Body Modification in Culture and Psychiatry*. Baltimore, MD: Johns Hopkins University Press.

Featherstone, M. (1982). The Body in Consumer Culture, *Theory, Culture and Society* 1: 18–33.

Featherstone, M. and M. Hepworth (1991). The Mask of Ageing and the Postmodern Life Course. In M. Featherstone, M. Hepworth and B.S. Turner (eds), *The Body: Social Process and Cultural Theory*. London: Sage Publications.

Fechter, A.-M. (2007). *Transnational Lives: Expatriates in Indonesia*. Aldershot: Ashgate.

Feldman, A. (1991). *Formations of Violence: The Narrative of the Body and Political Terror in Northern Ireland*. Chicago, IL: University of Chicago Press.

Fernández, N. (1999). Back to the Future? Women, Race, and Tourism in Cuba. In K. Kempadoo (ed.), *Sun, Sex and Gold: Tourism and Sex Work in the Caribbean*. Lanham, MD: Rowman and Littlefield.

Fernández-Kelly, M.P. (1983). *For We Are Sold, I and My People: Women and Industry in Mexico's Frontier*, SUNY Series in the Anthropology of Work. Albany: State University of New York Press.

Finklehor, D. (1984). *Child Sexual Abuse: New Theory and Research*. New York: Free Press.

Finsch, O. (1961 [1893]). *Ethnological Experiences and Materials from the South Seas*, trans. Benjamin Keen. New Haven, CT: Human Relations Area Files.

Flowers, P., C. Marriott and G. Hart (2000). 'The Bars, the Bogs, and the Bushes': The Impact of Locale on Sexual Cultures, *Culture, Health & Sexuality* 2(1): 69–86.

Folch-Lyon, E., L. Macorra and S.B. Shearer (1981). Focus Group and Survey Research on Family Planning in Mexico, *Studies in Family Planning* 12(12): 409–32.

Forrest, D. (1993). 'We're Here, We're Queer, and We're Not Going Shopping': Changing Gay Male Identities in Contemporary Britain. In A. Cornwall and N. Lindisfarne (eds), *Dislocating Masculinity: Comparative Ethnographies*. London and New York: Routledge.

Fortier, C. (2007). Blood, Sperm and the Embryo in Sunni Islam and in Mauritania: Milk Kinship, Descent and Medically Assisted Procreation, *Body and Society* 13(3): 15–36.

Foucault, M. (1979). *Discipline and Punish: The Birth of the Prison*, trans. Alan Sheridan. Harmondsworth: Penguin Books.

Foucault, M. (1981). *The History of Sexuality, Volume One: An Introduction*. Harmondsworth: Penguin Books.

Fox, K. (2004). *Watching the English: The Hidden Rules of English Behaviour*. London: Hodder and Stoughton.

Fox, R. (1978). *The Tory Islanders: A People of the Celtic Fringe*. Cambridge: Cambridge University Press.

Fox, R. (1980). *The Red Lamp of Incest*. London: Hutchinson.

Frank, K. (2002). *G-Strings and Sympathy: Strip Club Regulars and Male Desire*. Durham, NC: Duke University Press.

Frank, K. (2007). Thinking Critically about Strip Club Research, *Sexualities* 10(4): 501–17.

Frayser, S.G. (1985). *Varieties of Sexual Experience: An Anthropological Perspective on Human Sexuality*. New Haven, CT: HRAF Press.

Frembgen, J.W. (2008). Marginality, Sexuality and the Body: Professional Masseurs in Urban Muslim Punjab, *Asia Pacific Journal of Anthropology* 9(1): 1–28.

French, L. (1996). Border Trade: Thailand/Cambodia. Paper presented to the American Anthropological Association Annual Meeting, San Francisco, CA, 20–24 November 1996.

Freud, S. (1922). *Introductory Lectures on Psychoanalysis*. London: Allen and Unwin.

Freud, S. (1938). The Sexual Aberrations. In *Basic Writings of Sigmund Freud*, ed. and trans. A.A. Brill. New York: Modern Library.

Friedl, E. (1994). Sex the Invisible, *American Anthropologist* 96(4): 833–44.

Frost, H.G. (1983). *The Gentlemen's Club: The Story of Prostitution in El Paso*. El Paso, TX: Mangan Books.

Gagnon, J.H. (1968). Prostitution, *International Encyclopaedia of the Social Sciences* 12: 592–8.

Gaissad, L. (2009). Taming the Bush: Morality, AIDS Prevention and Gay Sex in Public Places. In H. Donnan and F. Magowan (eds), *Transgressive Sex: Subversion and Control in Erotic Encounters*. Oxford: Berghahn Books.

Gallen, M.E., L. Liskin and N. Kak (1986). Men – New Focus for Family Planning Programs, Johns Hopkins School of Public Health, Baltimore, MD, *Population Reports Series Journal* 33: 889–919.

García, L. (2009). Love at First Sex: Latina Girls' Meanings of Virginity Loss and Relationships, *Identities: Global Studies in Culture and Power* 16: 601–21.

Garreta, R. and A. Bartoll (2005). *Le Piège Afghan*. Paris: Dargaud.

Gaudio, R. (1994). Sounding Gay: Pitch Properties in the Speech of Gay and Straight Men, *American Speech* 69(1): 30–57.

Gay y Blasco, P. (1999). *Gypsies in Madrid: Sex, Gender and the Performance of Identity*. Oxford: Berg.

Gell, A. (1971). Penis Sheathing in a West Sepik Village, *Man* (NS) 6(2): 165–81.

Gell, A. (1975). *Metamorphosis of the Cassowaries: Umeda Society, Language and Ritual*. London: Athlone.

Gell, A. (1985). Style and Meaning in Umeda Dance. In P. Spencer (ed.), *Society and the Dance: The Social Anthropology of Process and Performance*. Cambridge: Cambridge University Press.

Gell, A. (1993). *Wrapping in Images: Tattooing in Polynesia*. Oxford: Clarendon Press.

Giddens, A. (1991). *Modernity and Self-Identity: Self and Society in the Late Modern Age*. Cambridge: Polity Press.

Giddens, A. (1993). *The Transformation of Intimacy: Sexuality, Love and Eroticism in Modern Societies*. Cambridge: Polity Press.

Gilman, S. (1985). Black Bodies, White Bodies: Toward an Iconography of Female Sexuality in Late Nineteenth-Century Art, Medicine and Literature. In H.L. Gates, Jr. (ed.), *'Race', Writing and Difference*. Chicago, IL, and London: University of Chicago Press.

Gilmore, D. (1988). *Carnival and Culture: Sex, Symbol and Status in Spain*. New Haven, CT: Yale University Press.

Gluckman, M. (1970 [1956]). *Custom and Conflict in Africa*. Oxford: Basil Blackwell.

Godelier, M. (2003). What Is a Sexual Act? *Anthropological Theory* 3(2): 179–98.

Goffman, E. (1965). Attitudes and Rationalizations Regarding Body Exposure. In M.E. Roach and J.B. Eicher (eds), *Dress, Adornment, and the Social Order*. New York: John Wiley.

González-López, G. (2005). *Erotic Journeys: Mexican Immigrants and Their Sex Lives*. Berkeley: University of California Press.

Goode, E. (2002). Sexual Involvement and Social Research in a Fat Civil Rights Organization, *Qualitative Sociology* 25(4): 501–34.

Goody, J.R. (1956). A Comparative Approach to Incest and Adultery, *British Journal of Sociology* 7: 286–305.

Gordimer, N. (1990). The Ingot and the Stick, the Ingot and the Gun: Mozambique-South Africa. In Richard Eyre, Nigel Hamilton, Nadine Gordimer, Richard Rodriguez and Frederic Raphael, *Frontiers*. London: BBC Books.

Gordon, S. (1983). *Off Balance: The Real World of Ballet*. New York: Pantheon.

Gottschall, J. (2004). Explaining Wartime Rape, *Journal of Sex Research* 41: 129–36.

Government of Northern Ireland (1972). *The Terror – and the Tears*. Government of Northern Ireland.

Green, S. (1997). *Urban Amazons: Lesbian Feminism and Beyond in the Gender, Sexuality and Identity Battles of London*. London: Macmillan Press Ltd.

Greenberg, D.F. (1985). Why Was the Berdache Ridiculed? *Journal of Homosexuality* 11(3/4): 179–89.

Greenhalgh, S. (1994). Controlling Births and Bodies in Village China, *American Ethnologist* 21(1): 3–30.

Greenhalgh, S. and E. Winckler (2005). *Governing China's Population: From Leninist to Neoliberal Biopolitics*. Stanford, CA: Stanford University Press.

Gregor, T. (1985). *Anxious Pleasures: The Sexual Lives of an Amazonian People*. Chicago, IL: University of Chicago Press.

Gross, J. (1993). Where 'Boys Will Be Boys' and Adults Are Befuddled, *New York Times*, 29 March.

Gruenbaum, E. (1996). The Cultural Debate over Female Circumcision: The Sudanese Are Arguing This One out for Themselves, *Medical Anthropology Quarterly* 10: 455–75.

Gutiérrez, R. (1996). The Erotic Zone: Sexual Transgression on the US–Mexican Border. In A.F. Gordon and C. Newfield (eds), *Mapping Multiculturalism*. Minneapolis: University of Minnesota Press.

Halberstam, J. (1998). *Female Masculinity*. Durham, NC: Duke University Press.

Haller, D. (2000). The Smuggler and the Beauty Queen: The Border and Sovereignty as Sources of Body Style in Gibraltar. In H. Donnan and D. Haller (eds), Special Issue on 'Borders and Borderlands: An Anthropological Perspective', *Ethnologia Europaea* 30(2): 57–72.

Hallpike, C.R. (1969). Social Hair, *Man* (N.S.) 4: 254–64.

Hammers, C. (2009). An Examination of Lesbian/Queer Bathhouse Culture and the Social Organization of (Im)Personal Sex, *Journal of Contemporary Ethnography* 38(3): 308–35.

Handy, E.S.C. (1978 [1927]). *Polynesian Religion*. Honolulu: Bishop Museum (reprint, Millwood: Kraus).

Hann, C. and I. Bellér-Hann (1998). Markets, Morality and Modernity in North-East Turkey. In T.M. Wilson and H. Donnan (eds), *Border Identities: Nation and State at International Frontiers*. Cambridge: Cambridge University Press.

Hann, C. and I. Hann (1992). Samovars and Sex on Turkey's Russian Markets, *Anthropology Today* 8(4): 3–6.

Hanna, J.L. (1987). *To Dance Is Human: A Theory of Nonverbal Communication*. Chicago, IL: University of Chicago Press.

Hanna, J.L. (1988). *Dance, Sex and Gender: Signs of Identity, Dominance, Defiance and Desire*. Chicago, IL: University of Chicago Press.

Hannerz, U. (1996). *Transnational Connections: Culture, People, Places*. New York: Routledge.

Hansen, C., C. Needham and B. Nichols (1991). Pornography, Ethnography, and the Discourses of Power. In B. Nichols (ed.), *Representing Reality*. Bloomington: Indiana University Press.

Hansen, L. (2001). Gender, Nation, Rape: Bosnia and the Construction of Security, *International Feminist Journal of Politics* 3(1): 55–75.

Harding, J. (1998). *Sex Acts: Practices of Femininity and Masculinity*. London: Sage.

Harper, E.B. (1964). Ritual Pollution as an Integrator of Caste and Religion, *Journal of Asian Studies* XXIII: 151–97.

Harrigan, J. (2008). Proxemics, Kinesics and Gaze. In J. Harrigan, R. Rosenthal and K. Scherer (eds), *New Handbook of Methods in Nonverbal Behavior Research*. Oxford: Oxford University Press.

Harris, R. (1972). *Prejudice and Tolerance in Ulster: A Study of Neighbours and 'Strangers' in a Border Community*. Manchester: Manchester University Press.

Hart, A. (1994). Missing Masculinity? Prostitutes' Clients in Alicante, Spain. In A. Cornwall and N. Lindisfarne (eds), *Dislocating Masculinity: Comparative Ethnographies*. London: Routledge.

Hart, A. (1995). Re-constructing a Spanish Red-Light District: Prostitution, Space and Power. In D. Bell and G. Valentine (eds), *Mapping Desire: Geographies of Sexualities*. London: Routledge.

Hart, K. (2005). *The Hit Man's Dilemma: Or, Business, Personal and Impersonal*. Chicago, IL: Prickly Paradigm Press.

Harter, P. (2004). Mauritania's 'Wife-Fattening' Farm, *BBC News*, 26 January. URL: http://news.bbc.co.uk/1/hi/world/africa/342(9903).stm.

Hayes, R. (1975). Female Genital Mutilation, Fertility Control, Women's Roles and the Patrilineage in Modern Sudan: A Functional Analysis, *American Ethnologist* 2: 617–33.

Heap, C. (2009). *Slumming: Sexual and Racial Encounters in American Nightlife, 1885–1940*. Chicago, IL: University of Chicago Press.

Hearn, J. and W. Parkin (1987). 'Sex' at 'Work': The Power and Paradox of Organisation Sexuality. Brighton: Wheatsheaf Books.

Hegley, J. (1997). *The Family Pack*. London: Methuen.

Heise, L.L. (1997). Violence, Sexuality, and Women's Lives. In R.N. Lancaster and M. de Leonardo (eds), *The Gender/Sexuality Reader*. New York: Routledge.

Helliwell, C. (2000). 'It's Only a Penis': Rape, Feminism and Difference, *Signs* 25(3): 789–816.

Herdt, G. (1981). *Guardians of the Flutes: Idioms of Masculinity – A Study of Ritualised Homosexual Behaviour*. New York: McGraw-Hill.

Herdt, G. (1982). Fetish and Fantasy in Sambia Initiation. In G. Herdt (ed.), *Rituals of Manhood*. Berkeley: University of California Press.

Herdt, G. (1984). Preface. In G. Herdt (ed.), *Ritualized Homosexuality in Melanesia*. Berkeley: University of California Press.

Hermanowicz, J.C. (2002). The Great Interview: 25 Strategies for Studying People in Bed, *Qualitative Sociology* 25(4): 479–99.

Herold, E., R. García and T. De Moya (2001). Female Tourists and Beach Boys: Romance or Sex Tourism? *Annals of Tourism Research* 28(4): 978–97.

Hershman, P. (1974). Hair, Sex and Dirt, *Man* (N.S.) 9: 274–98.

Herzfeld, M. (1985). *The Poetics of Manhood: Contest and Identity in a Cretan Mountain Village*. Princeton, NJ: Princeton University Press.

Herzfeld, M. (1987). *Anthropology through the Looking Glass: Critical Ethnography in the Margins of Europe*. Cambridge: Cambridge University Press.

Hill, D. (ed.) (1978). *The Shape of Sex to Come: Stories by Moorcock, Silverberg, Aldiss and Others*. London: Pan Books.

Hine, D.C. (1997). Rape and the Inner Lives of Black Women in the Middle West: Preliminary Thoughts on the Culture of Dissemblance. In R.N. Lancaster and M. de Leonardo (eds), *The Gender/Sexuality Reader*. New York: Routledge.

Hirsch, J.S. and H. Wardlow (eds) (2006). *Modern Loves: The Anthropology of Romantic Courtship and Companionate Marriage*. Ann Arbor: University of Michigan Press.

Ho, P.S.Y. and A.K.T. Tsang (2000). Negotiating Anal Intercourse in Inter-racial Gay Relationships in Hong Kong, *Sexualities* 3(3): 299–323.

Hodes, M. (1993). The Sexualization of Reconstruction Politics: White Women and Black Men in the South after the Civil War. In J.C. Fout and M.S. Tantillo (eds), *American Sexual Politics: Sex, Gender, and Race since the Civil War*. Chicago, IL: University of Chicago Press.

Hodes, M. (1997). *White Women, Black Men: Illicit Sex in the Nineteenth Century South*. New Haven, CT: Yale University Press.

Hodge, G.D. (2001). Colonization of the Cuban Body: The Growth of Male Sex Work in Havana, *NACLA Report on the Americas* 34(5): 20–8..

Hoffman, Howard (n.d.). *Howard Hoffman… On Life*. http://serendip.brynmawr.edu/exhibitions/hoffman/h012.html (accessed 19 February 2010).

Hogbin, I. (1970). *The Island of Menstruating Men*. Scraton, NJ: Chandler.

hooks, b. (1992). *Black Looks: Race and Representation*. Boston, MA: South End Press.

Hosken, F.P. (1981). Towards a Definition of Women's Rights, *Human Rights Quarterly* 3(2): 1–10.

Howard, S. (1986). Fig Leaf, Pudica, Nudity and Other Revealing Concealments, *American Imago* 43(4): 289–93.

Howes, D. (2005). Introduction: Empires of the Senses. In D. Howes (ed.), *Empire of the Senses*. Oxford: Berg.

Hrdlicka, A. (1925). Relation of the Size of Head and Skull to Capacity in the Two Sexes, *American Journal of Physical Anthropology* 8: 249–50.

Hughes, D.M. (2000). 'Welcome to the Rape Camp': Sexual Exploitation and the Internet in Cambodia, *Journal of Sexual Aggression* 6: 29–51.

Huseby-Darvas, E.V. (1999). Deconstructing and Reconstructing My Desexualised Identity. In F. Markowitz and M. Ashkenazi (eds), *Sex, Sexuality and the Anthropologist*. Urbana: University of Illinois Press.

Inhorn, M. (2007). Masturbation, Semen Collection and Men's IVF Experiences: Anxieties in the Muslim World, *Body and Society* 13(3): 37–53.

Jackson, Peter (1999). Commodity Cultures: The Traffic in Things, *Transactions of the Institute of British Geographers* 24(1): 95–108.

Jackson, Peter A. and G. Sullivan (eds) (1999). *Lady Boys, Tom Boys, Rent Boys: Male and Female Homosexualities in Contemporary Thailand*. London: Haworth Press.

Jackson, Phil (2004). *Inside Clubbing: Sensual Experiments in the Art of Being Human*. Oxford: Berg.

Jackson, S. (2008). Ordinary Sex, *Sexualities* 11: 33–7.

Jankowiak, W. (ed.) (1995). *Romantic Passion: A Universal Experience?* New York: Columbia University Press.

Jankowiak, W. (ed.) (2008). *Intimacies: Love and Sex across Cultures*. New York: Columbia University Press.

Jankowiak, W. and L. Mixson (2008). 'I Have His Heart, Swinging Is Just Sex': The Ritualization of Sex and the Rejuvenation of the Love Bond in an American Spouse Exchange Community. In W. Jankowiak (ed.), *Intimacies: Love and Sex across Cultures*. New York: Columbia University Press.

Jankowiak, W. and T. Paladino (2008). Desiring Sex, Longing for Love: A Tripartite Conundrum. In W. Jankowiak (ed.), *Intimacies: Love and Sex across Cultures*. New York: Columbia University Press.

Jeffrey, L.A. (2002). *Sex and Borders: Gender, National Identity, and Prostitution Policy in Thailand*. Vancouver: University of British Columbia Press.

Jeffreys, S. (1997). *The Idea of Prostitution*. Melbourne: Spinifex Press.

Jeffreys, S. (2005). *Beauty and Misogyny: Harmful Cultural Practices in the West*. London: Brunner/Routledge.

Jeffreys, S. (2009). *The Industrial Vagina: The Political Economy of the Global Sex Trade*. London: Routledge.

Jenkins, J. (1991). The State Construction of Affect: Political Ethos and Mental Health among Salvadoran Refugees, *Medicine, Culture and Psychiatry* 15: 139–65.

Jenkins, J. (1998). The Medical Anthropology of Political Violence: A Cultural and Feminist Agenda, *Medical Anthropology Quarterly* 12(1): 122–31.

Jervis, J. (1999). *Transgressing the Modern: Explorations in the Western Experience of Otherness*. Oxford: Blackwell.

Johnson, M. (1997). *Beauty and Power: Transgendering and Cultural Transformation in the Southern Philippines*. Oxford: Berg.

Johnston, J. (1971). *Marmelade Me*. New York: Dutton.

Jolly, M. and L. Manderson (eds) (1997). *Sites of Desire, Economics of Pleasure: Sexualities in Asia and the Pacific*. Chicago, IL, and London: University of Chicago Press.

Kaeppler, A. (1985). Structured Movement System in Tonga. In P. Spencer (ed.), *Society and the Dance: The Social Anthropology of Process and Performance*. Cambridge: Cambridge University Press.

Kaplan, E.A. (1983). *Women and Film: Both Sides of the Camera*. London and New York: Methuen.

Kazantzakis, N. (1965). *Journey to the Morea*. New York: Simon and Schuster.

Kelleher, P., C.M. O'Connor and J. Pillinger (2009). Globalisation, Sex Trafficking and Prostitution – The Experiences of Migrant Women in Ireland. URL (accessed 5 June 2009): http://www.immigrantcouncil.ie/images/2973_traffickingreport(0409).pdf

Kelly, P. (2008). *Lydia's Open Door: Inside Mexico's Most Modern Brothel*. Berkeley: University of California Press.

Kelsky, K. (1996). Flirting with the Foreign: Interracial Sex in Japan's 'International' age. In R. Wilson and W. Dissanayake (eds), *Global/Local: Cultural Production and the Transnational Imaginary*. Durham, NC: Duke University Press.

Kemp, T. (1936). *Prostitution: An Investigation of Its Laws Especially with Regard to Its Hereditary Factors*. Copenhagen: Levi and Munksgaard.

Kempadoo, K. (2001). Freelancers, Temporary Wives, and Beach-Boys: Researching Sex Work in the Caribbean, *Feminist Review* 67: 39–62.

Kennedy, D. (2005). *The Highly Civilized Man: Richard Burton and the Victorian World*. Cambridge, MA: Harvard University Press.

Kensinger, K. (1995). *How Real People Ought to Live: The Cashinahua of Eastern Peru*. Prospect Heights, IL: Waveland Press.

Keough, L.J. (2004). Driven Women: Reconceptualizing Women in Traffic through the Case of Gagauz Mobile Domestics, *Focaal: European Journal of Anthropology* 43: 14–26.

Kibby, M. and B. Costello (2001). Between the Image and the Act: Interactive Sex Entertainment on the Internet, *Sexualities* 4(3): 353–69.

Kilpatrick, D.G., C.N. Edmunds and A.K. Seymour (1992). *Rape in America: A Report to the Nation*. Arlington, VA: The National Victim Center.

Kirtsoglou, E. (2004). *For the Love of Women: Gender, Identity and Same-Sex Relations in a Greek Provincial Town*. London: Routledge.

Knopp, L. (1995). Sexuality and Urban Space: A Framework for Analysis. In D. Bell and G. Valentine (eds), *Mapping Desire: Geographies of Sexualities*. London: Routledge.

Kondo, D. (2005). The Tea Ceremony: A Symbolic Analysis. In D. Howes (ed.), *The Empire of the Senses*. Oxford: Berg.

Köpping, K.P. (1998). Bodies in the Field: Sexual Taboos, Self-Revelation and the Limits of Reflexivity in Anthropological Fieldwork (and Writing), *Anthropological Journal of European Cultures* 7(1): 7–26.

Koritz, A. (1997). Dancing the Orient for England: Maud Allen's the Vision of Salome. In J. Desmond (ed.), *Meaning in Motion: New Cultural Studies of Dance*. Durham, NC: Duke University Press.

Koskoff, E. (1997). Miriam Sings Her Song: The Self and Other in Anthropological Discourse. In R.A. Solie (ed.), *Musicology and Difference: Gender and Sexuality in Music Scholarship*. Berkeley: University of California Press.

Krafft-Ebing, R. von (1965 [1931]). *Psychopathia Sexualis*. New York: Physicians and Surgeons Book Co.

Krawenkel, H. (1981). Facing the Ugly Truth about Tourism, *Bangkok Post*, 14 August, p. 4.

Kressel, G. (1981). Sororicide/Filiacide: Homicide for Family Honour [with Comments and Reply], *Current Anthropology* 22(2): 141–58.

Kristiansen, I. (2009). Managing Sexual Advances in Vanuatu. In H. Donnan and F. Magowan (eds), *Transgressive Sex: Subversion and Control in Erotic Encounters*. Oxford: Berghahn Books.

Kubik, G. (1977). Patterns of Body Movement in the Music of Boys' Initiation in South-East Angola. In J.R. Blacking (ed.), *The Anthropology of the Body*. New York: Academic Press.

Kulick, D. (1995). Introduction: The Sexual Life of Anthropologists. In D. Kulick and M. Willson (eds), *Taboo: Sex, Identity and Erotic Subjectivity in Anthropological Fieldwork*. London: Routledge.

Kulick, D. (1996). Causing a Commotion: Public Scandal as Resistance among Brazilian Transgendered Prostitutes, *Anthropology Today* 12(6): 3–7.

Kulick, D. (1997). A Man in the House: The Boyfriends of Brazilian *Travesti* Prostitutes, *Social Text* 15(3/4): 133–60.

Kulick, D. (2000). Gay and Lesbian Language, *Annual Review of Anthropology* 29: 243–85.

Kulick, D. (2003a). Sex in the New Europe, *Anthropological Theory* 3(2): 199–218.

Kulick, D. (2003b). No. In D. Cameron and D. Kulick (eds), *The Language and Sexuality Reader*. London: Routledge.

Kulick, D. (2006). Theory in Furs: Masochist Anthropology, *Current Anthropology* 47(6): 933–52.

Kulick, D. and M. Willson (eds) (1995). *Taboo: Sex, Identity and Erotic Subjectivity in Anthropological Fieldwork*. London: Routledge.

Kuntsman, A. (2003). Double Homecoming: Sexuality, Ethnicity, and Place in Immigration Stories of Russian Lesbians in Israel, *Women's Studies International Forum* 26(4): 299–311.

Kuntsman, A. (2008). The Soldier and the Terrorist: Sexy Nationalism, Queer Violence, *Sexualities* 11(1/2): 142–70.

Kunzle, D. (1982). *Fashion and Fetishism: A Social History of the Corset – Tight-Lacing and Other Forms of Body Sculpture in the West*. Totowa, NJ: Rowman and Littlefield.

Kutsche, P. (1998). A Mudfight in Same-Sex Research, *American Ethnologist* 25(3): 495–8.

Laber, J. (1993). Bosnia: Questions about Rape, *New York Review of Books*, 25 March, pp. 3–6.

La Fontaine, J. (1990). *Child Sexual Abuse*. London: Polity Press.

Lambevski, S.A. (1999). Suck My Nation – Masculinity, Ethnicity and the Politics of (Homo)Sex, *Sexualities* 2(4): 397–419.

Lambevski, S.A. (2005). Bodies, Schizo Vibes and Hallucinatory Desires – Sexualities in Movement, *Sexualities* 8(5): 570–86.

Lancaster, R.N. and M. di Leonardo (eds) (1997). *The Gender/Sexuality Reader: Culture, History, Political Economy*. London: Routledge.

Langdon-Davies, J. (1928). *Lady Godiva: The Future of Nakedness*. New York: Harper.

Langdridge, D. (2006). Voices from the Margins: Sadomasochism and Sexual Citizenship, *Citizenship Studies* 10(4): 373–89.

Langdridge, D. and T. Butt (2004). A Hermeneutic Phenomenological Investigation of the Construction of Sadomasochistic Identities, *Sexualities* 7(1): 31–53.

Laqueur, T. (1987). *The Making of the Modern Body: Sexuality and Society in the Nineteenth Century.* Berkeley: University of California Press.

Laqueur, T. (1990). *Making Sex: Body and Gender from the Greeks to Freud.* Cambridge, MA, and London: Massachusetts University Press.

Lawson-Burke, M.E. (1998). Marshall Islands. In A. Kaeppler and J.W. Love (eds), *The Garland Encyclopaedia of World Music*, Vol. 9. New York and London: Garland Publishing Inc.

Leach, E.R. (1958). Magical Hair, *Journal of the Royal Anthropological Institute* 88: 147–64.

Leach, E.R. (1972 [1964]). Anthropological Aspects of Language: Animal Categories and Verbal Abuse. In W.A. Lessa and E.Z. Vogt (eds), *Reader in Comparative Religion: An Anthropological Approach.* New York: Harper and Row.

Leach, J. (2002). Drum and Voice: Aesthetics and Social Process on the Rai Coast of Papua New Guinea, *Journal of the Royal Anthropological Institute* 8(4): 713–34.

Lemert, E. (1951). *Social Pathology.* New York: McGraw Hill.

Lerner, G. (1986). *The Creation of Patriarchy.* New York: Oxford University Press.

Levin, D.M. (ed.) (1993). *Modernity and the Hegemony of Vision.* Berkeley: University of California Press.

Levitt, E.E., C. Moser and K.V. Jamison (1994). The Prevalence and Some Attributes of Females in the Sadomasochistic Subculture: A Second Report, *Archives of Sexual Behaviour* 23: 465–73.

Lewin, E. and W.L. Leap (1996a). Introduction. In E. Lewin and W.L. Leap (eds), *Out in the Field: Reflections of Lesbian and Gay Anthropologists.* Urbana, IL: University of Illinois Press.

Lewin, E. and W.L. Leap (eds) (1996b). *Out in the Field: Reflections of Lesbian and Gay Anthropologists.* Urbana, IL: University of Illinois Press.

Lewis, J.L. (2000). Sex and Violence in Brazil: *Carnaval, Capoeira,* and the Problem of Everyday Life, *American Ethnologist* 26(3): 539–57.

Liechty, M. (2005). Carnal Economies: The Commodification of Food and Sex in Kathmandu, *Cultural Anthropology* 20(1): 1–38.

Lindegaard, M.R. and A.-K. Henriksen (2009). Sexually Active Virgins: Negotiating Adolescent Femininity, Colour and Safety in Cape Town. In H. Donnan and F. Magowan (eds), *Transgressive Sex: Subversion and Control in Erotic Encounters.* Oxford: Berghahn Books.

Lindholm, C. (2001). *Culture and Identity: The History, Theory and Practice of Psychological Anthropology.* Boston: McGraw Hill.

Lindquist, J. (2002). The Anxieties of Mobility: Development, Migration, and Tourism in the Indonesian Borderlands. Doctoral dissertation, Department of Social Anthropology, Stockholm University, Sweden.

Littlewood, R. (1997). Military Rape, *Anthropology Today* 13(2): 7–16.

Loudon, J.B. (1977). On Body Products. In J.R. Blacking (ed.), *The Anthropology of the Body*. London: Academic Press.

Luibhéid, E. (2002). *Entry Denied: Controlling Sexuality at the Border*. Minneapolis: University of Minnesota Press.

Lunsing, W. (1999). Life on Mars: Love and Sex in Fieldwork on Sexuality and Gender in Urban Japan. In F. Markowitz and M. Ashkenazi (eds), *Sex, Sexuality and the Anthropologist*. Urbana, IL: University of Illinois Press.

Luo, T.-Y. (2000). 'Marrying My Rapist?!': The Cultural Trauma among Chinese Rape Survivors, *Gender and Society* 14(4): 581–97.

Lutkehaus, N. (1995). *Zaria's Fire: Engendered Moments in Manam Ethnography*. Durham, NC: Carolina Academic Press.

Lutkehaus, N. (1998). Gender in New Guinean Music. In A. Kaeppler and J.W. Love (eds), *The Garland Encyclopaedia of World Music*, Vol. 9. New York and London: Garland Publishing Inc.

Lyons, A. and H.D. Lyons (2004). *Irregular Connections: A History of Anthropology and Sexuality*. Lincoln: University of Nebraska.

Lyons, M. (1996). Foreign Bodies: The History of Labour Migration as a Threat to Public Health in Uganda. In P. Nugent and A.I. Asiwaju (eds), *African Boundaries: Barriers, Conduits and Opportunities*. London: Pinter.

McCallum, C. (1994). Ritual and the Origins of Sexuality in the Alto Xingu. In P. Gow and P. Harvey (eds), *Sex and Violence: Issues in Representation and Experience*. London: Routledge.

MacCannell, D. (1973). Staged Authenticity: Arrangements of Social Space in Tourist Settings, *American Journal of Sociology* 79(3): 589–603.

MacClancy, J. (1988). Going Nowhere: From Melanesia to the Mediterranean, *Journal of the Anthropological Society of Oxford* XIX(3): 233–40.

MacClancy, J. (1996). Popularizing Anthropology. In J. MacClancy and C. McDonaugh (eds), *Popularizing Anthropology*. London: Routledge.

McFarlane, J., B. Parker, K. Soeken and L. Bullock (1992). Assessing for Abuse during Pregnancy: Severity and Frequency of Injuries and Associated Entry into Prenatal Care, *Journal of the American Medical Society* 267(23): 3176–78.

McGeoch, P. (2007). Does Cortical Reorganisation Explain the Enduring Popularity of Foot-binding in Medieval China? *Medical Hypotheses* 69(4): 938–41.

Machado, M.A. (1982). Booze, Broads, and the Border: Vice and U.S.–Mexican Relations, 1910– 1930. In C.R. Bath (ed.), *Change and Perspective in Latin America*. El Paso, TX: Center for Inter-American and Border Studies.

McIntosh, J. (2006). Moving through Tradition: Children's Practice and Performance of Dance, Music and Song in South-Central Bali. Unpublished doctoral dissertation, Queen's University, Belfast.

Mackie, G. (1996). Ending Footbinding and Infibulation: A Convention Account, *American Sociological Review* 61(6): 999–1017.

Mackinlay, E. (1998). Gulf of Carpentaria. In A. Kaeppler and J.W. Love (eds), *The Garland Encyclopaedia of World Music*, Vol. 9. New York and London: Garland Publishing Inc.

MacKinnon, C.A. (1982). Feminism, Marxism, Method and the State: An Agenda for Theory, *Signs* 7(3): 515–44.

McMaster, G.R. (1995). Borderzones: The 'Injun-uity' of Aesthetic Tricks, *Cultural Studies* 9(1): 74–90.

McRobbie, A. (1991). *Feminism and Youth Culture: From 'Jackie' to 'Just Seventeen'.* Basingstoke: Macmillan.

Mageo, J.M. (1991). Ma'I aitu: The Cultural Logic of Possession in Samoa, *Ethos* 19: 352–83.

Mageo, J.M. (1994). Hairdos and Don'ts: Hair Symbolism and Sexual History in Samoa, *Man* (N.S.) 29(2): 407–32.

Magowan, F. (2007). *Melodies of Mourning: Music and Emotion in Northern Australia.* Oxford: James Currey Publishers.

Magowan, F. (2009). Courting Transgression: Customary Law and Sexual Violence in Aboriginal Australia. In H. Donnan and F. Magowan (eds), *Transgressive Sex: Subversion and Control in Erotic Encounters.* Oxford: Berghahn.

Malinowski, B. (1932). *The Sexual Life of Savages in North-Western Melanesia*, 3rd edn with a special foreword. London: Routledge and Kegan Paul.

Malinowski, B. (1955). *Sex and Repression in Savage Society.* New York: Meridian Books.

Malinowski, B. (1961 [1922]). *Argonauts of the Western Pacific.* New York: E.P. Dutton.

Malinowski, B. (1967). *A Diary in the Strict Sense of the Term.* Introduction by Raymond Firth. London: Routledge and Kegan Paul [reprinted in 1989 by Stanford University Press].

Manderson, L. (1992). Public Sex Performances in Patpong and Explorations of the Edges of Imagination, *Journal of Sex Research* 29(4): 451–75.

Manderson, L. (1995). The Pursuit of Pleasure and the Sale of Sex. In P. Abramson and S. Pinkerton (eds), *Sexual Nature, Sexual Culture.* Chicago, IL: University of Chicago Press.

Manouchian, M. (1974). *Manouchian.* Paris: Les Éditeurs Français Réunis.

Margolis, M.L. and M. Arnold (1993). Turning the Tables? Male Strippers and the Gender Hierarchy in America. In B.D. Miller (ed.), *Sex and Gender Hierarchies.* Cambridge: Cambridge University Press.

Mariner, W. (1827). *An Account of the Natives of the Tonga Islands.* Comp. John Martin, 2 vols (3rd edn, Edinburgh: Constable).

Markowitz, F. and M. Ashkenazi (eds) (1999). *Sex, Sexuality, and the Anthropologist.* Urbana, IL: University of Illinois Press.

Mars, L. (1984). What Was Onan's Crime? *Comparative Studies in Society and History* 26(3): 429–39.

Marshall, J. (2003). The Sexual Life of Cyber-Savants, *Australian Journal of Anthropology* 14(2): 229–48.

Marshall-Dean, D. (1998). Yap. In A. Kaeppler and J.W. Love (eds), *The Garland Encyclopaedia of World Music*, Vol. 9. New York and London: Garland Publishing Inc.

Martin, E. (1989). *The Woman in the Body: A Cultural Analysis of Reproduction.* Milton Keynes: Open University Press.

Martin, E. (1997). The Egg and the Sperm: How Science Has Constructed a Romance Based on Stereotypical Male–Female Roles. In L. Lamphere, H. Ragone and P. Zavella (eds), *Situated Lives: Gender and Culture in Everyday Life*. London: Routledge.

Martínez, O.J. (1988). *Troublesome Border*. Tucson: University of Arizona Press.

Marwick, M. (1965). *Sorcery in Its Social Setting*. Manchester: University Press.

Marx, K. (1973). *Grundrisse: Foundations of the Critique of Political Economy*. New York: Vintage Books.

Masters, J. (1956). *Bhowani Junction*. London: Reprint Society.

Mayer, T. (ed.) (2000). *Gender Ironies of Nationalism: Sexing the Nation*. London: Routledge.

Mazzio, C. (2005). The Senses Divided: Organs, Objects and Media in Early Modern England. In D. Howes (ed.), *The Empire of the Senses*. Oxford: Berg.

Mead, M. (1950). *Sex and Temperament in Three Primitive Societies*. New York: Mentor Books.

Meigs, A. and K. Barlow (2002). Beyond the Taboo: Imagining Incest, *American Anthropologist* 104(1): 38–49.

Meredith, F. (2003). But What Are Tits Really for, and Whose Are They Anyway? *Fortnight Magazine* No. 410, pp. 14–15.

Mies, M. (1986). *Patriarchy and Accumulation on a World Scale: Women in the International Division of Labour*. London: Zed Books.

Millar, W. (2005). Darwin's Disgust. In D. Howes (ed.), *Empire of the Senses*. Oxford: Berg.

Miller, D. (1991). Absolute Freedom in Trinidad, *Man* 26(2): 323–41.

Miller, T.E. and A. Shahriari (2006). *World Music: A Global Journey*. London: Routledge.

Montgomery, H. (2001). *Modern Babylon? Prostituting Children in Thailand*. Oxford: Berghahn Books.

Montgomery, H. (2009a). What Constitutes Transgressive Sex? The Case of Child Prostitution in Thailand. In H. Donnan and F. Magowan (eds), *Transgressive Sex: Subversion and Control in Erotic Encounters*. Oxford: Berghahn Books.

Montgomery, H. (2009b). *An Introduction to Childhood: Anthropological Perspectives on Children's Lives*. Oxford: Wiley-Blackwell.

Mookherjee, N. (2006). 'Remembering to Forget': Public Secrecy and Memory of Sexual Violence in the Bangladesh War of 1971, *Journal of the Royal Anthropological Institute* 12: 433–50.

Moore, F. (2005). One of the Gals Who's One of the Guys: Men, Masculinity and Drag Performance in North America. In A. Shaw and S. Ardener (eds), *Changing Sex and Bending Gender*. Oxford: Berghahn.

Moore, H. (1994). *A Passion for Difference*. Cambridge: Polity Press.

Morgan, K.P. (1991). Women and the Knife: Cosmetic Surgery and the Colonisation of Women's Bodies, *Hypatia* 6(3): 25–53.

Morphy, H. (1990). *Ancestral Connections*. Chicago, IL: University of Chicago Press.

Mostov, J. (2000). Sexing the Nation/Desexing the Body: Politics of National Identity in the Former Yugoslavia. In T. Mayer (ed.), *Gender Ironies of Nationalism: Sexing the Nation*. London: Routledge.

Mottier, V. (1998). Sexuality and Sexology: Michel Foucault. In T. Carver and V. Mottier (eds), *Politics of Sexuality: Identity, Gender Citizenship*. London: Routledge.

Mulvey, L. (1975). Visual Pleasure and the Narrative Cinema, *Screen* 16(3): 6–18.

Murphy, A.G. (2003). The Dialectical Gaze: Exploring the Subject–Object Tension in the Performances of Women Who Strip, *Journal of Contemporary Ethnography* 32(3): 305–35.

Murray, S.O. (1996). Male Homosexuality in Guatemala: Possible Insights and Certain Confusions from Sleeping with the Natives. In E. Lewin and W.L. Leap (eds), *Out in the Field: Reflections of Lesbian and Gay Anthropologists*. Urbana, IL: University of Illinois Press.

Murray, S.O. (1997). Explaining away Same-Sex Sexualities: When They Obtrude on Anthropologists' Notice at All, *Anthropology Today* 13(3): 2–5.

Nagel, J. (2003). *Race, Ethnicity, and Sexuality: Intimate Intersections, Forbidden Frontiers*. New York: Oxford University Press.

Nagengast, C. (1997). Women, Minorities and Indigenous Peoples: Universalism and Cultural Relativity, *Journal of Anthropological Research* 53(3): 349–69.

Nanda, S. (1990). *Neither Man nor Woman: The Hijras of India*. Belmont, CA: Wadsworth Publishing.

Neveu-Kringelbach, H. (2007). 'Cool Play': Emotionality in Dance as a Resource in Senegalese Urban Women's Associations. In H. Wulff (ed.), *The Emotions: A Cultural Reader*. Oxford: Berg.

Newton, E. (1993). My Best Informant's Dress: The Erotic Equation in Fieldwork, *Cultural Anthropology* 8(1): 3–23.

Nichols, B. (1995). *Blurred Boundaries: Questions of Meaning in Contemporary Culture*. Bloomington: Indiana University Press.

Obermeyer C.M. (1999). Female Genital Surgeries: The Known, the Unknown, and the Unknowable, *Medical Anthropology Quarterly* 13(1): 79–106.

Obeyesekere, G. (1984). *Medusa's Hair*. Chicago, IL: University of Chicago Press.

O'Connell Davidson, J. (1998). *Prostitution, Power and Freedom*. Cambridge: Polity Press.

O'Connell Davidson, J. (2005). *Children in the Sex Trade*. London: Polity Press.

O'Connell Davidson, J. (2006). Will the Real Sex Slave Please Stand up? *Feminist Review* 83: 4–22.

Olujic, M. (1998). Embodiment of Terror: Gendered Violence in Peacetime and Wartime in Croatia and Bosnia-Herzegovina, *Medical Anthropology Quarterly* 12(1): 31–50.

Olumide, J. (2001). *Raiding the Gene Pool: The Social Construction of Mixed Race*. London: Pluto Press.

O'Merry, R. (1990). *My Wife in Bangkok*. Berkeley, CA: Asia Press.

Ortner, S.B. (1981). Gender and Sexuality in Hierarchical Societies. In S.B. Ortner and H. Whitehead (eds), *Sexual Meanings*. New York: Cambridge University Press.

Osella, C. and F. Osella (1998). Friendship and Flirting: Micropolitics in Kerala, South India, *Journal of the Royal Anthropological Institute* 4(2): 189–206.

Padilla, M.B., Hirsch, J.S., Muñoz-Laboy, M., Sember, R.E. and Parker, R.G. (eds) (2007). *Love and Globalization: Transformations of Intimacy in the Contemporary World*. Nashville, TN: Vanderbilt Press.

Parker, R.G. (1991). *Bodies, Pleasures and Passions: Sexual Culture in Contemporary Brazil*. Boston: Beacon Press.

Parker, R.G. (1999). *Beneath the Equator: Cultures of Desire, Male Homosexuality, and Emerging Gay Communities in Brazil*. New York: Routledge.

Parker, R.G. (2001). Sexuality, Culture, and Power in HIV/AIDS Research, *Annual Review of Anthropology* 30: 163–79.

Parker, R.G., G. Herdt and M. Carballo (1991). Sexual Culture, HIV Transmission and AIDS Research, *Journal of Sex Research* 28: 77–98.

Parker, R.G., K. Quemmel, M. Mota Guimares and V. Terto (1995). AIDS Prevention and Gay Community Mobilization in Brazil, *Development* 2: 49–53.

Parry, J.P. and M. Bloch (eds) (1989). *Money and the Morality of Exchange*. Cambridge: Cambridge University Press.

Peacock, J.L. (1968). *Rites of Modernization: Symbolic and Social Aspects of Indonesian Proletarian Drama*. Chicago, IL: University of Chicago Press.

Penttinen, E. (2006). *Globalisation, Prostitution and Sex Trafficking*. London: Routledge.

Perniola, M. (1989). Between Clothing and Nudity. In M. Feher with R. Naddaff and N. Tazi (eds), *Fragments for a History of the Human Body, Part Two*. New York: Zone.

Perry, E. (1985). 'Deviant' Insiders: Legalized Prostitutes and Consciousness of Women in Early Modern Seville, *Contemporary Studies in Society and History* 27(1): 138–58.

Pinard, S. (1991). A Taste of India. In D. Howes (ed.), *The Varieties of Sensory Experience*. Toronto: University of Toronto Press.

Pink, S. (1997). *Women and Bullfighting: Gender, Sex and the Consumption of Tradition*. Oxford: Berg.

Pitman, J. (2003). *On Blondes*. London: Bloomsbury.

Pitt-Rivers, J. (1977). *The Fate of Shechem or The Politics of Sex: Essays in the Anthropology of the Mediterranean*. Cambridge: Cambridge University Press.

Plummer, K. (1992). Speaking Its Name: Inventing a Lesbian and Gay Studies. In K. Plummer (ed.), *Modern Homosexualities: Fragments of Lesbian and Gay Experience*. London: Routledge.

Plummer, K. (1995). *Telling Sexual Stories: Power, Change and Social Worlds*. London: Routledge.

Polhemus, T. (1993). Dance, Sex and Gender. In H. Thomas (ed.), *Dance, Gender and Culture*. London Macmillan.

Polsky, N. (1967). *Hustlers, Beats and Others*. Chicago, IL: Aldine.

Porter, D.J. (1997). A Plague on the Borders: HIV, Development, and Traveling Identities in the Golden Triangle. In L. Manderson and M. Jolly (eds), *Sites of Desire, Economies of Pleasure: Sexualities in Asia and the Pacific*. Chicago, IL: University of Chicago Press.

Povinelli, E. (2006). *The Empire of Love: Toward a Theory of Intimacy, Genealogy, and Carnality*. Durham, NC: Duke University Press.

Prasad, M. (1999). The Morality of Market Exchange: Love, Money and Contractual Justice, *Sociological Perspectives* 42(2): 181–214.

Press, C. (1978). Reputation and Respectability Reconsidered: Hustling in a Tourist Setting, *Carribean Issues* 4(1): 109–20.

Reed, S. (1998). The Politics and Poetics of Dance, *Annual Review of Anthropology* 27: 503–32.

Reiss, I. (1986). *Journey into Sexuality: An Exploratory Voyage*. Englewood Cliffs, NJ: Prentice Hall.

Richardson, D. (2000). *Rethinking Sexuality*. London: Sage Publications.

Richters, J. (2007). Through a Hole in a Wall: Setting and Interaction in Sex-on-Premises Venues, *Sexualities* 10(3): 275–97.

Rival, L. (2008). What Kind of Sex Makes People Happy? In R. Astuti, J.P. Parry and C. Stafford (eds), *Questions of Anthropology: Festschrift for Maurice Bloch*. Oxford: Berg.

Rival, L., D. Slater and D. Miller (1999). Sex and Sociality: Comparative Ethnographies of Sexual Objectification. In M. Featherstone (ed.), *Love and Eroticism*. London: Sage Publications.

Roebuck, J.R. and P.H. McNamara (1973). Ficheras and Free-lancers: Prostitution in a Mexican Border City, *Archives of Sexual Behavior* 2(3): 231–44.

Rofel, L. (2007). *Desiring China: Experiments in Neoliberalism, Sexuality and Public Culture*. Durham, NC: Duke University Press.

Ronai, C.R. (1992). The Reflexive Self through Narrative: A Night in the Life of an Erotic Dancer/Researcher. In C. Ellis and M.G. Flaherty (eds), *Investigating Subjectivity: Research on Lived Experience*. London: Sage.

Ronai, C.R. and C. Ellis (1989). Turn-ons for Money: Interactional Strategies of the Table Dancer, *Journal of Contemporary Ethnography* 18(3): 271–98.

Rosaldo, R. (1989). *Culture and Truth: The Remaking of Social Analysis*. Boston, MA: Beacon Press.

Roscoe, P. (1994). Amity and Aggression: A Symbolic Theory of Incest, *Man* (N.S.) 29: 49–76.

Rubin, G. (1975). The Traffic in Women: Notes on the 'Political Economy' of Sex. In R. Reiter (ed.), *Toward an Anthropology of Women*. New York: Monthly Review Press.

Sacks, O. (2005). The Mind's Eye: What the Blind See. In D. Howes (ed.), *The Empire of the Senses*. Oxford: Berg.

Sahlins, M. (1985). *Islands of History*. Chicago, IL: University of Chicago Press.

Said, E. (1978). *Orientalism*. New York: Pantheon Books.

Salzinger, L. (2000). Manufacturing Sexual Subjects: 'Harassment', Desire and Discipline on a Maquiladora Shopfloor, *Ethnography* 1(1): 67–92.

Sánchez Taylor, J. (2001). Dollars Are a Girl's Best Friend? Female Tourists' Sexual Behaviour in the Caribbean, *Sociology* 35(3): 749–64.

Sanday, P. (1981). The Socio-cultural Context of Rape: A Cross-Cultural Study, *Journal of Social Issues* 37(4): 5–27.

Sanday, P. (1986). Rape and the Silencing of the Feminine. In S. Tomaselli and R. Porter (eds), *Rape*. Oxford: Blackwell.

Sanday, P. (2002 [1983]). *Women at the Centre: Life in a Modern Matriarchy*. New York: Cornell University Press.

Sanday, P. (2007). *Fraternity Gang Rape: Sex, Brotherhood and Privilege on Campus*. New York: New York University Press.

Sanders, T. (2006). Sexing up the Subject: Methodological Nuances in Researching the Female Sex Industry, *Sexualities* 9(4): 449–68.

Sanders, T. (2008a). Male Sexual Scripts: Intimacy, Sexuality and Pleasure in the Purchase of Commercial Sex, *Sociology* 42(3): 400–17.

Sanders, T. (2008b). A Tangle of Lust, Lace and Unintended Consequences, *Times Higher Education*, 11 December, p. 22.

Sanders, T. (2008c). *Paying for Pleasure: Men Who Buy Sex*. Cullompton, UK: Willan Publishing.

Santtila, P., N.K. Sandnabba, L. Alison and N. Nordling (2002). Investigating the Underlying Structure in Sadomasochistically-oriented Behaviour: Evidence for Sexual Scripts, *Archives of Sexual Behaviour* 31: 185–96.

Sartre, J.-P. (1943). *L'Etre et le Neant*, 3rd edn. Paris: Gallimard.

Sartre, J.-P. (1992 [1956]). *Being and Nothingness: A Phenomenological Essay on Ontology*. New York: Washington Square Press.

Savan, L. (1993). Commercials Go Rock. In S. Frith, A. Goodwin and L. Grossberg (eds), *Sound and Vision: The Music Video Reader*. London and New York: Routledge.

Savell, K.L. (1996). Wrestling with Contradictions: Human Rights and Traditional Practices Affecting Women, *McGill Law Journal* 41: 781–817.

Savigliano, M. (1995). *Tango and the Political Economy of Passion: Tango, Exoticism and Decolonization*. Boulder, CO: Westview Press.

Scambler, G. (1997). Conspicuous and Inconspicuous Sex Work: The Neglect of the Ordinary and Mundane. In G. Scambler and A. Scambler (eds), *Rethinking Prostitution*. London: Routledge.

Schechner, R. (2001). Rasaesthetics, *Drama Review* 45(3): 27–50.

Scheper-Hughes, N. (1991). Virgin Territory: The Male Discovery of the Clitoris, *Medical Anthropological Quarterly* 5(1): 25–8.

Scheper-Hughes, N. and J. Devine (2003). Priestly Celibacy and Child Sexual Abuse, *Sexualities* 6(1): 15–40.

Scheper-Hughes, N. and M. Lock (1987). The Mindful Body: A Prolegomenon to Future Work in Medical Anthropology, *Medical Anthropology Quarterly* 1: 6–41.

Schick, I. (1999). *The Erotic Margin: Sexuality and Spatiality in Alterist Discourse*. London: Verso Press.

Schmidt, J. (2003). Paradise Lost? Social Change and Fa'afafine in Samoa, *Current Sociology* 5(3/4): 417–32.

Schneider, D. (1980). *American Kinship: A Cultural Account*. Chicago, IL: University of Chicago Press.

Schoepf, B. (1992). Women at Risk: Case Studies from Zaire. In G. Herdt and S. Lindenbaum (eds), *The Time of AIDS: Social Analysis, Theory and Method*. Newbury Park, CA: Sage Publications.

Schoepf, B. (1993). Gender, Development and AIDS: A Political Economy and Culture Framework. In R. Gallin, A. Ferguson and J. Harper (eds), *The Women and International Development Annual* 3: 53–85.

Schott, R. (1996). Gender and 'Postmodern War', *Hypatia* 11(4): 20–9.

Scott, J. (1995). Sexual and National Boundaries in Tourism, *Annals of Tourism Research* 22(2): 385–403.

Sedgwick, E.K. (1985). *Between Men: English Literature and Male Homosocial Desire*. New York: Columbia University Press.

Seidman, S. (1991). *Romantic Longings: Love in America, 1830–1980*. New York: Routledge.

Seifert, R. (1996). The Second Front: The Logic of Sexual Violence in Wars, *Women's Studies International Forum* 19(1–2): 35–43.

Seizer, S. (1995). Paradoxes of Visibility in the Field: Rites of Queer Passage in Anthropology, *Public Culture* 8: 73–100.

Sellon, E. (1863–4). On the Phallic Worship of India, *Memoirs of the Anthropological Society of London* 1: 327–34.

Seremetakis, C.N. (1996). In Search of the Barbarians: Borders in Pain, *American Anthropologist* 98(3): 489–511.

Shalhoub-Kevorkian, N. (2002). Femicide and the Palestinian Criminal Justice System: Seeds of Change in the Context of State Building? *Law and Society Review* 36(3): 577–606.

Shand, A. (1998). The Tsifte-teli Sermon: Identity, Theology and Gender in Rebetika. In W. Washabaugh (ed.), *The Passion of Music and Dance: Body, Gender and Sexuality*. Oxford: Berg.

Shay, A. (1995). Bazi-ha-ye Nameyeshi: Iranian Women's Theatrical Plays, *Dance Research Journal* 27(2): 16–24.

Shokeid, M. (1995). *A Gay Synagogue in New York*. New York: Columbia University Press.

Shore, B. (1981). Sexuality and Gender in Samoa: Conceptions and Missed Conceptions. In S.B. Ortner and H. Whitehead (eds), *Sexual Meanings: The Cultural Construction of Gender and Sexuality*. Cambridge: Cambridge University Press.

Shore, B. (1989). Mana and Tapu. In A. Howard and R. Borofsky (eds), *Developments in Polynesian Ethnology*. Honolulu: University Press of Hawaii.

Shweder, R. (1996). The View from Manywheres, *Anthropology Newsletter* 37(9): 1.

Siegel, E. (1984). *Movement Therapy: The Mirror of Ourselves: A Psychoanalytic Approach*. New York: Human Science.

Sigel, L. (2002). *Governing Pleasures: Pornography and Social Change in England 1815–1914*. New Brunswick, NJ: Rutgers University.

Simmel, G. (1971 [1907]). Prostitution. In D.N. Levine (ed.), *Georg Simmel: On Individuality and Social Forms*. Chicago, IL: University of Chicago Press.

Simon, W. and J.A. Gagnon (1999 [1984]). Sexual Scripts. In R. Parker and P. Aggleton (eds), *Culture, Society and Sexuality: A Reader*. London: Routledge.

Skinner, J. (2003). At the Busk and after Dusk: Ceroc and the Construction of Dance Times and Places, *Focaal: European Journal of Anthropology* 42: 109–19.

Skinner, J. (2008). Women Dancing Back-and-Forth: Resistance and Self-Regulation in Belfast Salsa, *Dance Research Journal* 40(1): 65–77.

Smart, C. (1995). *Law, Crime and Sexuality: Essays in Feminism*. London: Sage.

Smith, B.B. (1998). Nauru. In A. Kaeppler and J.W. Love (eds), *The Garland Encyclopaedia of World Music*, Vol. 9. New York and London: Garland Publishing Inc.

Smith, H.E. (1971). Thai-American Intermarriage in Thailand, *International Journal of Sociology of the Family* 1: 127–36.

Snyder, C., W.J. Gabbard, J. Dean May and N. Zulcic (2006). On the Battleground of Women's Bodies: Mass Rape in Bosnia-Herzegovina, *Affilia* 21: 184–95.

Soupault, P. (1928). *Terpsichore*. Paris: Emile Hazan.

Spencer, P. (ed.) (1985). *Society and the Dance: The Social Anthropology of Process and Performance*. Cambridge: Cambridge University Press.

Stallybrass, P. and A. White (1986). *The Politics and Poetics of Transgression*. Ithaca, NY: Cornell University Press.

Stokes, M. (1994). Local Arabesk, the Hatay and the Turkish Syrian Border. In H. Donnan and T.M. Wilson (eds), *Border Approaches: Anthropological Perspectives on Frontiers*. Lanham, MD: University Press of America.

Stoler, A.L. (1989). Making Empire Respectable: The Politics of Race and Sexual Morality in 20th-Century Colonial Cultures, *American Ethnologist* 16(4): 634–60.

Stoler, A.L. (1991). Carnal Knowledge and Imperial Power: Gender, Race, and Morality in Colonial Asia. In M. di Leonardo (ed.), *Gender at the Crossroads of Knowledge: Feminist Anthropology in the Postmodern Era*. Berkeley: University of California Press.

Stoler, A.L. (1992). Sexual Affronts and Racial Frontiers: European Identities and the Cultural Politics of Exclusion in Colonial Southeast Asia, *Comparative Studies in Society and History* 34(3): 514–51.

Stoller, P. (1989). *The Taste of Ethnographic Things: The Senses in Anthropology*. Philadelphia: University of Pennsylvania Press.

Stone, A.L. (2007). Sexuality and Social Change: Sexual Relations in a Capitalist System, *American Anthropologist* 109(4): 753–5.

Storr, M. (2003). *Latex and Lingerie: Shopping for Pleasure at Ann Summers Parties*. Oxford: Berg.

Strathern, M. (1979). The Self in Self-Decoration, *Oceania* 49: 241–57.

Strathern, M. (1990). *The Gender of the Gift: Problems with Women and Problems with Society in Melanesia*. Studies in Melanesian Anthropology, Vol. 6. Berkeley: University of California Press.

Strong, T. (1998). Orientalism. In S.J. Cohen (ed.), *International Encyclopaedia of Dance*, 6 Vols. Oxford: Oxford University Press.

Synnott, A. (1993). *The Body Social: Symbolism, Self and Society*. London: Routledge.

Taylor, G.W. and J. Ussher (2001). Making Sense of S&M: A Discourse Analytic Account, *Sexualities* 4(3): 293–314.

Taylor, P. (1997). *Behind the Mask: The IRA and Sinn Fein*. New York: TV Books.

Thomas, D.Q. and R.E. Ralph (1993). Rape in War: Challenging the Tradition of Impunity, *SAIS Review* 14(1): 81–99.

Thompson, S. (1990). Putting a Big Thing into a Little Hole: Teenage Girls' Accounts of Sexual Initiation, *Journal of Sex Research* 27(3): 341–61.

Thomson, B. (1908). *The Fijians: A Study of the Decay of Custom*. London: Heinemann.

Thornton, R.J. (2008). *Unimagined Community: Sex, Networks, and AIDS in Uganda and South Africa*. Berkeley, CA: University of California Press.

Tobin, J. (1998). Tango and the Scandal of Homosocial Desire. In W. Washabaugh (ed.), *The Passion of Music and Dance: Body, Gender and Sexuality*. Oxford: Berg.

Totman, R. (2003). *The Third Sex: Kathoey, Thailand's Ladyboys*. London: The Souvenir Press.

Truong, T.-D. (1990). *Sex, Money and Morality: Prostitution and Tourism in South-east Asia*. London: Zed Books.

Turner, T. (1980). The Social Skin. In T. Cherfas and R. Lewin (eds), *Not Work Alone: A Cross Cultural View of Activities Superfluous to Survival*. London: Temple Smith.

Turner, V. (1967). *The Forest of Symbols: Aspects of Ndembu Ritual*. Ithaca, NY: Cornell University Press.

Turner, V. (1968). *The Drums of Affliction*. Oxford: Clarendon Press.

Turner, V. (1969). *The Ritual Process*. Chicago, IL: University of Chicago Press.

Turner, V. (1982). *From Ritual to Theater*. New York: Performing Arts Journal Publications.

Tuzin, D. (2006). Base Note: Odor, Breath and Moral Contagion in Ilahita. In J. Drobnick (ed.), *The Smell Culture Reader*. Oxford: Berg.

Ucko, P. (1970). Penis Sheaths: A Comparative Study, *Proceedings of the Royal Anthropological Institute* (The Curl Lecture 1969): 24–67.

Urla, J. and A. Swedlund (1995). The Anthropometry of Barbie: Unsettling Ideals of the Feminine Body in Popular Culture. In J. Terry and J. Urla (eds), *Deviant Bodies: Critical Perspectives on Difference in Science and Popular Culture*. Bloomington: Indiana University Press.

Uygun, B.N. (2004). Post-socialist Scapes of Economy and Desire: The Case of Turkey, *Focaal: European Journal of Anthropology* 43: 27–45.

Valdez Santiago, R. and E. Shrader Cox (1992). *La violencia hacia la mujer Mexicana como problema salud publica: La incidencia de la violencia domestica en una microregion de Cuidad Nexahualcoyotl*. Mexico City: CECOVID.

Van Gulik, R.H. (1961). *Sexual Life in Ancient China*. Leiden: E.J. Brill.

Vason, G. (1810). *An Authentic Narrative of Four Years Residence on Tongataboo*, ed. S. Piggott. London: Longman.

Vila, P. (2000). *Crossing Borders, Reinforcing Borders: Social Categories, Metaphors, and Narrative Identities on the US–Mexico Frontier*. Austin: University of Texas Press.

Vila, P. (2005). *Border Identifications: Narratives of Religion, Gender, and Class on the US–Mexico Border*. Austin: University of Texas Press.

Virgili, F. (2002). *Shorn Women: Gender and Punishment in Liberation France*. Oxford: Berg.

Wade, P. (1993). Sexuality and Masculinity in Fieldwork among Columbian Blacks. In D. Bell, P. Caplan and W.J. Karim (eds), *Gendered Fields: Women, Men, and Ethnography*. London: Routledge.

Walkowitz, J. (1980). *Prostitution and Victorian Society: Women, Class and the State*. Cambridge: Cambridge University Press.

Wallace, M. (1990 [1979]). *Black Macho and the Myth of the Superwoman*. London: Verso.

Ward, H. and S. Day (2006). What Happens to Women Who Sell Sex? Report of a Unique Occupational Cohort, *Sexually Transmitted Infections* 82: 413–17.

Wardlow, H. (2002). Giving Birth to Gonolia: 'Culture' and Sexually Transmitted Diseases among the Huli of Papua New Guinea, *Medical Anthropology Quarterly* 16(2): 151–75.

Wardlow, H. (2004). Anger, Economy and Female Agency: Problematizing 'Prostitution' and 'Sex Work' among the Huli of Papua New Guinea, *Signs: Journal of Women in Culture and Society* 29(4): 1017–40.

Wardlow, H. (2006). *Wayward Women: Sexuality and Agency in a New Guinea Society.* Berkeley: University of California Press.

Wardlow, H. (2008). She Liked It Best When She Was on Top: Intimacies and Estrangements in Huli Men's Marital and Extramarital Relationships. In W. Jankowiak (ed.), *Intimacies: Love and Sex across Cultures.* New York: Columbia University Press.

Warring, A. (2006). Intimate and Sexual Relations. In R. Gildea, O. Wieviorka and A. Warring (eds), *Surviving Hitler and Mussolini: Daily Life in Occupied Europe.* Oxford: Berg.

Washabaugh, W. (ed.) (1998). *The Passion of Music and Dance: Body, Gender and Sexuality.* Oxford: Berg.

Weeks, J. (1993). *Sex, Politics and Society: The Regulation of Sexuality since 1800.* London and New York: Longman.

Weinberg, T. (2005). Sadomasochism and the Social Sciences: A Review of the Sociological and Social Psychological Literature. In P. Kleinplatz and C. Moser (eds), *Sadomasochism: Powerful Pleasures.* Binghamton, NY: Harrington Park Press.

Weinberg, T. (2009). Sacher-Masoch, Leopold Ritter von. URL: http://www2.hu-berlin.de/sexology/gesund/archiv/sen/ch22.htm.

Weiner, A. (1988). *The Trobrianders of Papua New Guinea.* New York: New York University.

Weitzer, R. (2000a). Why We Need More Research on Sex Work. In R. Weitzer (ed.), *Sex for Sale: Prostitution, Pornography, and the Sex Industry.* London: Routledge.

Weitzer, R. (ed.). (2000b). *Sex for Sale: Prostitution, Pornography, and the Sex Industry.* London: Routledge.

Wekker, G. (2006). *The Politics of Passion: Women's Sexual Culture in the Afro-Suriname Diaspora.* New York: Columbia University Press.

Werbner, R. (1984). World Renewal: Masking in a New Guinea Festival, *Man* (N.S.) 19(2): 267–90.

Werbner, R. (1989). *Ritual Passage, Sacred Journey.* Manchester: Manchester University Press.

Westermarck, E. (1926). *A Short History of Marriage.* New York: Macmillan.

Westhaver, R. (2006). Flaunting and Empowerment: Thinking about Circuit Parties, the Body, and Power, *Journal of Contemporary Ethnography* 35(6): 611–44.

Weston, K. (1991). *Families We Choose: Lesbians, Gays, Kinship.* New York: Columbia University Press.

Weston, K. (1993). Lesbian/Gay Studies in the House of Anthropology, *Annual Review of Anthropology* 22: 339–67.

Whelan, F. (2000). *The Complete Guide to Irish Dance.* Belfast: Appletree.

Whitehead, H. (1981). The Bow and the Burden Strap. In S.B. Ortner and H. Whitehead (eds), *Sexual Meanings.* New York: Cambridge University Press.

Whiteley S. (1997). Little Red Rooster v. The Honky Tonk Woman. In S. Whiteley (ed.), *Sexing the Groove: Popular Music and Gender.* London: Routledge.

Whiteley, S. (2000). *Women and Popular Music.* London: Routledge.

Wickstrom, S. (2005). The Politics of Forbidden Liaisons: Civilization, Miscegenation, and Other Perversions, *Frontiers* 26(3): 168–98.

Wiegman, R. (1993). The Anatomy of Lynching. In J.C. Fout and M.S. Tantillo (eds), *American Sexual Politics: Sex, Gender, and Race since the Civil War.* Chicago, IL: University of Chicago Press.

Wiener, M.J. (2007). Dangerous Liaisons and Other Tales from the Twilight Zone: Sex, Race, and Sorcery in Colonial Java, *Comparative Studies in Society and History* 49(3): 495–526.

Wieringa, S. (2005). Globalisation, Love, Intimacy and Silence in a Working Class Butch/Fem Community in Jakarta. ASSR Working Paper 05/08 Amsterdam School for Social Science Research. URL: http://www.assr.ni./.

Wikan, U. (1977). Man Becomes Woman, *Man* 12(2): 304–19.

Wikan, U. (1978). The Omani Xanith, *Man* 13(4): 667–71.

Wilkinson, E. (2009). Perverting Visual Pleasure: Representing Sadomasochism, *Sexualities* 12(2): 181–98.

Williams, J. (1984 [1830–2]). *The Samoan Journals of John Williams*, ed. R.M. Moyle. Canberra: Australian National University Press.

Wilson, T.M. and H. Donnan (2006). *The Anthropology of Ireland*. Oxford: Berg.

Wilton, T. (1996). Which One's the Man? The Heterosexualisation of Lesbian Sex. In D. Richardson (ed.), *Theorising Heterosexuality*. Buckingham: Open University Press.

Wimmer, A. (2008). Elementary Strategies of Ethnic Boundary Making, *Ethnic and Racial Studies* 31(6): 1025–55.

Wolf, A.P. (1966). Childhood Association, Sexual Attraction, and the Incest Taboo: A Chinese Case, *American Anthropologist* 68(4): 883–98.

Wood, G. (2001). Sex and the City, *Observer Magazine*, 1 April, pp. 21–3.

Wright, R. (1966 [1940]). *Native Son*. New York.

Wulff, H. (2003). The Irish Body in Motion: Moral Politics, National Identity and Dance. In N. Dyck and E. Archetti (eds), *Sport, Dance and Embodied Identities*. Oxford: Berg.

Wulff, H. (2007). *Dancing at the Crossroads: Memory and Mobility in Ireland*. Oxford: Berghahn Books.

Yanagisako, S. (2002). *Producing Culture and Capital: Family Firms in Italy*. Princeton, NJ: Princeton University Press.

Yelvington, K.A. (1996). Flirting in the Factory, *Journal of the Royal Anthropological Institute* 2: 313–33.

Young, A. (2000). *Women Who Became Men: Albanian Sworn Virgins*. Oxford: Berg.

Young, R.J.C. (1995). *Colonial Desire: Hybridity in Theory, Culture and Race*. London: Routledge.

Zeldin, T. (1995). *An Intimate History of Humanity*. London: Minerva.

Žižek, S. (1991). *Looking Awry: An Introduction to Jacques Lacan through Popular Culture*. Cambridge, MA: MIT Press.

INDEX